D1221288

Quest for Eros

Quest for Eros

Browning and 'Fifine'

Samuel B. Southwell

THE UNIVERSITY PRESS OF KENTUCKY

Many of the Browning letters are quoted, by permission, from Edward C. McAleer, ed., *Learned Lady: Letters from Robert Browning to Mrs. Thomas Fitzgerald* (Cambridge, Mass.: Harvard University Press, 1966), and from Elvan Kintner, ed., *The Letters of Robert Browning and Elizabeth Barrett, 1845-1846* (Cambridge, Mass.: The Belknap Press of Harvard University Press, 1969).

Library of Congress Cataloging in Publication Data

Southwell, Samuel B
    Quest for Eros.

    Includes bibliographical references and index.
    1. Browning, Robert, 1812-1889. Fifine at the
fair.   I. Browning, Robert, 1812-1889. Fifine at
the fair. 1980.   II. Title.
PR4222.F53S6   821'.8   79-4945
ISBN 0-8131-1399-7

Copyright © 1980 by The University Press of Kentucky

Scholarly publisher for the Commonwealth,
serving Berea College, Centre College of Kentucky,
Eastern Kentucky University, The Filson Club,
Georgetown College, Kentucky Historical Society,
Kentucky State University, Morehead State University,
Murray State University, Northern Kentucky University,
Transylvania University, University of Kentucky,
University of Louisville, and Western Kentucky University.

Editorial and Sales Offices: Lexington, Kentucky 40506

821
B886fizs
c.1

For my mother
Lucile Beall Southwell

281524

Contents

Acknowledgments

I wish to express my appreciation to the University of Houston for grants permitting completion of the manuscript and supporting publication; to William Jerome Crouch and Katharine H. Shaw at the University Press of Kentucky for expert editing; to E. V. Quinn, of Balliol College, for providing me a copy of the manuscript of *Fifine at the Fair*; and to the Humanities Research Center of The University of Texas at Austin and to John Murray for permissions to quote from Browning's works and papers.

I am grateful to Oscar Maurer, under whom I studied Victorian literature, and to Morse Peckham for his scholarship and for a gift of time and advice to a stranger. Among graduate students from whom I have learned are Charlene Chesnut, whose paper on *Fifine* deepened my interest in the poem, and Dianna Mullin Vitanza, whose master's thesis helped me to understand "Fra Lippo Lippi." Friends and colleagues who have given me important help are Earl L. Dachslager, John McNamara, George Y. Trail, James D. Welch, and William C. Wright. I am especially indebted to Helen M. Barthelme, Alfred R. Neumann, Nicholas W. Quick, and Irving N. Rothman. Graver debts are to Lucile, who taught me to read with care, and to Mary, Michael, and Teresa, who sustain larger meanings.

1
Introduction

Opinion concerning Robert Browning's *Fifine at the Fair* suggests that a clear and coherent reading of the poem must overcome formidable obstacles but will be worthwhile. The magnitude of the problem was vividly reflected in the earliest critical response. A writer for the *Westminster Review* commented that "the subject matter" would "have made the epic of the present day" if it had been "treated as Browning could treat it, and as he has treated it here in many passages." The writer continued: "We believe that he has put more substance into *Fifine at the Fair* than into any other poem. But for the ordinary reader it might just as well have been written in Sanscrit."[1]

Most of Browning's contemporaries were bewildered by the poem,[2] but recent comment has emphasized its significance and its excellence. Roma King considers it one of the four works most important for understanding Browning, the other three being *Sordello, The Ring and the Book,* and *Parleyings with Certain People of Importance in Their Day.* In the opinion of Morse Peckham these poems are, quite simply, "Browning's four greatest works."[3] An exhaustive reading will bear out current opinion in ways that have not been explicitly anticipated. A measure of the poem's value is suggested by the fact that it embodies the climactic development of Browning's intellectual experience. Its significance for the study of Browning consists partly in its providing a perspective which will illuminate the structure and development of Browning's work as a whole. To understand the central structure of his poetry is to read much of Browning's work anew.

For Browning the composition of *Fifine* had about it the spontaneity of authentic creation. He wrote to Isabella Blagden: "I have been hard at work, the poem *growing* under me and seeming worth attending to: it is *almost* done."[4] There is perhaps a note of reservation here—the poem "seeming worth attending to"—which we will come to understand. But the poem seemed to Browning to have a special importance. He told his old friend Alfred Domett that although he was "doubtful as to its reception by the public," the poem was "the most metaphysical and boldest he had written since Sordello."[5] Thinking especially perhaps of the extreme complexity he had achieved, Browning took pride in the work. Near the end of the poem he seems to step outside its margins to comment: "Here's his book, and now perhaps you see / At length what poetry can do!" (CXVI, 1995-96).[6] After the most sympathetic critics had thrown up their hands and the poem failed publicly, Browning made his last comments on the poem in the form of two quotations from Greek drama which he wrote on the manuscript before presenting it to Balliol College. We will come to see that these quotations were carefully selected as expressions of the significance of the poem for Browning. DeVane translated the Greek quotations as follows:

And reading this doubtful word he has dark night before his eyes, and he is nothing clearer by day.

To what words are you turned, for a barbarian nature would not receive them. For bearing new words to the Scaeans you would spend them in vain.[7]

The second quotation obviously expresses Browning's bitterness at the reception of *Fifine*. What has not been recognized is the validity of the implied claim that *Fifine* is "new words"—that it gives expression to a cluster of conceptions radically new and deeply disturbing even for so audacious a mid-Victorian as Browning. The first quotation, passing strange as it may seem, records an aspect of Browning's own response to his achievement. A major concern of the study undertaken here will be to demonstrate that what brought "dark night before his eyes" was light, that in *Fifine at the Fair* Browning's intellect illuminated a realm which his temperament would not permit him to deny but which it could not assimilate. Browning's explosive energies engender here their most radical implications, issuing in a conception of human culture, veiled in symbol, which Victorian reticence made almost unthinkable and which would be realized and overtly articulated by other thinkers only in the twentieth century.

Yet if personal needs had not been powerfully at work in the poem, there would have been no light. Indeed, the poem may in a sense be called an epic of the second half of the nineteenth century, but because it lies close to Browning's secret life it is in part a crippled epic. For related reasons, it may be structurally the most complex and difficult long poem in the language, *Sordello* notwithstanding.

Complexity evolves in part from extreme tension between the poem's larger elements—the dramatic framework, the symbolic development, and the pattern of direct statement. The poem is also informed, and to some degree distorted, by a striking conflict between intellect and temperament. These tensions are implicated in a pervasive strategy of disguise. Within the context of such pressures the poem achieves some of the most intense poetry and some of the most plangent lyricism in all Browning's work. So one may recognize not only a strange element of failure but also a rare kind of virtuosity. As a technical performance *Fifine at the Fair* is in some respects Browning's supreme achievement. Nevertheless, it presents a problem which affects its claim to autonomy as a work of art and which eventually determines the critical approach capable of dealing with the poem in its entirety. To seek unity in the isolated text leads inevitably to the conclusion that a hypothesis is missing. That conclusion rests upon considerations the introduction of which early in the study will be burdensome to the reader but will ease his progress thereafter. It will be helpful to observe first the form of the poem and the content of its dramatic action.

Superficially, the form of the poem is the dramatic monologue, but this form is a very frail external framework for what actually happens in the poem. The headnote is a quotation from Molière's *Don Juan* and within the poem the wife, the not-quite-silent auditor, is named Elvire, as in Molière. The speaker refers to himself at one point as "Don and Duke" (XII, 129) and is presumably Don Juan. But his relationship to the character of Molière's play and to the Don Juan of legend is extremely tenuous, its limitations defined by the frailty of the dramatic action.

The speaker invites Elvire to go with him to the fair at Pornic. They are suddenly at the fair and the speaker's discourse begins. He is at first intrigued by the happy criminality of the lives of the itinerant entertainers at the fair. He is especially attracted by one of them, Fifine, a gypsy dancing girl. Insofar as the remainder of the poem (and that is to say most of it) may be characterized as relevant to the dramatic content, it consists of the speaker's effort to justify to the wife his interest in Fifine. (What occurs in this discourse is referred to, appropriately, as a quest. Exploration of the nature and result of the quest is a primary concern of this study.) At the fair we catch a few glimpses of Fifine. Twice during the poem the wife is imagined as objecting to the speaker's arguments, the speech enclosed in quotation marks. Less than halfway through the poem (LXII), we are aware that at sunset man and wife have departed the fair and are returning home. From the speaker's discourse there emerge brief indications of scenes along the way. Always the scenery serves the symbolic development. The scene treated most fully, that of "an ancient stone monument," is very hazy, partly because it is viewed near the end of dusk and partly because in response to symbolic exigencies it is obscurely dichotomized as two different monuments of radically different shapes. At one point the speaker engages the attention of a peasant boy whose comments we hear though they merely extend the symbolic development of the speaker's discourse. Eventually we learn that the speaker and wife have returned home. In the very last section of the poem (CXXXII), a passage of only fifteen lines, the dramatic element takes on its most vivid expression. The scene is ugly, the speaker giving a pretext for leaving to see Fifine but suggesting that he may not return. These last fifteen lines of the poem provide the only thematic reason for identifying the speaker with the legendary Don Juan, and in the epilogue we learn that this Don Juan has been painfully faithful after all. Such a summary of the action of the poem in isolation from the context exaggerates an element that is effectively absorbed in the internal poetry.

Browning divided the 2,355 alexandrine lines of the main body of the poem into 132 sections, varying in length from 1 1/2 to 102 lines. These divisions represent relatively small organic units in a very complex text. For the purpose of reference throughout this study, the sections will be grouped into six larger elements which will be referred to as "parts."

The six parts, with some working titles to facilitate reference, are as follows: part 1 (Modalities of Woman), prologue and sections I-XXXIV; part 2 (The Elegiac Process), sections XXXV-LX; part 3 (Affirmation of the World and the Flesh), sections LXI-LXXX; part 4 (Translation of the Quest into Mind), sections LXXXI-LXXXVIII; part 5 (The Cultural Vision), sections LXXXIX-CXXVI; part 6 (Abandonment of the Quest), sections CXXVII-CXXXII and epilogue.[8]

The question of the poem's unity is fundamental, and the first point to be emphasized is that its unifying elements are varied and complex. The most conspicuous device for giving thematic unity to the poem is a reference to a Greek play. Near the end of part 2 Browning quotes a line, first in Greek, then in his translation, from the *Prometheus Bound* of Aeschylus. The line, which will be referred to hereafter as the pivotal motto of the poem, is in Browning's translation: "God, man, or both together mixed" (LIX, 907). Later in the poem, at the end of part 5, the phrase occurs three times, twice in English, once in Greek (CXXIV, 2188; CXXV, 2210 and 2216). The phrase, seeming almost irresponsibly cryptic in its first appearance, links a crucial vision of heaven in part 2 with an earthly vision achieved as the culmination of the quest. While its unifying function is clear, the phrase seems awkwardly adapted to the purpose of the poem and quite fortuitous in its first, abrupt appearance. Browning apologizes: "For fun's sake, where the phrase has fastened, leave it fixed" (LIX, 906). Within the context of the poem, we will not find any special reason for this use of *Prometheus Bound* in a central unifying function. The fact is significant, and we will come to understand why the pivotal motto seems less organic than other unifying elements.

The prologue and the epilogue, though they may seem at first incidental to the poem, are profoundly integral with it. The prologue epitomizes the poem and the epilogue is its inevitable sequel. A single thematic link is crucial: the prologue and epilogue deal directly with a departed soul, a wife no longer living; the dead woman emerges repeatedly at the symbolic level of the poem. Imagery of the sea, though it is in abeyance in the climactic part 5, unites the poem from the beginning to end as well as linking it with the prologue. The poem moves from dualistic to monistic assumptions; this basic progression is accompanied by a succession of symbols for spirit which have increasing material density: light in part 2, air in part 3, water in part 5. In a related progression, dominant images integrate the various parts: light in part 2, water in part 3, stone in part 5. In part 5 the quest is translated into the realm of intellect; the poem makes a new beginning and when it does so, the vegetation and insect imagery with which the poem began is echoed and transformed (LXXXIX). Conspicuous at the beginning of the poem are the related images of tent and tower. These images occur again at the beginning of part 5, and their configuration is duplicated in the images of dolmen and menhir at the center of the poem's basic symbolic statement. The symbolism of tent and tower and of dolmen and menhir is the same. The image of Fifine, conspicuous in part 1 where she is associated with a question (XV, 149), is in part 5 the center of an epiphany which implies an answer (XCI). In a basic artistic strategy the poem recounts and adapts from the *Helen* of Euripides the legend that Helen went not to Troy but to Egypt, whence she returned to Greece with her husband, Menelaus (XXVII). The Helen story is echoed in part 2 in a passage about Eidotheé and again in part 4 when husband and wife are imagined as returning after a separation and being reunited in Athens (LXXXIII). The references to the Helen and Menelaus story in its narrative content may seem digressive at the dramatic level, but even at this level they are clearly part of an effort to unify. A conceptual rationale evolved in Christian imagery in the crucial vision of heaven (LIX) in part 2 is translated into pagan imagery in part 4. Architecture shaken and endangered at the end of part 3 anticipates the collapse of architecture in part 5 and the thematic associations are the same. Fundamental to the poem is a psychological assimilation of woman as sexual being which is initiated in the symbolic movement of part 1. It is paralleled by a comparable intellectual assimilation in part 5.

Both the intensity of the poetry and pervasive unifying elements indicate the presence in the poem of a powerfully integrative energy incompatible with a digressive style or an episodic plan, and yet we must recognize in the poem important elements which cannot be unified with the rest of the poem on the basis of the text alone.

Stated in the most general terms, the internal incoherence of *Fifine at the Fair* is manifest chiefly in the circumstance that while the symbolic development is essentially consistent in itself, it cannot be made consistent with the poem's dramatic elements. In the dramatic situation a speaker addresses a living wife; recurrent in the poem is the conception of a beloved woman who has died. Though this conception is consistent with the prologue and the epilogue, and though the poet is aware of the problem, and attempts to resolve it, the dramatic situation offers no explanation for it. One might attempt to reconcile this conception to the dramatic situation by a hypothesis concerning the speaker's hostility to the dramatic wife, but such an attempt will be frustrated by the nature of the imagery related to the beloved woman who has been lost. In one passage she emerges in imagery of death which is positively necrotic; she grows into life by a process of memory and becomes the object of an expression of love the genuineness of which cannot be questioned (XXXVII-XXXIX). At three points, separated within the text, the image of the lost beloved includes the imagery of a "rillet" or brook. In the first instance, the image is associated with young love and the deepening of spiritual into sensual love (XXXII, 453-54). The second instance suggests love in its maturity (XXXIX, 620-22). The third instance, unmistakably touched with grief, depicts symbolically the death of the beloved (LXXIII).

Early in the poem, Browning undertakes what will be referred to as "the strategy of the phantom wife" (XXVII). The purpose of this strategy is to achieve a refraction of the identity of Elvire which will permit the speaker to consider and address her in two modes, one of them corresponding to the experience of love reflected in the

conception of the dead beloved, the other expressing frustrations of
the present. Only by this very audacious strategy does the poem
become possible at all. It is a device mediating between the symbolic and dramatic components of the poem. The device provides continuity between the symbolic development of the central poem and
the dead wife of the prologue and epilogue, but nothing in the dramatic element of the poem will make this continuity intelligible.
The facts are that at the dramatic level the wife is living but much
of the symbolic development is concerned with a woman who is
dead. The poem does not identify the dead woman in any way. The
incongruity is fundamental, as may be seen in connection with the
development of the strategy of the phantom wife.

The strategy of the phantom wife is developed in the course of a
symbolic episode which will be referred to as "the pageant of wom-
en worthies" (XIX-XXXIII), the imagined participants in which
represent modalities of woman in subjective experience. The participants in the pageant are Helen, Cleopatra, a "Saint" viewed on the
top of a church steeple and in her shrine below, the wife explicitly
designated as "phantom wife," and Fifine. In the development of
this pageant the "Saint," in spite of the ascetic associations of sainthood, represents young love in that moment when spiritual passion
deepens into physical passion. Next in sequence is the phantom
wife, who represents mature love inclusive of the matrimonial
stresses subversive of love. It becomes clear that the sequence of
"Saint" and "phantom wife" (XXXII-XXXIII) represents the continuity of a single experience. This sequence contemplates, as though
subliminally, experience spanning part of a lifetime. The symbolic
development of which these sequences are a part culminates in the
vision in which the speaker is united in heaven with the lover who
has preceded him there (LIX). Inevitably we become aware of a
symbolic process which may be called elegiac in the sense that the
purpose of elegy is both reconciliation to and realization of a death.
The elegiac process is further evidence of the thematic irrelevance
of the symbolic development to the living wife of the dramatic
structure.

The dramatic elements are also essentially irrelevant to major
thematic aspects of the poem. An invariable pattern frequently re-

peated is that in which expressions of love are followed by expressions of hostility and anger. This pattern would seem to require for its explanation the ambivalence of a particular psychic organization experiencing inhibition and frustration. We would expect such a distinctive psychic condition to be a marked trait of a character fully developed and vividly portrayed. The character of the speaker, however, remains vague and shadowy. The paucity of characterization in the poem has been repeatedly observed, and this condition can puzzle the reader.[9] The identification of the speaker as Don Juan though tenuous is unmistakable, and yet it is understandable that Edward Dowden should find the designation of the speaker as Don Juan a misnomer and Roma King should find it misleading.[10] The truth is that diverse identifications of the speaker seem to cancel each other out. Despite the formal identification of the speaker as Don Juan, the ostensible purpose of his discourse throughout the poem is to justify simply a passing interest in Fifine, a faint infidelity of the imagination. One reason the character tends to disappear is that this ostensible purpose gives way to larger and more interesting themes. In another sense, the character is forgotten both in the intensity of the poetry and in the magnitude of the symbolism that emerges in his discourse. This is not properly a failure of characterization. Radically limited characterization is a requirement of the plan of the poem, for the dramatic elements of the poem are only a disguise and a subordinate framework for the symbolic development that is the poem's real substance. Our understanding gains nothing from an effort to explain the pattern of love and hostility by reference to the psychological organization of the speaker.

Although the pattern in which expressions of love are followed by expressions of hostility will be referred to hereafter as "the ambivalent pattern," the pattern lacks an important characteristic of ambivalence: in every instance the two expressions, of love and of hostility, are each discrete; they do not influence and modify each other but appear to be unrelated, and consequently the reader will be surprised and confused by their conjunction. Furthermore, the ambivalent pattern is usually without dramatic consequence. In its climactic occurrence at the end of part 3 it is as though a singer has a temper tantrum on stage and then abruptly resumes her song. The diverse experiences of love and hostility must arise from reactions to some single circumstance by radically distinct modes of imagination which are nowhere identified or accounted for within the poem.

Directly related to the ambivalent pattern is another major characteristic. The central experience of the poem, referred to as the quest (CXXIX, 2292), is sustained throughout most of the poem. Despite the rather strange interruptions by the ambivalent pattern there is an essentially continuous sense of forward movement, of hope and anticipation. But in the final sections of the poem (CXXVII-CXXXII) the quest is abandoned and the text fails to justify or make intelligible this radical turn. The poem celebrates lyrically (CXXIV) the intellectual achievement in which the quest culminates. After the speaker has abandoned the quest, he explicitly affirms that the intellectual achievement of the quest is valid and that it by no means implies the renunciation which is its sequel (CXXVIII, 2247-52). After the renunciation, rationalizations based upon the accomplished fact attempt to justify it (CXXVIII, 2257-81). That these rationalizations are inadequate is suggested by the fact that the renunciation is unstable. What has been given up in the quest is recalled with a sense of grief (CXXXI, 2321-24) and the renunciation is repeatedly associated with death (CXXIX, CXXX, CXXXI). Then in the final lines with a recurrence of the ambivalent pattern, the renunciation is in turn renounced. But there is yet another turn, and renunciation, in despair, is the theme of the epilogue. Obviously, powerful psychological forces are at work, but despite this, or perhaps because of it, the character of the speaker remains nebulous.

There are yet other problems. The dramatic elements of the poem may not be dismissed. The discursive spirit of the dramatic monologue is overwhelmed in an efflorescence of symbolism and in this sense the dramatic monologue collapses; yet its formal character is rigorously maintained. Only the speaker speaks; we hear what others say and what other characters imagine yet other characters to say, but their words are always in quotation marks or in quotations marks within quotation marks. It is at this formal level that the speaker has his identity as Don Juan. If we accept the dramatic elements at face value or even if we take the additional step of translating Don Juan into a man who wishes to justify a fancied infidelity and whose interest in Fifine is only intellectual, much of the poem will remain digressive—for instance, the following: a depiction of three drawings in the sand said to represent "my three prime types of beauty," but relevant to no conceivable aesthetic theory (XLVII, XLVIII, XLIX); a protracted image of the poet Arion in triumph, this image associated with patently deliberate sexual imagery (LXXVIII); a passage recalling the counsel of Eidotheé to Menelaus as she assists him in his escape from the isle (LII, 780-87); an identification of Elvire with Horace and the speaker's characterization of himself as "your Virgil of a spouse" (LXXXII-LXXXIII). There is the additional difficulty that certain passages which seem at first coherent with the dramatic circumstance turn out to be irrelevant to it when we examine carefully the substance of their argument.

To interpret means to explain the relationships of parts to each other and to a whole. Interpretation is necessarily interpretation of a unit. The effort to interpret must always begin with the assumption of the unity of what we find in the text. That operational canon is so basic that we may abandon it only with bad conscience, but in studying *Fifine* we will do so inevitably or we will remain content with generalized assertions which cannot be proved. Despite varied and complex elements tending to unity, *Fifine at the Fair* is not a unit, not a whole. It is a part, integral with a whole that extends beyond it. Various of its parts manifest no relationship whatsoever to other parts and with reference to the text alone they are inexplicable. A hypothetical whole may be achieved by combining the content of the text with an assumed dynamism in the relationship between the poet and the developing text. Within the resulting hypothetical whole all the parts become coherent with each other and with the whole. The coherence of the resulting whole gives to the hypothesis a claim to validity, the basis of which is more circumstantial than that of most assumptions underlying literary criticism.

The relationship which must be assumed to have existed between the poet and the text is as follows: the quest developed as a partial and disguised objectification of an incipient emotional reorientation, filled with hope but carrying the seeds of its failure. The poet reacted repeatedly to the developing symbolism, recording his reaction in the text while refusing to provide objective representation of the total experience from which his reaction arose. The incompleteness of *Fifine at the Fair* as the objective representation of a subjective condition and process must be considered an artistic flaw of magnitude though the work is a lavish display of artistic power. The dramatic structure is a device for disguise and distancing, but the symbolic substance overwhelms the tensions in which Browning attempted during most of his career to separate his art and his life. The poem represents an extraordinary, perhaps a unique, interplay of the realms of artistic imagination and personal experience. The poem explicitly recognizes this interplay, as will be demonstrated in later chapters. Browning's intimate and disruptive participation in the process of the poem arises from the fact that the substance of *Fifine* was of the greatest personal importance to him but incompatible with his art as developed in the great dramatic monologues of the middle period and *The Ring and the Book*.

The hypothesis fundamental to the study may be stated as follows: Despite the strains of the last years of his marriage, Browning dearly loved his wife.[11] In the London years following Elizabeth's death, her absence, despite his perpetual round as a dinner guest, filled his solitude with an aching loneliness, but a sense of loyalty to her became identified with profound inhibitions from which he suffered all his life and from which he longed fervently to escape. Thus the powerful influence of her memory involved a deep ambivalence, in recurrent moments of intense recollection bringing back to him the warmth and strength of love, but more generally seeming to frustrate the need of that warmth and strength in the daily substance of his life. *Fifine at the Fair* expresses, and in some large measure constitutes, Browning's effort to escape the combined and undifferentiated effects of memory and inhibition while yet remaining loyal to the memory of Elizabeth. Finally, in the last lines of the epilogue, the poem records the failure of that effort.

It is difficult to find words for description of the goal of the quest which are consonant with the Victorian milieu from which

Browning momentarily escaped and with that aspect of the twentieth century toward which he moved. Plato's terms may help. We
may say that the quest is the pursuit of Eros. We may choose to
think of Eros in his more general aspect as him by whom "all is
bound together."[12] Then we may say that the object of the quest is a
condition of health in which there will be repaired a debilitating divorce between Eros and Aphrodite, specifically, "the common
Aphrodite." The divorce is experienced primarily as personal and
psychological. Stated in other terms, the quest in *Fifine* is a final as-
sault upon the problem Browning analyzed in his explanation of
the failure of Sordello. In a remarkable description of repression in
book VI of *Sordello*, Browning used the term *soul* as we would use
the unconscious:[13]

> . . . *let the Soul attempt sublime*
> *Matter beyond its scheme and so prevent*
> *Or more or less that deed's [joy's] accomplishment,*
> *And Sorrow follows: Sorrow to avoid—*
> *Let the Employer match the thing Employed,*
> *Fit to the finite his infinity.* (VI, 494-99)

> . . . *the Body was to be so long*
> *Youthful, no longer—but, since no control*
> *Tied to that Body's purposes his Soul,*
> *It chose to understand the Body's trade*
> *More than the Body's self.* (508-12)

> *The soul must needs instruct its weak compeer,*
> *Run o'er its capabilities and wring*
> *A joy thence it holds worth experiencing—*
> *Which, far from half discovered even,—lo*
> *The minute's gone, the body's power's let go.* (516-20)

> *And the result is, the poor Body soon*
> *Sinks under what was meant a wondrous boon,*
> *Leaving its bright accomplice all aghast.* (547-49)

> *Must life be ever but escaped, which should*
> *Have been enjoyed? nay, might have been and would,*
> *Once ordered rightly, and a Soul's no whit*
> *More than the Body's purpose under it.* (561-64)

The main development of *Fifine* is a process of realization bringing eventually a liberation of the unconscious to which Browning could give intellectual and imaginative assent but to which he could not adjust the pattern of his life. There resulted, nevertheless, a magnificent intellectual achievement and a rare manifestation of the nature of art illuminated by its failure.

The procedure of applying the basic hypothesis of this study is subject to a number of caveats. The poem is not being approached for its biographical interest; rather, recourse has been made to biography to achieve a perspective in which the poem becomes fully coherent. Accordingly, it is not within the scope of the study to take interest in the cause of the inhibitions assumed in its basic hypothesis beyond pointing out that various explanations are available.[14] Furthermore, this study is not an effort at depth analysis. I assume that the considerable amount of sexual symbolism in the poem is readily comprehensible from the simplest and most limited knowledge of the nature of symbolism and that Browning used this symbolism in full consciousness of its meaning, though he probably assumed that it would evade conscious recognition by most of his readers.

The essential biographical significance of the poem is neither simple nor obvious, and Roma King is certainly right in arguing against the idea "that Elvire *is* Elizabeth or that Don Juan is Browning."[15] Such naïve identification is not to be expected in such a poem. The characters are fictional points in an emotional pattern. This study argues that the pattern was of crucial personal importance for Browning and that recognition of this is essential to understanding the poem. It will be conclusively demonstrated that Elizabeth is pervasively present in the poem in a way that has not been previously suspected. The dramatic wife, the phantom wife, and in some sense Fifine, all represent some aspect of the meaning of Elizabeth for Browning in the early seventies. This is true though the eventual achievement of the poem transcends personal meaning.

The biographical significance of *Fifine* has been sentimentalized and distorted, but some of its dimensions have been reliably recognized from the first, especially the relationship of Elizabeth to the prologue and the epilogue, which seems all but obvious.[16] As the result of the work of W. O. Raymond, any treatment of the poem must confront the significance for it of Louisa Lady Ashburton. Professor Raymond points to the close coincidence in time between the writing of *Fifine* and Browning's relationship with Lady Ashburton. The crucial episode in this relationship may not yet be fully understood, notwithstanding the recent effort of William Whitla to clarify it. We have Browning's testimony that he proposed to Lady Ashburton, accompanying his proposal, directly or indirectly, by an explanation that his "heart was buried in Florence, and the attractiveness of marriage with her lay in its advantage to Pen."[17] This seems incredible, and yet it may have the ring of that letter in which Browning first broached the question of marriage to Elizabeth, reassuring her and perhaps himself: "I would be no more than one of your brothers—*no more.*' "[18] Whatever the nature of the proposal, Lady Ashburton reacted in anger and the resulting alienation between the two was permanent and embittered on both sides. According to Raymond, Browning in later years interpreted this episode as a betrayal of his loyalty to the dead Elizabeth. It is certain that for the rest of his life Browning's references to Lady Ashburton and the episode with her were brutal—"that contemptible Lady Ashburton" (1874), "her character as a calumniator" (1886), "an odious experience" (1886), "a hateful subject" (1887).[19] Raymond, with DeVane's approval, proposes that "the elaborate similes and metaphors of *Fifine* . . . are often linked in thought and mood with Browning's dark brooding over his recent innocent but bitterly regretted lapse of constancy."[20] Raymond is not specific about "the elaborate similes and metaphors" but his interpretation would seem to be undeniable if it is applied only to a single brief passage of the poem in section CXXIX. This passage, however, follows the abandonment of the quest, and only by recognizing that fact can Raymond's interpretation be made consistent in any measure with the present reading of the poem. To assume, as Raymond suggests, that Browning's remorse over his "lapse of constancy" was the basic impulse of the poem is to leave it in irremediable disarray and to totally obscure its achievement.

It is quite possible that Browning's relationship to Lady Ashburton informs the entire body of the poem, but what the main body of it reflects is something quite opposite to a "bitterly regretted lapse of constancy." It is quest for Eros. The quest fails; then there occurs a fleeting regret of the lapse of constancy, this all but lost in the instability of the renunciation.

The point of importance here is that all possible interpretations of the Lady Ashburton affair thus far proposed lend credibility to the hypothesis necessary to a coherent reading of the poem. The second lady Ashburton reflected in portraits and written records was as unlike Elizabeth Barrett as can be imagined. She was a vital, vigorous woman of feminine abundance and striking, sensual beauty. She was a widow when Browning knew her and very rich. Browning proposed to her in September 1869 with disastrous effect. At her initiative, they met again at her home at Loch Luichart on October 2, 1871, but they were not reconciled. Some weeks later, in December 1871, Browning began writing *Fifine at the Fair*.[21] If Lady Ashburton was associated in Browning's mind with Fifine, then a part of her meaning for him was the possibility of the fulfillment of a very great need—a need which conceivably any number of women might have fulfilled.

In any event, we do not need Lady Ashburton to understand the meaning of Fifine. It is sufficient that Fifine is, as DeVane says, "the perfect representative of the flesh.[22] But to understand Browning's treatment of the wife Elvire, we must understand his relationship to Elizabeth, and the most persuasive external evidence supporting a biographical reading of the poem is in its relationship to the love letters of the Browning courtship, a relationship which will be examined in detail in chapter 2, below.

Further consideration may be given now to separate elements essential to understanding the poem. Attention has been called to the strategy of the phantom wife, a strategy for refraction of the identity of the wife in dichotomous images of "the phantom wife" on the one hand and on the other "the tearful true Elvire" (XXVII, 326). The distinction corresponds to two dominant modalities in which the speaker experiences the wife, and in order to illuminate the significance of this dichotomization a distinction will be maintained throughout this study between "the phantom wife" and "the dramatic wife." It is a generally valid rule of the poem that the phantom wife is the wife spoken about and the dramatic wife is the wife spoken to. The phantom wife is described; she is the wife who is seen. The dramatic wife is the wife who speaks. It is essential to the writer's strategy, however, that the distinction be sometimes blurred and it is essential to the experience of the poem that eventually the phantom wife and the dramatic wife are unified in a single image (CXXX). The refraction of identity is fundamental to the poem.

The phantom wife, the wife who is described, discussed, and reflected in poetic images, is the Elizabeth of the past in all the sympathetic aspects in which Browning can remember her. She is an object of love. The dramatic wife is the Elizabeth of the present identified with an element of psychic inhibition. She is an object of hostility. The phantom wife is part of the symbolic development of the speaker's discourse. When he turns on his companion in contempt or anger, we are drawn quickly back to the dramatic level of the poem. If we read the poem as fundamentally dramatic, this turn will be bewildering and may seem an expression of sophistry. It is in reality the expression of a spiritual ordeal. The refraction of the identity of the wife is the primary means by which the dramatic structure is subordinated to the thematic development which it disguises and thus makes possible.

The dramatic structure, however frail, stands between the reader and the meaning of the poem. Another obstacle also intrudes. Three distinct elements of the poem may be designated as dramatic, symbolic, and discursive. The basic development of the poem is in symbolism, but between symbolic movements, there are intervals of discursive comment. The subject is often the nature of truth, and at crucial points the apparent effect of the discussion is to negate the implications of associated symbolism. This effect is due to an inversion of the meaning of words to the extent that "truth" is represented, in effect, by the word "lie" (LXXVI, LXXXVI, CXXIV). The poem can be made fully understandable only by clarification of this extraordinary circumstance, which is the purpose of chapter 3. The inversion of terms is part of an effort to reconcile tensions between intellect and temperament which are fundamental to the poem and also unquestionably a part of the poem's strategy of disguise. It also reflects a verbal tendency evident in Browning as early as *Sordello*.[23] The depth of Browning's need for disguise in *Fifine* is reflected in the fact that the poem's extraordinary intellectual realization is expressed only symbolically and is never given abstract articulation.

After examining the relevance of the love letters to *Fifine* in chapter 2 and distinguishing the various meanings of "truth" in the poem in chapter 3, the study will proceed to a close sequential reading of the poem. Then chapter 10 will describe the basic structure of Browning's poetry and indicate the unique relationship of *Fifine* to that structure. The concluding chapter will touch upon the relationship of the poem to the cultural history of the time.

2

'Fifine' and the Love Letters

The fundamental argument for the hypothesis basic to this study is that this hypothesis, and it alone, can give coherence to the poem and that it will explain all the facts embodied in the poem. This is a powerful and perhaps a sufficient argument. However, the hypothesis may be further strengthened if its implications are consistent with the poet's experience as reflected in documentary evidence external to the poem.

The hypothesis assumes psychological factors which imply that in the poem the poet lived once again through essential elements of an earlier experience necessarily related to the love letters written some thirty years previously. It is therefore highly probable that there should be similarities of some sort between *Fifine* and the letters. Parallels are in fact so striking as to suggest not only that there is a thematic correspondence but also that Browning had been reading the letters at about the time that he began writing *Fifine*.

As had been indicated, the conception of the phantom wife provides an essential key to the poem. The conception of Elizabeth as a phantom, or as an imagined presence, is frequent in the letters: "How often, how *always* I turn in the dusk and *see* the dearest real Ba with me."[1] Association of the phantom with dusk is echoed in *Fifine* (CXXX). Usually in the letters the phantom Ba is imagined as sitting in a gondola chair in the young Browning's room at home, and this may provide for the poet a concealed element of continuity in the Venetian dream vision beginning in section XCIV of *Fifine*. In one form or another the notion of Ba as phantom, as imagined presence, occurs in letters of both Robert and Elizabeth at least eleven times over a period of eight months.[2]

The phantom wife of the poem as participant in an imagined pageant of "well-sung women worthies" (XIX, 208) is identified with a saint: "Pish! Whatever Saint you please" (XX, 228). She is seen first "cold pinnacled" on the spire of a church. Elizabeth, nervous about concealing her relationship to Robert in a forthcoming carriage drive with her cousin and benefactor Mr. Kenyon, wrote as follows: "*Ora pro me* in Mr. Kenyon's carriage to-day. . . . I shall feel all the while as if set on a vane on the top of St. Paul's . . . can you fancy the feeling?"[3]

The Saint on her spire has been "conversant with naught but wind and rains" (XX, 233); in her shrine below she is all but overwhelmed with snow. In the letters, bad weather—snow and especially the east wind—came to be symbolically identified with Elizabeth's bad health, and fair weather with her hope for recovery. Robert wrote to her, "You shall laugh at east wind yet as I do."[4] Elizabeth, apologizing for an expression of pessimism, explained, "The sense of mortality, and discomfort of it, is particularly strong when east winds are blowing and waters freezing." As the portrait of the Saint develops in *Fifine*, words are attributed to her which are totally fortuitous in context·and can have no purpose other than symbolic identification. She says, " 'I looked for scarce so much from earth!' " (XX, 236). Thus is paraphrased what Elizabeth repeatedly avowed of Robert's love. Elizabeth wrote, "I had done *living*, I thought, when you came and sought me out."[5] As though further to symbolize the identity of the Saint, the poet has her comment on the nudity of Fifine, " 'She must have stripped herself only to clothe the poor' " (XX, 245). This can only reflect Browning's growing conviction in the years following Elizabeth's death of her essential naïveté.[6] Another image in the poem which must be applied to the phantom wife as an aspect of Elizabeth is that of Eidotheé, whose name means divine idea and who is represented first as a sculpture by Michelangelo (LII) but then conceived more abstractly as an idealization of one beloved, an idealization especially distinguished from the objective reality of that person, and retained as a possession of the soul when the beloved has been lost (LVII). In the letters, Elizabeth treats repeatedly the notion that what Robert loves is an idealization: "You see in me what is not:—*that* I know."[7] The dramatic wife of the poem twice makes the same protest, in sections XL and LIII. Elizabeth writes as follows: "I thought you did not love me at all—you loved out into the air, I thought —a love *a priori*, as the philosophers might say, and not by *induction* any wise!" Robert, undaunted by possible errors of idealization, celebrated his possession of Elizabeth as a conception: "I have your memory, the knowledge of you, idea of you printing into my heart and brain,—on that, I can live my life."[8] A poetic elaboration of this sentence constitutes the treatment of Eidotheé in the poem (LVII). Both here and elsewhere (LII) Eidotheé is associated with sculpture. Elizabeth explained the powerful impression of sculpture on her as follows: "Then there is a great deal, of course, in that grand white repose! Like the Ideas of the Platonic system, those great sculptures seem."[9]

The Eidotheé sequence (LII-LIX) culminates in a vision in which the speaker is reunited with the lost lover in heaven. The dominant imagery here is that of varicolored hues of the world fusing in the white light of heaven (LIX). This imagery appears first in the letters and later in the essay on Shelley and in *The Ring and the Book*. Robert wrote to Elizabeth: "You speak out, *you*,—I only make men & and women speak—give you truth broken into prismatic hues, and fear the pure white light, even if it is in me: but I am going to try." Somewhat later Elizabeth, with percipient hesitation, encouraged Robert to express himself directly in nondramatic poetry: "How these broken lights and forms look strange and unlike now to me, when I stand by the complete idea. Yes, *now* I feel that no one can know you worthily by those poems. . . . *Now* let us have your own voice speaking of yourself—if the voice may not hurt the speaker—which is my fear."[10]

For Browning the white light of the artist would be, as F. R. G. Duckworth says, "the absolute truth or the whole truth," and thus, in the words of the Shelley essay, "not what man sees, but what God sees."[11] The speaker of *Fifine*, protesting his loyalty in elegiac tones, imagines joining his departed spouse in a fusion of the white light of heaven (LIX). Later, however, he relinquishes hope of knowledge of such truth in this world: "Why, reasonably, then / Comes the great clearing-up. Wait threescore years and ten!" (LXXXVI, 1515-16).

A number of especially vivid images are identical in the letters and the poem. An elegiac image in the poem is that of a pearl "let negligently slip away into the wave!" (XXXIX, 614). The pearl is one of Browning's images for Elizabeth: "So let me kiss you, my pearl of women." The possibility of one lover's losing the other is repeatedly imaged as losing a pearl or a "jewel" in the sea. Robert, reassuring Elizabeth who wanted him not to feel "entangled," writes, "My pearl lies in my hand—I may return it to the sea, if I will." In the letters, too, this loss is imagined as occurring carelessly, as in *Fifine*. Robert protests that he will not lose his "jewel" by letting it "drop into the sea through foolishly balancing it in my open hand over the water."[12] The imagery is made especially memorable by repetition in the letters of Elizabeth.[13]

In the poem a most unusual image depicts the relation of the soul to its material environment. This is the image of a piece of crystal which contains a drop of liquid at its center used by Druids, the poem says, for divination (CII, 1794-98). In the letters, Robert uses the image in characterizing the soul of Mr. Kenyon. Elizabeth repeats the image in her reply.[14]

The dominant imagery of *Fifine* is that of water and sea. This imagery is also conspicuous in the letters. It is sustained chiefly by the recurring image of the siren, derived from Landor's lines on Browning and eventually associated with Elizabeth and with what in Landor's lines comes to seem a prophecy of their flight to Italy.[15] Other water images present more specific parallels with the poem. On more than one occasion in the letters, water or the sea is associated with the inner being of Robert or Elizabeth. Robert asserts of himself that "underneath is a deep, a sea not to be moved." Elizabeth writes, "But deep down, deeper than the Sirens go, deep underneath the tides, *there*, I bless and love you." She had been "pure of wishes" but "now, they recoil back on me in a springtide . . flow back, wave upon wave, . . . till I should lose breath to speak them!"[16] The sea in *Fifine*, though abundantly rich in symbolism, is generally not associated with Elvire. The sea is the world of matter, "this wash o' the world" (LXVII, 1089). It is a source of vitality. Fifine as sexual vitality is associated with the sea—"the sea-Fifine"—and at one point the sea is the basis for intense sexual imagery (LXXVIII, 1309-20). As the realm of matter, the sea is also the element in which the lost beloved disappears—"only these atoms fleet, / Embittered evermore, to make the sea one drop / More big thereby" (LXXIII, 1210-12).

In contrast with the sea, the air above is spirit. The phantom wife is associated with air. Land is "the solid and safe" where "high and dry, we chafe / The body, and don the dress" (prologue). Land is associated with conventionality and with resignation and as such is associated with Elvire as the dramatic wife. Land is sometimes a conclusion, a terminating point providing a stance from which one may take pride or exult in his encounter with the sea. The swimmer in *Fifine* may "by and by / Leave wholly for the land, and there laugh, shake me dry / To last drop, saturate with noonday" (LXVI, 1073-75). Similarly in the letters Robert says at the conclusion of a metaphorical swim, "You may put foot on land, and draw breath, and think what a deep pond you have swum across."[17]

The symbolism of the sea in *Fifine* is pervasively consistent until at a moment near the end of the poem Elvire, suddenly in contrast with "Fifine, the foam-flake, she," is identified with "the sea's self" (CXXIX, 2299). It is difficult to believe that in this temporary shift symbolism has not given way to the memory of the letters. Robert had written, "My life and love flow steadily under all those bubbles." Of Elizabeth he said, "But *you* are the real deep wonder of a creature,—and I sail these paper boats on you rather impudently. But I always mean to be very grave one day."[18] The complete passage in which Elvire is suddenly identified with the sea reads as follows:

> Fifine, the foam-flake, she: Elvire, the sea's self, means
> Capacity at need to shower how many such!
> And yet we left her calm profundity, to clutch
> Foam-flutter, bell on bell, that, bursting at a touch,
> Blistered us for our pains. But wise, we want no more
> O' the fickle element. Enough of foam and roar!

> *Land-locked, we live and die henceforth: for here's the*
> *villa-door.* (CXXIX, 2299-305)

There are other parallels between the poem and the love letters. The "primæval monument" as developed in section CXXIV is perhaps colored by a memory of Stonehenge of whose "vague grand massiveness" Elizabeth wrote in her letter of Janaury 4, 1846. Elizabeth is symbolized by a butterfly in the prologue and thus Robert symbolizes her in a letter.[19] A number of images in the poem would seem to be distortions or transformations of images reflected from the letters, and in such instances, as in others, reference to the letters provides important keys to the poem. In the poem the word "Iostephanos," meaning "violet-crowned," appears as a place-name, the place having no existence outside the poem. The significance of Browning's use of the word is heightened by the fact that he used it as a name for a person in *Balaustion's Adventure*, a work directly associated with Elizabeth.[20] In the letters it appears, in Greek, as an adjective. Elizabeth referring to Browning's play *Luria* and to violets which Robert had left in a chair and which she had sat on, said, "If you have killed Luria as you helped to kill my violets, what shall I say, do you fancy?"[21] Thus the violets are united verbally with death. In the next sentence but one she uses the Greek, phrase for "violet-crowned muses"—(iostephanoi mousai). In the poem the phrase becomes a private code contributing to intense complexity of statement. To understand the passage in which the word appears, it is necessary to have in mind a number of previous developments in the poem. The speaker's ultimate loyalty to the wife has been symbolized in the conception of their eventual reunion in the afterlife (LIX). The Île Noirmoutier, across a stretch of water from Pornic, has been developed as a symbol of the obscure goal of death (LXIII, 986-90). In the lines preceding the passage to be quoted below, departure of the husband from the wife has been paralleled with the farewell to Virgil in Horace's *Ode* 1.3, the speaker in *Fifine* becoming "Your Virgil of a spouse" (LXXXII, 1438-41, and LXXXIII, 1446). Thus the speaker and the wife are cast as poets. In Browning's version, however, both poets are departing, at first separately, with a spiritual goal represented by Athens, then together from Pornic Town, and now as they have just "the strait to cross" their goal is the Île Noirmoutier, the dark convent, but it now has another name and the dark goal of death is somehow imbued with the spiritual triumph of poetry.

> Embark I trust we shall
> Together some fine day, and so, for good and all,
> Bid Pornic Town adieu, —then, just the strait to cross,
> And we reach harbor, safe, in Iostephanos! (LXXXIII, 1458-61)

In connection with other images from the letters distorted in the poem, it is important to keep in mind the deep ambivalence toward Elizabeth which informs the poem. In such passages as that on Iostephanos quoted above there is a tender and passionate love for the memory of Elizabeth, but in others there is a mordant anger of instincts frustrated by loyalty to a woman dead for a decade.

In an early letter, after the seriousness of Robert's intention had become quite clear, Elizabeth wrote: "You may force me to *feel*; . . . but you cannot force me to *think* contrary to my first thought . . . that it were better for you to forget me at once in one relation. And if better for *you*, can it bad for *me*?—which flings me down on the stone-pavement of the logicians."[22]

In some of the turns of his later ambivalence it must have seemed indeed to Browning that it would have been better. But he had not forgotten her then and it seemed that he could not now. He was growing old in the tangles of an inhibition in which her memory was implicated. In the Venetian dream vision, the speaker refers to old age, and there suddenly intrudes a remarkable simile:

> but, Age reduced to simple greed and guile,
> Worn apathetic else as some smooth slab, erewhile
> A clear-cut man-at-arms i' the pavement, till foot's tread
> Effaced the sculpture, left the stone you saw instead, —
> Was not that terrible beyond the mere uncouth? (XCV, 1703-7)

It would seem that here, as in the "Parleying with Frances Furini,"[23] and elsewhere in *Fifine*, symbols which were earlier related to female figures now refer to Browning himself.

The links discussed thus far between the poem and the letters provide an essential background for the most important link of all and one which does much to illuminate one of the most important facets of the poem. Elizabeth had produced a translation of *Prometheus Bound*, which was published in 1833 and reviewed in *Athenaeum* just nine weeks before an encouraging notice of *Pauline* appeared there.[24] Elizabeth recognized the deficiencies of this translation and at the time Robert met her had all but completed another. There are repeated references to the play and Elizabeth's new translation throughout their correspondence. The first occurs in Elizabeth's third letter, and the last, twelve days before the marriage. The play was one of the earliest literary interests they shared. In her fifth letter Elizabeth told Robert of the new translation and of a plan for "a monologue of Aeschylus."[25] It may have been Robert who eventually carried out this plan in the poem "Aeschylus' Soliloquy"—the authorship is not clear. In her sixth letter Elizabeth, as though eager for a subject with which to engage Robert's attention, asked his opinion on a critical point in *Prometheus*. He answered with enthusiasm and assurance, and in the same letter he told her of a plan he had had "once upon a time" to "restore" the *Prometheus Firebearer* as Shelley did the *Unbound* and described at length the story as he had imagined it. He thought that Elizabeth might be tempted by the theme; in her next letter she demurred.[26] Somewhat later, Browning read the manuscript of Elizabeth's new translation and she was both grateful for, and embarrassed by, the pages of comment he produced.[27] Elizabeth's second translation was not published until 1850, the year Robert published *Christmas-Eve and Easter-Day*, and so as a continuing potentiality the work remained for years in some measure a common literary interest for the Brownings, but to Robert reading or remembering the love letters, *Prometheus Bound* was more than a literary interest. Associations with the play were very personal, for from the very beginning and throughout the letters the play was a source of metaphor for the lovers writing to each other about each other and about themselves. In her third letter Elizabeth said of Browning's career that he had "not yet reached the prelude," taking the words somewhat awkwardly from Prometheus's comment in reciting the woes of Io.

In her fifth letter, writing in praise of Robert's dramatic powers, she took a phrase from the play: "but you ride your own faculty as Oceanus did his sea-horse 'directing it by your will.' "[28] Although for Robert on one occasion Elizabeth becomes, playfully, the "Ever-wandering Io," his use of lines from the play tends either to be impersonal or to place him at the center of the Aeschylean story in parallels between himself and the hero.[29] In the later stage of the courtship Robert used Promethean lines of proud defiance. Recalling Elizabeth's long-sustained insistence that he should abandon the courtship, he quoted, in Greek, "Thus upon scorners I retort their scorn."[30] Two weeks before the marriage Robert found it necessary to urge upon Elizabeth an early date for the marriage to avoid traveling in bad weather. He expressed his impatience under the restraining pressure of relatives and friends by quoting, again in Greek:

> *Oh, think no more*
> *That I, fear-struck by Zeus to a woman's mind*
> *Will supplicate him, loathed as he is,*
> *With feminine upliftings of my hands*
> *To break these chains. Far from me be the thought!* [31]

The lines will seem more apt when it is realized that the chains are an echo of the terms in which Elizabeth had finally accepted Robert's irrevocable commitment to her. The passage in which she did so might be taken as a foreshadowing of the present reading of *Fifine*. She casts Robert as Prometheus and herself as the silent character who helped Hephaestus chain Prometheus to the rock:

And therefore, as you have these thoughts reasonably or unreasonably, I shall punish you for them at once, & "chain" you . . (as you wish to be chained), chain you, rivet you—do you feel how the little fine chain twists round & round you? do you hear the stroke of the riveting?—& you may *feel that* too. Now it is done—now, you are chained—Bia has finished the work . . *I, Ba!* (observe the anagram!) and not a word do you say, O Prometheus, though you have the conscience of it all, I dare say. Well!—you must be pleased. . . . as it was "the weight of too much liberty" which offended you: & now you believe, perhaps, that I trust you, love you, & look to you over the heads of the whole living world, without any one head needing to stoop,—YOU MUST, if you please, because you belong to me now & shall believe as I choose.[32]

By inference, the poem's use of a direct quotation from the play gives rise to the image of the bound Prometheus as a central symbol. This symbol is generated by what has been called the pivotal motto of the poem. It is used five times in two particular places in the poem, quoted in each instance first in Greek then in translation. The phrase is used in connection with two culminating passages, the vision of heaven climaxing the elegiac movement of part 2 (LIX) and the dream vision of part 5 which formulates symbolically the central intellectual realization of the poem (CXXIV, CXXV). In the second instance the phrase is followed by what is the most nearly explicit statement of the intellectual import of the poem. In Aeschylus the phrase is part of the first speech of Prometheus, which occurs early in the play. At the end of the first part of his speech, Prometheus detects the approach of a presence. He cries out questioning the nature and purpose of the being which approaches. The phrase as it first occurs in *Fifine*, at the end of the vision of heaven, is as follows:

Theosutos e broteios eper kekramene,—
(For fun's sake, where the phrase has fastened, leave it fixed!
So soft it says,—"God, man, or both together mixed"!) (LIX, 905-7)

The alternatives—"God, man, or both together mixed"—pose a question which is not at all clear at the time of the first appearance of the phrase but which in Browning's context may be formulated in this way: What is the nature of consolation necessary to human vitality? Is it exclusively divine in its origin? Do both matter and spirit converge in vital experience? Does all depend eventually on physical fulfillment, on the gratification of man by woman in the flesh? The cryptic partial answer, insofar as it is ever explicit, may be indicated in connection with another parallel between the poem and the letters.

In Aeschylus it is the sea nymphs whose approach Prometheus had detected. They say to him:

> *Fear not: this is a company of friends*
> *that comes to your mountain with swift*
> *rivalry of wings.*
> *Hardly have we persuaded our Father's*
> *mind, and the quick-bearing winds*
> *speeded us hither. The sound*
> *of stroke of bronze rang through our cavern*
> *in its depths and it shook from us*
> *shamefaced modesty; unsandaled*
> *we have hastened on our chariot of wings.*[33]

In a tender passage, expressing love and gratitude for love, Elizabeth compared herself to the unsandaled ocean nymphs who came to console Prometheus:

> Yet when you tell me that I ought to know some things, tho' untold, you are wrong, & speak what is impossible. My imagination sits by the roadside $\alpha\pi\epsilon\delta\iota\lambda os$ [unsandaled] like the startled sea nymph in Aeschylus, but never dares to put one unsandalled foot, unbidden,—& never (I write the simple truth) even as the alternative of the probability of your ceasing to care for me, I have touched (untold) on the possibility of your caring *more* for me . . never! That you should *continue* to care, was the utmost of what I saw in that direction. So, when you spoke of a "strengthened feeling," judge how I listened with my heart—judge![34]

Browning's use of the same Aeschylean passage suggests another dimension of the meaning of Fifine. Fifine is the symbolic object of the fundamental impulse of the poem—male loneliness, the need of woman. The poem, in its deep ambivalence, makes abundantly clear that Elizabeth could have fulfilled this need, that the memory of her, stiffened now as a restraining influence, was also redolent of love and fulfillment. So Fifine, in a sense, represents an aspect of Elizabeth—Elizabeth as living sensual being. But Elizabeth is dead. Near the end of the poem the speaker, submitting to the spiritual hegemony of the phantom wife, pleads: "Be but flesh and blood, and smile to boot." Precisely because she continued to live for Browning as a spiritual reality, her nature as physical, sensual being was emphasized by absence. It will be understandable, and it is only superficially ironic, that a link between the letters and the poem becomes in part a link between Elizabeth and Fifine, as will be demonstrated in a passage to be examined in a later chapter.

The love letters draw our attention to yet another interest intimately related to the courtship, and one that provides additional perspective on *Fifine*. Browning was writing "The Flight of the Duchess" during the first part of the courtship. There are references to the poem in thirty-three letters over a period of eleven months. When Browning gave Elizabeth a finished draft, she proposed a total of seventy-three changes, of which Browning adopted all but four.[35] It has been suggested that Browning and Elizabeth should be considered coauthors of the poem and that the poem was a part of Browning's strategy of courtship.[36] In any event, the poem is a kind of prothalamium and its importance for the experience of the courtship is unquestionable. Therefore parallels between this poem and *Fifine* are of special interest.

The following elements occur in both *Fifine* and "The Flight of the Duchess": a) a duke who abuses his wife, b) a tall woman in ill health who obstructs love, c) a conspicuous expression of anger toward the woman who obstructs love, d) a gypsy who serves as an agent of liberation and the realization of love, e) the association of repression and debilitating influence with a false society, f) the identification of liberation and the realization of love with the achievement of reality, g) symbolization of reality in stone or stony land as a salient aspect of landscape, h) identification of an aspect of landscape with female sexuality, i) an image of the female object of love in a fetal position, j) a conception of sexual union and social unity as continuous, k) the image of a tree and a vine as representing the relation of lovers, l) a conception of the pursuit of love as a quest (a pilgrimage in "Flight of the Duchess"), m) association of the realization of love with pagan ritual, n) a vision of lovers reunited in heaven.

So extensive are the parallels between the poems as to encourage a comparison between their artistic techniques, specifically the technique of distancing. A primary means of accomplishing this in *Fifine* is that of suggesting by use of the headnote that the speaker is Don Juan. The primary means of distancing in "Flight" is the use of unusual rhyme and rhythm, which Elizabeth thought reflected a Greek influence.[37] The irregular rhyming is emphatic and awkward, bordering constantly on humor. It is strangely discordant with the substance of the poem. Butler's *Hudibras* may be at work here, but one may easily imagine that the more direct influence is the *Don Juan* of Lord Byron.

The links with the love letters, with *Prometheus Bound*, and with "The Flight of the Duchess" make unquestionable the personal significance of *Fifine at the Fair* to Browning and the presence of Elizabeth at the heart of the poem.

3
Truth

Before proceeding to a sequential examination of the poem, it is necessary to examine that aspect of it which presents the single greatest obstacle to a consistent reading. An acute difficulty lies in Browning's treatment of words and ideas involved in his conception of truth. The basic realizations of the poem are achieved through symbolism. With care, one can understand the symbolic development. But in passages where the speaker pauses in a kind of interlude to comment on a symbolic realization which has gone before or is to follow, we seem to confront semantic chaos. Browning's extreme practice in this respect suggests varied pressures making for complexity.

Most of the crucial developments of the poem give rise to a deep ambivalence and a radical conflict between intellect and temperament. This "boldest" of poems since *Sordello* is charged with a need for certainty which repeatedly expresses itself in emphatic declarations which the context seems sooner or later to invalidate. The poem pretends to metaphysics and deals in metaphysical conceptions, but its mode of operation is essentially intuitive. Intuition tends to passionate affirmations of conceptions dimly perceived. There are also the conflicting temperamental needs, often observed in Browning, both for secrecy and on the other hand for dogmatic, even obstreperous assertion. Henry James's story "The Private Life" is based upon the deep duality between man and poet which James observed in Browning. In a unique way Browning as poet and Browning as man are both present in *Fifine*. We must recognize, too, the reality of censorship in Victorian society, an influence with which Browning deals indirectly but bitterly and at some length in *Fifine*. All these factors may contribute to obscurity and to apparent confusion in the poem.

It is certainly significant that the intellectual realization of the poem, a conception which has had crucial importance in the twentieth century, is expressed only in symbolism so complex that it may not be fully understood in a first sequential reading. Passages of discursive reasoning occur repeatedly in the poem, with expression tending often to epigrammatic conciseness, but this conception, the culmination of the central development of the poem, is never given explicit articulation. Yet the immediate sequel to the development of this conception is a joyous celebration of discovery (CXXIV). We seem to witness expectation of public acclaim for a discovery that remains a secret and an insistence upon the social acceptability of a shocking proposal—shocking for the Victorian reader if he could have understood it.

Despite the conflicting elements within the poem, its central development is consistent. Apparent inconsistencies and resulting obscurity may be in part resolved on the basis of two considerations. To begin with, the poem is a quest; it is fundamentally developmental and there is no inconsistency in the fact that a position taken at one point is later contradicted. Furthermore, we must acknowledge the nature of the psychic and intellectual experience reflected here. We are not only told that truth is intuitive; we seem to experience the intuition from which a great symbolic realization arises. It is easy to imagine that knowledge from so intimate a source as intuition, and knowledge not permitted to escape from the secret world of symbol into the public world of discursive articulation, must seem to be a part of one's person, a part of his organism, and inevitably consistent with old habits of affirmation. Debarred from the reifying realm of public articulation, such knowledge must seem certain and yet strangely tenuous, its power of asserting its implications diminished by its exclusion from communal consciousness. In a passage introductory to the culminating realization of the poem, the speaker says, "I gave no idle guess / But gained a certitude, I yet may hardly keep" (1580-81).

With such considerations in mind we may more readily accept

the specific difficulties in the speaker's use of the basic words "true" and "truth."[1] They appear for a combined total of thirty-seven times. Conspicuously they appear in juxtaposition with their opposites, as in "the true and the false." The effect is an expectation of precision in metaphysical argument, but, as has been suggested, the underlying significance of these emphatic juxtapositions is a wish for certainty. Such words undergo chimerical changes, examination of which will throw some light on related difficulties and at the same time provide a further preview of the poem. Special attention must be given to the use of the words "true" and "truth" and to the meaning of truth as indicated in other contexts.

Basic to the elegiac movement in part 2 is the conception that the source of truth on earth is human subjectivity: "In the seeing soul, all worth lies" (LV, 824). This is made to seem consistent with a depiction of heaven (LIX) in accord with the dualistic Christian tradition adjusted on neoplatonic lines. Here the refracted variety of colors of the world are blended in "achromatic white," the white light as observed heretofore, which often represents truth in Browning's poetry and which is inevitably associated with "the pure white light of truth" the achievement of which, according to Elizabeth, would permit Browning to speak in his own voice. Later, in part 3, the speaker adapts this dualistic conception to an explanation of the meaning of matter and spirit for life in the world. The image he uses is that of a swimmer floating in a bay. The water represents matter, the "wash o' the world" (LXVII, 1089); the air above the sea represents spirit. Matter and the world are "the false"; spirit is "true" (LXV, 1041). This is the meaning usually denoted by the juxtaposition of the words "true" and "false" in the first half of the poem. It is unquestionably the meaning of any association of Fifine, "the sea-Fifine," with the false. The association is Platonic, not moralistic. To associate Fifine with "the false" serves the surface moral issue at the dramatic level but the essential meaning is that she is flesh and blood of this world. Even within the vision of heaven in part 2 there is a marked deterioration of the dualism necessary to such a vision, and in the course of the poem that dualism essentially disappears.

The dualism of part 2 is essentially symbolic, serving poetic and personal needs of the moment. To say this is to acknowledge that Browning's belief at the time of the writing of *Fifine* was essentially the same as that expressed in the "Parleying with George Bubb Dodington," where these words appear: "Exact the thing I call / Man's despot, just the Supernatural." I. e., belief in the supernatural is oppressive. Nothing of the supernatural intervenes in the order of nature or in human life. The assumptions of Browning's analyses of nature and the human psyche are naturalistic. A fact tending to confusion is Browning's proclivity to see all existence as numinous. He was apparently at all times willing to hypothesize a Something beyond, but except possibly for a few years before and after 1850, the Something was always definitely beyond, and Browning insisted, nowhere more emphatically than in *Fifine*, that we know nothing about the beyond.[2]

Throughout the poem, but especially in connection with the early dualism, the words "true" and "false" refer to inner and outer conditions. The culminating movement of the poem in part 5 achieves a monistic conception of the world, and accordingly we find new words for the inner and outer nature of men and things. In place of the juxtaposition of "the true" and "the false," there is the juxtaposition of "glories" and "shames," (CVIII, 1874, and CXVII, 2005) or in one instance, of "glory" and "stain" (CX, 1893-94). However, these "glories" and "shames" are "one stuff miscalled by different names" (CVIII, 1875). The knowledge achieved is of "truth inside, and outside, truth also" (CXXIV, 2182). The words "true" and "false" are given new meanings in the conception of "falsehood that is change, as truth is permanence" (CXXIV, 2183). We may be confused by the persistence of the use of these terms, first introduced in a dualistic context, unless we understand that the passage is a celebration of the monistic conception symbolically realized in part 5. The "permanence" here is the invariability of a power that resides in all things working in their forms a continuity of change. Eventually in the celebration of the "truth" of part 5, the word takes on its simplest modern meaning as fidelity in reporting the way things are. This truth, being universal and intuitively perceived,

"sets aside speech, act, time, place, indeed, but brings
Nakedly forward now the principle of things
Highest and least." (CXXIV, 2205-7)

Yet another meaning of truth appears in part 3. In the elaboration of the swimmer imagery here, the dualism it earlier represented, and thus the significance of the words "true" and "false," is
markedly qualified in accord with the more generally monistic tendency of Browning's thought. In this we confront a paradoxical relationship between what Browning tended to believe and the way
he insisted on feeling. The speaker explains that we are capable of
only so much knowledge of spirit as "to illude with hope" that we
may someday be absorbed into immortality. (Even this limited affirmation is equivocal, for the phrase "illude with hope" is at least
in some measure self-contradictory. One of the meanings of "illude" is to delude with false hopes.) Any effort to achieve spirituality which has spirituality as its conscious goal or which functions in
a medium or by an instrumentality assumed to be itself of a spiritual nature is self-defeating; it is "foiled by the very effort,
sowse, / Underneath ducks the soul, her truthward yearnings
dowse / Deeper in falsehood!" (LXV, 1049-51).[3] The further development of this idea is incompatible with the subjectivism elaborated in part 2 and that subjectivism was the basis for the conjecture
of the vision of heaven and the dualism which it represented. A
thesis of the swimmer imagery is quite simply that any exertion of
energy in the only realm available to life, the realm of matter, has
spiritual implications: "Move a mere hand to take waterweed, jelly-
fish, / Upward you tend!" (LXV, 1056-57). But the essential point is
driven home: "And yet our business with the sea / Is not with air,
but just o' the water, watery" (LXV, 1057-58).

The dualism of the swimmer imagery seems thus to be radically
qualified. This is in accord with the fact that the dualistic conceptions of part 2 are symbolic and with the fact that the arguments
of part 3 have been undertaken in default of a more dependable
approach to truth. "Words," the speaker said at the beginning,
"struggle with the weight / So feebly of the False, thick element be-

tween / Our soul, the True, and Truth" (LXI, 943-45). Music, the speaker argues, is the language of the truth.

With the restrictions of the dualistic implications of the swimmer imagery, there is suddenly introduced a new and entirely different meaning of "true" and "truth":

Now, there is one prime point (hear and be edified!)
One truth more true for me than any truth beside—
To-wit, that I am I, who have the power to swim. (LXVI, 1063-65)

The implications of this sense of ontological certainty will be examined more fully in a later chapter.[4] This "truth" more true than any other, this emphatic sense of self, is close to the heart of the poem. Early in the poem, the speaker proclaims that Fifine "shall make my thoughts be surer what they mean!" (XV, 149). Somewhat later (XIX, 199) these words are repeated. Fifine will provide, not the content of thought, but its affective value. Within the experience of the speaker, however, there are two special sources of this "truth" which is a certainty of self. They are "Elvire, Fifine," the first as the wife of memory, the phantom wife. The speaker says that they "convince unreasonable me / That I am, anyhow, a truth, though all else seem / And be not" (LXXX, 1357-59). To Elvire, conceived as the phantom wife, he says,

I can stand
Still, and let truth come back,—your steadying touch of hand
Assists me to remain self-centred, fixed amid
All on the move. (LXXX, 1360-63)

Then the speaker expresses his expectation of the same "truth" from Fifine before turning back to console Elvire, who becomes suddenly again the dramatic wife:

When, where, and how it is I shall see truth return,
That I expect to know, because Fifine knows me!—
How much more, if Elvire! (LXXX, 1369-71)

Somewhat later there is a moment darkly calm with anticipation of death—"How quickly night comes." It is like one of those moments more conspicuous in the latter part of the poem when there is a fusion of the characters of the dramatic and phantom wives. The speaker addresses Elvire gently:

> *Are you unterrified?*
> *All false, all fleeting too! And nowhere things abide,*
> *And everywhere we strain that things should stay,—the one*
> *Truth, that ourselves are true.* (LXXXIV, 1468-71)

Clearly, after the collapse and disappearance of the dualistic conception informing parts 2 and 3, the universe of the speaker is one in which there is external to the individual no general source of ontological support. In such a world, says J. Hillis Miller, speaking of the Victorian world, only in a relationship to another person can the individual come to know "the profound depths which are the secret ground of . . . selfhood."[5] We will therefore be impressed with the genuineness of the word "truth" at the last of those moments when in the realm of imagination the quest for Fifine has been fleetingly won. The speaker's imagination, unimpeded by earlier inhibiting elements, penetrates a symbolic realm of female secrecy to image Fifine in undress and young sensuality. Her meaning for him is that which proves "when finger finds out finger in the dark / O' the world, there's fire and life and truth there" (XCI, 1604-5).

After the speaker has entered into the intellectual adventure that makes up part 5 he pauses to rejoice in his analytic powers, comparing them to those of a chemist "tracing each effect back to its cause" (CIII, 1810). He is elated for two reasons. The specific conception of the organic, psychological, and cultural unity of man which he is in the process of elaborating symbolically would seem unquestionably to be original with Browning. (For possible influences see below, chap. 11.) If understood, it would have been Browning's original contribution to human thought and from any point of view it must be considered a conception of the first magnitude. Its achievement by a mid-Victorian seems almost incredible.

It is probable that in the realm of experience it came to seem an uncertain speculation. Browning could not test it. He could not even permit himself to give it explicit formulation. So it was "a certitude I yet may hardly keep" (XC, 1581). Yet it is a certitude, and in the poem pride in the development of the idea is unmistakable. The other reason for the speaker's pleasure is that this conception is a persuasive justification of Fifine; it is the climactic effort of the quest. Both a sense of intellectual achievement and a sense of achieving a basic human relationship are reflected as the speaker exults in his knowledge of his own being: "Just so I glut / My hunger both to be and know the thing I am" (CIII, 1814-15). This sense of self, of certainty of being, is the meaning consistently associated with truth. It is the meaning of a passage halfway through part 4 when the speaker at a point of frustration between the claims of the flesh and of the phantom wife, asserts, "I need to be proved true" (LXX, 1155). His condition is compared to "Descents to Hell" in which "nothing so confirms / One's faith in the prime point that one's alive, not dead" as when he confronts a "phantom" there, "male enemy or friend, / Or merely stranger-shade" (LXX, 1155-59).

The sense of self, of ontological certainty, is, of course, a condition emotionally or intuitively experienced. It is coherent with Browning's conception of intuition as the source of truth and this conception of truth accounts for the primacy he gives to music as a mode of expression. Music is associated with what may be referred to as the moments of truth experienced in *Fifine*. At the beginning of part 3 and serving as a thematic prelude to the rest of the poem, there is a passage of extraordinary poetry in which the human condition is experienced in unity with life and death, and nature expressed in animal existence (LXII-LXIII). In the beginning of this passage the speaker imagines sound—"Harmonics far and faint." It is a sound of "Reverberated notes whence we construct the scale / Embracing what we know and feel and are!" (LXII, 970-71). The climactic development of part 3 is the Arion passage (LXXVIII) celebrating sexual vitality and artistic power. After being saved from the sea by a dolphin ("the exquisite sea-thing"—"True woman creature"), Arion sings in Corinth. The power of his music menaces the architecture (which in part 5 collapses before a comparable force):

> *The pillar nods,*
> *Rocks roof, and trembles door, gigantic, post and jamb,*
> *As harp and voice rend air—the shattering dithyramb.*
>   (LXXVIII, 1301-3)

Part 5, the sustained symbolic elaboration of the basic intellectual achievement of the poem, invokes Schumann's *Carnaval* (XCI). At the end of part 5, the "truth" which has been realized is characterized as music. It is "some imperial chord" which "subsists, / Steadily underlies the accidental mists / Of music springing thence" (CXXIV, 2175-77).

In consonance with their intuitive origin, all these intimations of truth are expressed symbolically and are never given discursive formulation. The content of truth is utterly confined to the realm of symbol even though the speaker is repeatedly discursive on the nature of truth in the abstract. The somatic and instantaneous origin of truth is expressed with rigorous consistency. Truth is intuitive. It is also sensate. Dependence upon verbal communication poses a danger of accepting mankind's opinion of itself. In the dream-vision of Venice which makes up the first half of part 5, the crowd in Saint Mark's square is "dumb as death." "They spoke; but,—since on me devolved / To see, and understand by sight,—the vulgar speech / Might be dispensed with" (XCVIII, 1726-28). The explanation is that " 'Who sees not, hears and so / Gets to believe; myself it is that, seeing, know' " (1731-32). At the end of the dream-vision the speaker says "I ought / To simply say—'I saw,' each thing I say 'I thought' " (CXVIII, 2012-13).[6]

The conception of truth as intuitive is essential to Browning's emphasis upon the perception of truth as occurring at "the happy moment." The phrase occurs twice in widely separated passages, both of which are extremely difficult discursions on the nature of truth. Both passages reflect a tendency to gather under a single conception the various meanings of truth. This may perhaps be justified on the argument that all kinds of truth are unified in being perceived intuitively. In any event both of the "happy moment" passages are related to the intuitive realization elaborated symbolically in part 5, and both are of greatest interest when seen in this larger context.

The first passage, section LXXXVI, standing twenty-four lines before the depiction of an intuitive experience fundamental to the poem's ultimate thesis, culminates in the conception of the possibility that partial truths, known in this world, will give rise eventually to ultimate vision of truth, though the passage ends in laconic disparagement of the hope. The idea of partial truths, the relativism pervading all of Browning's thought, remains.[7] Tacit dismissal of the ultimate metaphysical possibility is preparatory to the earthly vision that is to follow.

The second happy moment passage, section CXXIV, follows immediately the symbolic elaboration of that earthly vision and is a joyous celebration of discovery. The closing lines of the passage affirm the truth of the earthly vision. Truth, says the speaker,

> *is forced*
> *To manifest itself through falsehood; whence divorced*
> *By the excepted eye, at the rare season, for*
> *The happy moment, truth instructs us to abhor*
> *The false, and prize the true, obtainable thereby.*
> *Thus do we understand the value of a lie.* (CXXIV, 2195-200)

The two passages on the happy moment enclose the earthly vision, as preparation for it and then as triumphant coda.

The most difficult passages dealing with conceptions of truth remain. The passage now to be examined will be interpreted as a statement on the ill effects of the poet's conforming to that Victorian censorship which forbade frank treatment of the sensual and sexual aspects of life. We will find this passage intelligible only if we remember the radical conversion of vocabulary which Browning has achieved. Especially in connection with art, the tendency to designate the outer aspects of things as "the false," "falsehood," and "lie" persists in all parts of the poem. This vocabulary, it will be recalled, is not moralistic but metaphysical in the Platonic sense that considers this world—matter and the flesh—false and unreal. The wording of the passage indicates a conception of poetry as presenting another kind of falseness in that it is imitation and employs a mask. This technical kind of disguise will be brought into close relationship with yet another kind of disguise which is directly concerned with morality. Conformity is characterized as a "vile disguise" (LXXVI, 1250). So poetry, inherently a kind of disguise, can in addition be guilty of a "vile disguise" which is a deformity, and by contrast, imitation of the natural man would be graceful. The speaker admonishes, "Mimic grace, / Not make deformity your mask" (1258-59). The sentence which will now be quoted accepts the possibility that frank treatment of physical life may result in some measure of moral temptation but considers this a lesser evil, for artistic candor can exalt an aspect of life which concealment would debase. In this sentence "falsehood" has become a code word for frank treatment of physical life, and "lie" may also be a code word with the same meaning, though it can well refer to the essential relationship of art to reality or simply to the essential nature of art as does the word "lie" in other contexts:

> And e'en should falsehood tempt
> The weaker sort to swerve, —at least the lie's exempt
> From slur, that's loathlier still, of aiming to debase
> Rather than elevate its object. (LXXVI, 1255-58)

In yet other contexts the poem treats the outer and inner aspects of art, which are made to coincide with aspects of change and permanence. The speaker experiences in music "still the certainty of change, / Conviction we shall find the false, where'er we range, / In art no less than nature" (XCIII, 1677-79). Because this and other similar assertions are so emphatic it is necessary to stress that they in no way qualify the conception of art as the medium of truth and of music as the art best serving truth because most consonant with the intuitive nature of its perception.

Art is "false" when considered in relationship to the reality which it imitates. It is in this sense that poetry is a "mask" and a "lie." The dream pageant of women worthies is conceived at one point as a dramatic performance: " 'T is not fit your phantom leave the stage" (XXXVIII, 580). It is perhaps with this notion of dramatic performance in mind that the speaker addressing the dramatic wife early in the poem refers to the figures of the dream pageant—"those the false, by you and me the true" (XXVI, 302). Later in the poem, with reference to the actors among the performers at the fair, the speaker comments that the appeal of dramatic action depends upon its not being confused with reality. He imagines the actors prefacing their performance with the words " 'A lie is all we do or say' " (LXXXV, 1477). A kind of explanation is offered: "To feign, means—to have grace / And so get gratitude!" (1482-83). The idea that the illusion which does not delude is itself a source of grace, or a kind of truth, is suggested in a cryptic sentence of the greatest importance for the present analysis: "The histrionic truth is in the natural lie" (1492). This makes sense if we recognize that the words "truth" and "lie" are here interchangeable. The phrase "natural lie" refers not to a failure of mimesis or science; it refers to the lie that is in the nature of things, which, if it is recognized, takes on the value of histrionic truth—the feigning and the grace.

To understand Browning's radical use of terms related to conceptions of truth is indispensable for reading the poem.

4

Modalities of Woman

In the headnote to *Fifine at the Fair* Browning quotes and translates a passage from Molière's *Don Juan* (I, 3), in which Donna Elvira asks her husband, Don Juan, for an explanation of his strange behavior and indicates in ironic tones her expectation that he will respond in spurious protestations of his love. The effect from the outset is to skew our expectations of credibility in the speaker of *Fifine*. While this is definitely Browning's purpose, we will be struck by the dissimilarity between Molière's Don Juan and the speaker of the poem. A parallel that does exist between them is not at all concerned with the legendary role of Don Juan as rampant seducer. Don Juan's reply to Donna Elvira, which Browning does not quote, is not the lie she ironically anticipates. He does not tell her that he still loves her. He tells her with brutal frankness that he does not. Then he lies about the reason. His reason, he says, is religion: "J'ai fait réflexion que, pour vous épouser, je vous ai dérobée à la clôture, d'un convent, que vous avez rompu des voeux qui vous engageoient autre part, et que le Ciel est fort jaloux de ces sortes de choses. Le repentir m'a pris, et j'ai craint le courroux céleste; j'ai cru que notre mariage n'étoit qu'un adultère déguisé, qu'il nous attireroit quelque disgrâce d'en haut, et qu'enfin je devois tâcher de vous oublier, et vous donner moyen de retourner à vos premières chaînes."[1] The brutality of this, the cynicism that is obscene because it is obvious, is paralleled in the closing lines of *Fifine*, and there only, when the speaker gives the wife a transparent pretext for returning to the fair to seek out Fifine and makes it clear that he may not return. Only in these final lines does there emerge the probability of an actual infidelity which would give the speaker anything in common with the legendary character of Don Juan. And yet we will come almost imperceptibly to realize that the real problem of the speaker is the pretended problem of Don Juan—that is his beloved is "bound elsewhere" and that he must try to forget.

It can hardly be without significance that Browning's translation of the final clause of the headnote, while expanding to fit his hexameter line, has changed the meaning by giving a new emphasis to the final word. Molière's clause involves only the idea of separation by death: "*et que rien n'est capable de vous détacher de moi que la mort?*" Browning's translation envisions the possibility that death may not only separate the lovers but bring the end of love:

> *nor aught in nature can avail*
> *To separate us two, save what, in stopping breath,*
> *May peradventure stop devotion likewise—death!*

The question implicit in the psychological conflicts of the poem concerns the status and claim of love when the lovers are separated by death. This question is also implicit in the prologue, subtitled "Amphibian."[2]

The prologue is built upon the metaphor longest sustained within the poem, that of the swimmer in the sea, the water representing human life on earth and the air above representing the realm of spirit. A butterfly in the air above the swimmer is "like soul and nought beside" and represents

> *a certain soul*
> *Which early slipped its sheath,*
> *And has for its home the whole*
> *Of heaven.*

The idea of death and loss so introduced conditions and strengthens its introduction within the poem, especially when it occurs in connection with the corresponding imagery of sea and air (see LXVII, 1089-102).[3] In both the prologue and the main body of the poem the biographical reference seems inescapable, and this is consistent with the fact that the prologue is a limited and rarefied epitome of the poem, foreshadowing it and conditioned by it.

The first six lines of the prologue are as follows:

> *The fancy I had today,*
> > *Fancy which turned a fear!*
> *I swam far out in the bay,*
> > *Since waves laughed warm and clear.*
>
> *I lay and looked at the sun,*
> > *The noon-sun looked at me:*

In the prologue the swim in the bay corresponds to the experience embodied in the entire poem. The mutual recognition of sun and swimmer corresponds to the stark discovery in the quest of naked fundamentals of the human condition. The "fancy" corresponds to the intellectual realization symbolically achieved in part 5. This astonishing achievement is transformed into a "fancy" within a special perspective by the complex pressures described at the beginning of the preceding chapter.

Only in the prologue are we given a direct suggestion of the psychological forces underlying the renunciation, which occurs in part 6. Within the poet's immediate subjective experience, the conception of part 5 is a "fancy which turned a fear." In Browning's bitter inscription on the manuscript, that conception as the intellectual heart of the poem "brought dark night before his eyes."

In the prologue the sea, by juxtaposition with air, represents the condition of human life in the physical world. It is the realm of "one who, in the world / Both lives and likes life's way." The sea here, as in the body of the poem, is "the wash o' the world." The symbolism of the sea, however, is eventually particularized by its relationship to "land," a symbol which becomes increasingly conspicuous toward the end of the prologue as it does toward the end of the poem. The land, which represents "worldly noise and dust," is a realm both of desiccation and restriction. The "play" in the sea is that "of limbs that slip the fetters." To bathe in the sea is "to free oneself of tether," and swimming in the sea is a condition of one "emancipate." Thus the prologue enunciates the fundamental motif of the poem, announced in the opening sections—a passionate desire for freedom. But each of the symbols, land and sea, involves an ambivalance. The sea is the realm where "emancipate through passion / And thought," we achieve poetry which "we substitute, in a fashion / For heaven." Yet in this realm of passion and thought, we may not only "tire" but "dread the surge." The ambivalence associated with land is the corollary of that associated with sea. The dry realm of restriction, of "fetter," is also "land the solid and safe." After the challenge, after the beauty and freedom of the sea, when "we tire or dread the surge," we must "confess" that we "welcome again" the land. The final movement of the prologue from sea to land again occurs also at the end of the poem, even though the purpose of both the prologue and the poem may be stated symbolically as a vindication and celebration of the sea. In the poem the abnegation of the sea is attended by regret, but before that abnegation occurs, and while the vindication of that symbolized by the sea is in process, there occurs a note of weariness (see CXXI), which obviously parallels the "If we tire" of the prologue.

Within the poem, land is associated with renunciation of the quest and this renunciation is repeatedly associated with death: "Land-locked, we live and die henceforth" (CXXIX, 2305). The association of death with abnegation of the sea would seem to be a corollary of a tendency of the prologue to throw into question the conception of the separate realm of spirit symbolized by the air overhead.

In connection with the image of the butterfly—the soul "which early slipped its sheath"—the separation of the realms of earth and spirit is given unusual emphasis, and this separation is imagined as inalterable. The speaker says of the butterfly,

> *I never shall join its flight,*
> *For, naught buoys flesh in air.*
> *If it touch the sea—good night!*
> *Death sure and swift waits there.*

In the next stanza the symbolism of spirit is maintained while the conception of spirit is subverted by countervailing diction. The

image of butterfly is degraded as "insect" and a certain spuriousness
is permitted to infect the idea of spirit in the counter imagery desig-
nating flesh as "uncouth." Furthermore, aspiration of flesh beyond
the condition of "clay" is a matter, not of hope or potentiality, but
of pretending:

> *Can the insect feel the better*
> *For watching the uncouth play*
> *Of limbs that slip the fetter,*
> *Pretend as they were not clay?*

The realm of hope and potentiality in this poem is not spirit but
flesh. The idea of spirit is consistently treated in the prologue as hypothetical. The realm of spirit, basic to the central metaphor of the
prologue, is occupied by a being recently born into it—a "creature
dear as new." While the conception of the realm of spirit is nullified
by various verbal effects, the attitude toward the occupant of the
realm of spirit is strikingly ambiguous:

> *Undoubtedly I rejoice*
> *That the air comports so well*
> *With a creature which had the choice*
> *Of land once. Who can tell?*

"Undoubtedly" because it has in some sense been doubted?
Does he rejoice *because* she "had the choice of land once" and having chosen spirit is not to be lamented? And if the first sentence
means anything at all, does not the question throw everything in
doubt? Much of the ambivalence and the resulting ambiguity of the
poem is concentrated in this stanza. While the attitude toward the
spiritual being is ambiguous, a negative attitude toward the realm
of spirit, where one would presumably join the soul departed,
emerges in wording which also renders dubious the existence of
such a realm, making it a matter of report. The swimmer is

> *one who, in the world,*
> *Both lives and likes life's way,*
> *Nor wishes the wings unfurled*
> *That sleep in the worm, they say?*

The consistent devaluation of the conceptual basis of the central metaphor of the prologue suggests that the conception is not intended as having serious metaphysical implications and that it is a carefully designed function of a symbolic process. The same conclusion must be drawn concerning the spiritual symbolism of air and light within the body of the poem.

The prologue establishes its introductory and anticipatory function by wondering about "a certain soul" that "has for its home the whole of heaven." Does that soul "look beneath" and watch the swimmer? The same heavenly perspective is imagined in the passage initiating the strategy of the phantom wife within the body of the poem (see XXVII). The question is expanded in the final stanza of the prologue:

> *Does she look, pity, wonder*
> *At one who mimics flight,*
> *Swims—heaven above, sea under,*
> *Yet always earth in sight?*

Thus the prologue contributes to the development of the question which is implicit in the headnote and informs the entire poem: What is the status and claim of love when the lovers are separated by death? The importance of the question is greater because the product of the "noon-disport" in the sea is a "fancy which turned a fear."

At the beginning of the main body of the poem the speaker, in an exuberant mood, is departing with Elvire to see the performers who have arrived for the fair at Pornic: "O trip and skip, Elvire! Link arm in arm with me! / Like Husband and like wife, together let us see. . . ." (I, 1-2). The effect of the phrase "Like husband and like wife" is to suggest here at the very beginning a dislocation of the identity of Elvire which will be developed later in the conception of the phantom wife and which is fundamental to the extremely complex strategy of the poem. Other aspects of this strategy are also set in movement at once, by lines that establish basic unifying imagery and begin elaboration of that established in the prologue.

The speaker suddenly stops to observe the newly completed structures of the fair:

> *Now, who supposed the night would play us such a prank?*
> *—That what was raw and brown, rough pole and shaven plank,*
> *Mere bit of hoarding, half by trestle propped, half tub,*
> *Would flaunt it forth as brisk as butterfly from grub?*
> *This comes of sun and air, of Autumn afternoon,*
> *And Pornic and Saint Gille, whose feast affords the boon—*
> *This scaffold turned parterre, this flower-bed in full blow,*
> *Bateleurs, baladines!* (II, 5-12)

The "scaffold," harsh, unattractive, faintly obscene, has been made
graceful as though by flowers, epitomizing a transformation which
continues through the entire course of the poem. The direction of
that transformation is also established, for the soul image of the
butterfly in the prologue has been despiritualized by the carnival
setting and by its earthy origin "from grub." The passage will be
echoed at the beginning of the culminating movement of the poem
in part 5 and there the remembered imagery will evince a remarkable densification of materiality (see LXXXIX). The bateleurs and
baladines are associated here with the transformation of "scaffold
turned parterre." Characterization of the performers by these flow-
erlike words establishes a symbolic strategy of the greatest structural and substantive importance. The words have similar meanings.
Bateleur (which is French, not English) means juggler, buffoon,
mountebank, ropedancer. *Baladine* (rare in English, *baladin* in
French) can mean mountebank, buffoon, but also theatrical or public dancer and ballad maker. Basic flower symbolism is associated
from the first with the troupe of performers at the fair. On one
hand the symbolism declares both the compelling beauty and the
epistemological duplicity of natural existence, in accord with which
the physical aspect of human life becomes later both "truth" and
"lie." On the other hand the symbolism declares—secretly, in the
sense that symbol is secret—the essential, the natural, innocence of
the performers of the fair. Hence the vindication of the performers,
of their "criminality," is not a perverse intellectual casuistry but is
inherent in the texture of the poem.

The speaker next refers to the arrival on the previous evening of the wandering troupe. He describes their curiosities—their "six-legged sheep" and their "ape of many years"—and the female members of the troupe:

> *Or, best, the human beauty, Mimi, Toinette, Fifine,*
> *Tricot fines down if fat, padding plumps up if lean,*
> *Ere, shedding petticoat, modesty, and such toys,*
> *They bounce forth, squalid girls transformed to gamesome boys.*
> (III, 23-26)

Mimi and Toinette will not be mentioned again. Fifine will become a central symbol of the poem. Her "shedding . . . modesty" here is most significant, as it echoes a line from the first chorus of *Prometheus Bound*, a passage from Aeschylus which will be echoed more fully near the end of part 5 of *Fifine* (CXXV, 2214-23).[4] Thus, from the earliest lines of the poem there are verbal associations with the play.

In this same passage the attitude of the speaker is curious but detached, the idle curiosity of the townsman for the carnival, and in the wording of the final line—"squalid girls" and "gamesome boys"—there is an expression of antipathy. Then suddenly, in a second pulsation of the transformational progress of the poem, this antipathy is attributed by implication to the town and it is rejected with zest:

> *No, no, thrice, Pornic, no! Perpend the authentic tale!*
> *'T was not for every Gawain to gaze upon the Grail!*
> *But whoso went his rounds, when flew bat, flitted midge,*
> *Might hear across the dusk,—where both roads join the bridge,*
> *Hard by the little port,—creak a slow caravan,*
> *A chimneyed house on wheels; so shyly-sheathed, began*
> *To broaden out the bud which, bursting unaware,*
> *Now takes away our breath, queen-tulip of the Fair!* (IV, 27-34)

With the reference to Gawain and the Grail in the second line a tension basic to the poem is established in the opposition of a spiritual ideal to the sensuousness and freedom—"the human beauty"—of

the girls of the group of entertainers. When the initial flower imagery is repeated at the beginning of the final movement of the poem,
there will also be repeated the imagery of the chimneyed house on
wheels linked again with the meaning of Fifine, the "queen-tulip of
the Fair" (see XCI, 1588-93). The meaning of Fifine will be then expanded to make explicit the speaker's personal, sexual reaction to
her as well as the philosophical implications of that reaction. In the
lines just quoted, it suffices to note the continuation of the initial
flower imagery of transformation and its direct link here with
Fifine.

The power of the Fifine and lily-tulip imagery in the poem may
be underestimated if we neglect here the phrase "takes away our
breath." The force of this is developed in lines which give lyric expression to a longing for freedom—a basic impulse of the poem—
while establishing other essential symbols:

> *On terrace 'neath the tower, 'twixt tree and tree appeared*
> *An airy-structure; how the pennon from its dome,*
> *Frenetic to be free, makes one red stretch for home!*
> *The home far and away, the distance where lives joy.*
> *The cure, at once and ever, of world and world's annoy;*
> *Since, what lolls full in front, a furlong from the booth,*
> *But ocean-idleness, sky-blue and millpond-smooth?* (V, 36-41)

The tower and the tent will each be mentioned again in extremely important passages. The ocean imagery continues from the
prologue and is the most conspicuous imagery of the poem. The
parallel between Fifine and the ocean is not so clear at this point as
it becomes later in the poem, but that parallel is fundamental. Both
the "queen-tulip of the Fair" and the ocean are objects of the desire,
the need, which the poem is all about. Fifine is woman as sensual
being; the sea is the world, the condition of man's physical existence on earth. Eventually Fifine is available, permissible, to the
speaker only under the condition that the claims of the world and
the flesh may be justified. The entire movement of the poem is toward such a justification, but here the impulse of the movement is a
psychological need to which intellectual realization is subservient.

Impelled to joy, the speaker then turns to the social barriers defining the restrictions of his freedom and he identifies imaginatively
with those who live beyond these restrictions.

> *Frenetic to be free! And, do you know, there beats*
> *Something within my breast, as sensitive? —repeats*
> *The fever of the flag? My heart makes just the same*
> *Passionate stretch, fires up for lawlessness, lays claim*
> *To share the life they lead: losels, who have and use*
> *The hour what way they will, —applaud them or abuse*
> *Society, whereof myself am at the beck,*
> *Whose call obey, and stoop to burden stiffest neck!* (VI, 43-50)

The speaker now sustains (VII-XIII) intense fascination with the
idea of freedom and "lawlessness" represented by the itinerant performers of the fair.

The treatment of these "misguided ones who gave society the
slip" (VII, 65) is basic to the meaning of the poem. Their condition is
imagined as one of intense joy—"disgraced, they seem to relish life
the more" (55). If we lament the benefits of civilization they have
given up, why is it, asks the speaker, there "goes up so frank a
laugh?" (70). It is "as though they held the corn and left us only
chaff / From garners crammed and closed" (71-72). There follows a
bitter remark on the rewards of respectability: "And we indeed are
clever / If we get grain as good, by threshing straw forever!" (72-
73).[5] The speaker thus initiates an inquiry the goal of which will
later be fulfilled in a new understanding of human culture and a
conception of a form of culture capable of nourishing human joy.
The speaker's fascination arises from a need to comprehend "a
compensating joy, unknown and infinite" (XIII, 141).

The condition of the outcasts, being that of complete joy, is also
one of the most deliberate choice. They are "truants" and "purpose
yet to be" (VIII, 74). "A faithful few," they

> *combine*
> *To cast allegiance off, play truant, nor repine,*
> *Agree to bear the worst, forego the best in store*
> *For us who, left behind, do duty as of yore.* (VII, 51-54)

If one should attempt to reform the leader of the troupe, offering him every opportunity for a more respectable profession, "his thanks will be the roundest curse / That ever rolled from lip" (XII, 137-38). To the speaker in his fascination with deliberate choice of joy, it seems the "truants" have a special knowledge. They seem to say, " 'We know a secret passing praise / Or blame of such as you!' " (VII, 56-58). The intention of the speaker is to understand the secret:

> *I want, put down in black and white,*
> *What compensating joy, unknown and infinite,*
> *Turns lawlessness to law, makes destitution—wealth,*
> *Vice—virtue, and disease of soul and body—health?* (XIII, 140-43)

With this resolve, the speaker turns from the "truants" as a collectivity to the individual dancing girl, Fifine, "queen-tulip of the Fair," who, he says, will "make my thoughts be surer what they mean" (XV, 149). The treatment of Fifine cannot be considered apart from the meaning of those "who gave society the slip." This meaning begins to emerge in the nature of the transgressions of the "truants" as reflected in the imagination of the speaker.

More or less incidentially, we learn that the master of the troupe is guilty of cheating; his "six-legged sheep" and his "Twin-headed Babe" are false. Beyond this specific, the notion of criminality among the performers is quite generalized and emphasis is upon a mode of life vividly contrasting with the rigorous restrictions of Victorian middle-class society. The speaker contrasts the performers' life with his own submission to "Society, whereof myself am at the beck, / Whose call obey, and stoop to burden stiffest neck!" (VI, 49-50). The most significant characteristic of their troupe is frank sensuality. This is dramatized as the master of the troupe exhibits "his Graces," the women of his family, for public delectation—his sisters, his wife, and his daughter the trapeze performer, who may be Fifine, though in accord with the generalized symbolic value of the troupe, this is not made explicit. The trapeze performer wears little clothing:

No scrap of skirt impedes free passage through the air,
Till, plumb on the other side, she lights and laughs again,
That fairy-form, whereof each muscle, nay, each vein
The curious may inspect,—his daughter that he sells
Each rustic for five sous. (XI, 117-21)

Her nudity is contrasted with the multilayered propriety of Victorian petticoats—"as multiplied a coating as protects / An onion from the eye!" (XII, 132-33). The passage may be taken to mean that the master of the troupe "sells" his daughter in the sense that her public display of nudity has a commercial motive. The same suggestion occurs in a passage in which the speaker deals with the attitude of "quality (you and I)," of the "proud dames" of polite society, toward Fifine. One of his points is that they think they would not be able to "support the nods and becks / Of clowns that have their stare, nor always pay its price" (XXIV, 273-74). Again the sexual offense is immodesty—showing and seeing, not doing. The Victorian perspective with its elaborate sexual taboos and horror at their violation was notoriously disinclined to appreciate distinctions betweens degees of sin, and in a Victorian context we might take immodesty as sufficiently adequate indication for artistic purposes of more palpable crimes. Yet a passage apparently intended as a general characterization of the criminality of the group is strangely ambiguous. The speaker is fascinated by the relationship to society of the "misguided ones who gave society the slip" (VII, 65). The troupe as a collectivity is epitomized in the coquetry of an individual:

Still, truants as they are and purpose yet to be,
That nowise needs forbid they venture—as you see—
To cross confine, approach the once familiar roof
O' the kindly race their flight estranged: stand half aloof,
Sidle half up, press near, and proffer wares for sale
—In their phrase,—make, in ours, white levy of black mail.
They, of the wild, require some touch of us the tame,
Since clothing, meat and drink, mean money all the same.

(VIII, 74-81)

Here in an image applied to the group, there is prefigured the
later approach of Fifine (see XV, XXI, XXIII) with her tambourine as
receptacle for contributions from the observers of the show. Such is
the subtlety of the poem, but while Fifine participates in the character of the troupe as a whole, her own criminality is never particularized. Inevitably we find a suggestion of prostitution in the
speaker's suppression of "their phrase," but the phrase which he
substitutes—"white levy of black mail"—is ambiguous in a way
that a euphemism need need not be. When the phrase occurs again,
it serves the achievement of radical contrast between the "truants"
and society. The passage also reinforces the basic association between flowers, females, and the performers of the fair:

For, what they traffic in, consists of just the things
We,—proud ones who so scorn dwellers without the pale,
Bateleurs, baladines, white leviers of black mail,—
I say, they sell what we most pique us that we keep.
How comes it, all we hold so dear they count so cheap? (X, 99-103)

Repetition of the phrase would seem to indicate a value in its essential ambiguity. If we try to read the poem as realism, Fifine may
be a prostitute, but symbolically she is something else. There is no
interest in the poem in any specific criminality. The interest of the
poem, the fascination of the speaker, is in freedom from social restrictions and the achievement of a perspective from which certain
freedoms cease to be criminal at all. Symbolically, Fifine and the
itinerant troupe do not represent crime; they represent freedom and
especially sexual freedom. It is of fundamental importance that
none of the elaborate arguments of the poem can be considered to
have any special relevance to a justification of matrimonial infidelity or to any specific, conventional moral question whatsoever.

When the "faithful few combine / To cast allegiance off" (VII,
51-52) their escape from society is not an escape into criminality,
but an escape into joy and into nature. They are imagined as crying, " 'To the wood then, to the wild: free life, full liberty!' " (62).
They are seen in the countryside where "they rendezvous beneath
the inclement sky, / House by the hedge, reduced to brute com-

panionship" (63-64). It is when this is considered "wretchedness" that there "goes up so frank a laugh" (70). Throughout the poem there is a note of bitter frustration because for those who "stoop to burden stiffest neck" the garners are both "crammed" and "closed" (72).

The perspective of Victorian sexual morality persists in part 1 and deeply affects the portraits of the performing troupe and Fifine. The position of the speaker moves between various attitudes, now in momentary conformity with the Victorian perspective, now in mock conformity, now in protest. A corollary of his effort for freedom is a fundamental process which may be called the assimilation of Fifine. In the ultimate vision of Fifine the suggestion of prostitution is lost in the complete disappearance of all social definition. Ultimately she is simply female; she is youth and beauty; her meaning is sensual, personal, and metaphysical (see XCI). The process of achieving this vision is implicit in the entire development of the poem and is coherent with the intellectual assimilation achieved in part 5, but it is in part 1 that the assimilative process deals most directly with Fifine. As we have seen, the process of assimilation begins, not with Fifine in particular but with the troupe as a collectivity, making evident the symbolic continuity between Fifine and the troupe. The motive of their traffic with society is redeemed under beguiling imagery in the first lyric passage of the poem (IX, 82-98), a passage which separates the two passages quoted concerning white leviers of black mail. Their gains are compared to the remnants a bird of the countryside steals from city environs for the building of her nest. The nest is lovingly described. If you examine it carefully you discover the odds and ends which are

> *Filched plainly from mankind, dear tribute paid by town,*
> *Which proved how oft the bird had plucked up heart of grace,*
> *Swooped down at waif and stray, made furtively our place*
> *Pay tax and toll, then borne the booty to enrich*
> *Her paradise i' the waste; the how and why of which,*
> *That is the secret, there the secret that stings!* (IX, 93-98)

The passage symbolizes the meaning of the troupe for the speaker. They live in joy and beyond the restraints of civilization;

in acts of utter naturalness they make some small use of civilization, and in their image of joy they impose a beguiling demand; the
demand in its naturalness is innocent and they are thus white (innocent) leviers of black mail. In the image of the bird and her "paradise i' the waste" touched fragmentarily by civilization there is
prefigured an image which is the objective of the quest and toward
which the poem probes continuously—an elemental condition and
source of joy underlying the superficies of culture.

Fifine is first emphatically distinguished from the rest of the performers as emphasis is given to her central symbolic role in the
poem. The speaker cries: "This way, this way, Fifine! / Here's she,
shall make my thoughts be surer what they mean!" (XV, 148-49).
She is now for the first time individualized. Before portraying "the
gypsy's foreign self" the speaker exempts her from racial disqualifi-
cation: "Yet where's a woolly trace degrades the wiry hair?" (152).
There follows a joyous description of her dark beauty, her sensuality made solid and palpable by articulation of each feature—her
"Greek-nymph nose," her Hebrew eyes "That swim as in a sea, that
dip and rise and roll, / Spilling the light around!" (155-56). The description ends by pointing to a boylike quality, a slenderness which
attracted the speaker from the first, and by emphasizing the autonomous sufficiency of Fifine as a physical being. She is,

> *though mischievous and mean,*
> *Yet free and flower-like too, with loveliness for law,*
> *And self-sustainment made morality.*[6] (XVI, 173-75)

In the lines immediately following these Fifine is treated under
imagery comparable in its redemptive value to the bird imagery
under which the carnival troupe was described earlier. The central
lily imagery will within another fifty lines be echoed in a passage
redolent with personal echoes from the poet's past (see XX, 228-45).
In the passage now to be considered, the lily—with parallel implications for flowers elsewhere in the text (see LXXXIX)—is established as metaphor for woman in her specifically sexual definition.
Under this image the two antipodal emotional foci of the poem—
Elvire and Fifine—are brought together in symbolic antithesis and
tensions, and yet both are identified under the shape of the lily—

lilies of the North and the South, temperate and torrid, chaste and passionate:

> *A flaw*
> *Do you account i' the lily, of lands which travellers know,*
> *That, just as golden gloom supersedes Northern snow*
> *I' the chalice, so, about each pistil, spice is packed, —*
> *Deliriously-drugged scent, in lieu of odour lacked,*
> *With us, by bee and moth, their banquet to enhance*
> *At morn and eve, when dew, the chilly sustenance,*
> *Needs mixture of some chaste and temperate perfume?*
> *I ask, is she in fault who guards such golden gloom,*
> *Such dear and damning scent, by who cares what devices,*
> *And takes the idle life of insects she entices*
> *When, drowned to heart's desire, they satiate the inside*
> *O' the lily, mark her wealth and manifest her pride?* (XVII, 175-87)

The first two hundred lines of the poem have been filled with female images: Mimi, Toinette, Fifine shedding "modesty and such toys"; the "nest builder of the wood and wilde"; the "Graces in a group" paraded by the master of the troupe; the fairy form on the trapeze with "no scrap of skirt"; Fifine's portrait in detail; the lilies north and south. Except for brief prohibitive reflections of Elvire "chaste, temperate, and serene," the female has been experienced superficially in her externality, compellingly fleshly and sexual. Now, almost casually, the poem takes a momentous turn to explore the female as an inward experience. The speaker proposes as his imaginative vehicle "one pageant more . . . / O' the kind, sick Louis liked to see defile between / Him and the yawning grave, its passage served to screen" (XIX, 201-3). The speaker invites Elvire to witness an imaginary procession of "well-sung women-worthies" (208) of ancient fame. The purpose is to show how Fifine can make the speaker's "thoughts be sure of what they mean" (199). The women are imagined, at the beginning, as filing forth from "yonder tent," with the interior of which Fifine as sexual symbol is repeatedly associated hereafter in such a way that the tent becomes a symbolic veil of the female in her mode as concealed and secret being, the eventual imaginative penetration of the veil becoming one of the climactic developments of the poem (see XCI). We are to witness now in the pageant different aspects of woman refracted from the consciousness of the speaker. That the images have this character is reflected in the complex interrelations among the separate female figures.

The "well-sung" women who appear are Helen, Cleopatra, and the "Saint" of Pornic Church. Then Fifine brings up the rear and still somewhat later Elvire is imagined as joining the procession. The addition of Elvire to the pageant, however, is a distinctly separate psychological and artistic strategy, one having the greatest significance for the development of the poem, and the first four figures—Helen, Cleopatra, the Saint, and Fifine—are a psychological and affective unit. The unit is intensely symmetrical and complex. Helen and Cleopatra, of the ancient world, are laden with history, while the Saint and Fifine are part of the immediate present. Historical associations are conspicuously absent from the Saint. She is imagined in her immediate condition and efficacy. Helen and Cleopatra contrast as disparate aspects of woman. Helen's beauty is not specifically sensual; indeed metaphorical treatment leaves her a rather abstract figure—"mighty, like a moon / Outbreaking from a cloud" (XX, 212-13)—and her beauty is touched with moral value; it "casts o'er all the blood a candour from her brow" (217). Cleopatra's appeal is fundamentally sexual. Her most conspicuous aspect is her nudity—"Cleopatra! bared, the entire and sinuous wealth / O' the shining shape" (218-19). Her breasts encircled by jewels are elaborately described. About both Helen and Cleopatra there is something distinctly forbidding. Helen's beauty puts "harsh things in tune" but it does so to "magically bring mankind to acquiesce / In its own ravage" (214-15). The jewels about Cleopatra's breast are a "fire-frame." In her head "so high and haught" there is "a soul's predominance" except for "one thievish glance, / From back of oblong eye, intent to count the slain" (225-26). As will be seen later in the poem (XXXII, 415-47), both Helen and Cleopatra represent woman as embodying restrictive demands. In connection with the forbidding aspects of Helen and Cleopatra, one should keep in mind the deep ambivalence of the speaker toward both the

wife and Fifine. In this forbidding aspect the two classical figures
contrast with the Saint and Fifine, with whom in other respects
they correspond. The correspondence between the queen of Egypt
and Fifine, the gypsy dancing-girl, as symbols of female sexuality is
obvious.[7] The relationship between the Saint and other figures in
the poem is much more complex. Echoes in the description of the
Saint (228-45) of imagery associated with Elizabeth in the love letters have been pointed out in chapter 2: her position "aloft o' the
spire"; the clause "I looked for scarce so much from earth"; and her
generous naïveté toward the "unashamed" who "must have
stripped herself only to clothe the poor." Within the poem the Saint
is linked with Helen and, in more complex fashion, with the wife.

Helen and the Saint correspond in their contrast with the patent
sexuality of Cleopatra and Fifine. Helen shares in some measure the
Saint's role as an object of veneration whom mankind would "call
no curse upon but bless!" Both are also associated with night and
storm and are capable of benefic influences. Helen puts "harsh
things in tune." The Saint "prays calm the seas" (229) and, the peasants say, "Goes walking out to save from shipwreck" (231). Here
Browning may have had yet another association in mind, remembering that Helen became a goddess of sailors. Helen also has
significant associations with the wife. The image of the moon is associated with the wife regularly except in one extremely significant
case (see XCI) to be examined later and in the present instance of association with Helen, who, as we have seen, is "mighty, like a
moon / Outbreaking from a cloud." (The moon is always associated with Elizabeth in Browning's poetry, according to DeVane.)[8]
Furthermore, the extraordinary complexity of the poem may be
suggested by recalling that the storm tradition associated with
Helen was sent by Hera, the goddess of marriage, in disapproval of
the flight of Helen and Paris. When Browning writes that Helen
puts "harsh things in tune" he may have in mind that within a few
lines a legend concerning Helen will provide a major element in the
artistic strategy for resolution of the tensions posed by the Elvire-
Fifine polarity. When he writes that Helen can "magically bring
mankind to acquiesce / In its own ravage" (214-15), he may anticipate the eventual acquiescence of the speaker in the frustration of

his impulse for freedom (see CXXVIII, CXXIX, and epilogue). It is only on the basis of such consideration that much sense can be made of the phrase "(Beldame, a moment since)" in the following lines from the description of Helen:

> —*call no curse upon, but bless*
> *(Beldame, a moment since) the outbreaking beauty, now,*
> *That casts o'er all the blood a candour from her brow.* (215-17)

Thus the image of Helen may be seen as involved in a reconciliatory turn as the speaker approaches, beyond the intervening figure of the forbidding Cleopatra, the innocent and loving image of a childlike Saint whom the speaker experiences in a mode of memory and as beloved.

The Saint, like Helen, is to be associated with the wife, and here the links are more obvious. It is necessary, however, to anticipate further the development of the poem. Within a few lines a strategy will emerge for displacement of the identity of Elvire, conferring upon that identity a duality of modes, under which she will be referred to hereafter as "the dramatic wife" and "the phantom wife." Eventually the dramatic wife will be lost in the mode of the phantom wife, who in the epilogue appears quite simply as a ghost. The transmutation in this process is one of the most wonderful things in the poem. The Saint prefigures Elvire as the phantom wife.

It is sufficient for the moment to note the images associated with the Saint and involved in the transmutation. The Saint's position "aloft o' the spire" is said to be "nearer to God half-way / In heaven" (242-43). Later, Elvire will refer to herself as a meteor "half in heaven" (XXXIII, 502). The Saint is seen not only on the church spire. In another perspective of her there is established the image of snow, which in its eventual elaboration becomes symbolic of death:

> *the wintry snow that coats the pent-house of her shrine,*
> *Covers each knee, climbs near, but spares the smile benign.*
> (XX, 234-35)

The snow might have been imagined to conceal a detail concerning the Saint's garment. Its folds "flow down and multiply / Around her feet" (239-40). The lily imagery established heretofore as symbolic of female sexuality, is, in connection with the Saint, formalized in consonance with death and immortality. Her garment is "besprent with fleurs-de-lys" (239). The lily, the ascending snow, the folds of garment about the feet will be later focused with great intensity in a vision of the phantom wife (see XXXVIII, 601-8).

A point to be noted about the description of the Saint, for purposes of later contrast, is that it makes the Saint peculiarly dynamic. Among all the female figures in the poem, only Fifine is seen in so many activities. She "prays calm the seas"; she "goes walking out to save from shipwreck"; she is "conversant" though "with naught but winds and rains"; she speaks twice; she has "one long thin pure finger in the girth / O' the girdle" and one "pressed hushingly to lip"; and while they "made her march" in the pageant, she is concerned lest "some foundering ship / Might miss her from her post."

With the Saint portrayed, the speaker informs the wife that he will complete the masque and will present "not one more form" if she will "allow" an addition, "bringing up the rear / O' the bevy," a figure, her feet conspicuous unlike the Saint's:

> *who concludes the masque with curtsey, smile and pout,*
> *Submissive-mutinous? No other than Fifine*
> *Points toe, imposes haunch, and pleads with tambourine!*
>
> (XXI, 251-53)

The pageant as thus far developed is symbolically symmetrical. The Saint, who will be symbolically merged with the wife, and Fifine are foci of attraction. Associated with the Saint and Fifine respectively are Helen and Cleopatra in the relationship of shadow figures bearing ambivalent elements of demand and prohibition. The pageant embodies tensions basic to the poem.

That Browning has here achieved genuine depths of the unconscious is suggested by the fact that the figures of the first four-part stage of this pageant seem to reflect the characteristics of the myth-

ological figures who, according to Jung and his followers, correspond to the stages of the development of the anima in its growth to
maturity.[9] Different writers assign different mythological figures to
these four stages and the figures of the mythic symbolism overlap
in corresponding or comparable functions, but the following parallels may be suggested: Browning's Helen corresponds to Isis, associated with fruit, birth, rebirth, immortality (Helen may reflect
something also of Sophia, associated with vision, wisdom, inspira-
tion, ecstasy); Cleopatra corresponds to Hecate, associated with
sickness, extinction, dismemberment; the Saint corresponds to the
Virgin Mary, associated like Sophia with vision, wisdom, inspira-
tion, and ecstasy; Fifine corresponds to Lilith, associated with ecstasy, drunkenness, madness, impotence, stupor.[10] If Fifine may
reasonably be made to correspond to Lilith in her original role in
the pageant, later she becomes something else, as will be seen.

As the poem progresses we observe the compulsion of the
speaker to experience woman in a multiplicity of aspects. Among
these there is a basic polarity of effect at the dramatic level in the
opposition of Elvire and Fifine. Furthermore each of these poles of
meaning must also be experienced symbolically in diverse and conflicting modalities. The speaker's condition is a complex morass of
impulses, and the motive force of the poem is expressed in his effort
to extricate himself by achieving a decision and the serenity of
order and objectivity. Thus the first four-part panoply in the pageant of "women worthies" represents in some respects the goal of
the poem, though a goal which will be achieved only momentarily
and then relinquished in despair. Consummation of the effort will
require that the wife be experienced under the lineaments of the
Saint—an object of calm veneration, clearly conceived, formalized
in immortality, remote, exerting a benefic, saving influence on the
world, and, most important, reconciled, if only in naïveté, to the
"unashamed." Perhaps something of the failure of the speaker's
earthly quest—indeed, his earthy quest—may be seen in the peculiar dynamism of the image of the Saint. The poem achieves universal meaning precisely because it is intensely personal.

When Fifine has been added to the pageant, the speaker poses
the question in the mind of Elvire " 'Well, what's the meaning here,

what does the masque intend?' " (XXII, 254). He answers by requiring that Elvire become in imagination part of the pageant. Here the first step is taken in refraction of the image of the wife, establishing two modalities, one an image in life, the other in afterlife. The speaker does not simply ask Elvire to imagine herself part of the pageant. His words suggest the condition of an afterlife:

> *Task fancy yet again! Suppose you cast this clog*
> *Of flesh away (that weeps, upbraids, withstands my arm)*
> *And pass to join your peers, paragon charm with charm.*
>
> (XXIII, 257-59)

The speaker assures the wife that as "that yonder-you" she will "prove best of beauty there." She will "beat her who lured to Troy-town beach / The purple prows of Greece—nay, beat Fifine" (263-64). The irony and cynicism of this at the dramatic level of the immediate context are phenomena in the surface of the poem. And yet in the end, the wife will win, dominating the speaker's despair-filled consciousness. Now, as though to struggle against that antici-pated end, and with the wife included in the symbolic complex of the pageant, the speaker elaborates the image of Fifine, and she is seen in two modalities, both of which are prohibitive. The first mo-dality is social. The speaker enunciates an attitude which represents an aspect of the wife's perspective on Fifine and is based upon a middle-class Victorian equation of class with virtue. The speaker speaks for "quality (you and I)" who

> *once more compassionate*
> *A hapless infant, doomed (fie on such partial fate!)*
> *To sink the inborn shame, waive privilege of sex.* (XXIV, 270-72)

While emphasizing the scorn of "you, proud dames, whom des-tiny / Keeps uncontaminate from stigma of the stye" (276-77), the speaker takes up, and then questions, the sentimental rationaliza-tion of vice, which is a condescension of class and virtue:

> *You draw back skirts from filth like her*
> *Who, possibly, braves scorn, if, scorned, she minister*

To age, want, and disease of parents one or both;
Nay, peradventure, stoops to degradation, loth
That some just-budding sister, the dew yet on the rose,
Should have to share in turn the ignoble trade,—who knows?
                                                    (278-83)

The rationalization of Fifine may in some measure support the
process of her assimilation, but it sentimentalizes her and falsifies
her meaning for the speaker, for whom another view of her is necessary, and we move now to another modality of Fifine. This modality too is prohibitive, but the prohibition now is a psychological
projection. We seem to arrive here at what would be a key passage
for psychoanalytic study of the poem. If so, we witness an unusual
example of the power of the poem to release psychic forces and,
eventually, to open realms of mythic realization.

At the center of the scene is the tent, symbol of woman as secret. To the speaker's rhetorical question "Who knows?" he answers, "Ay, who indeed! Myself know nothing, but dare guess"
(XXV, 284). No sooner does he "guess" than what he guesses he sees.
He guesses "That off she trips in haste to hand the booty . . . yes"
(285). The passage as it continues is unique in the poem and extraordinary in any context. An image acknowledged as originating
in the mental processes of a character becomes a part of narrative
actuality. An image first guessed at—arising first in the imagination—is then seen. In the entrance to the tent there emerges an ominous figure of horrendous maleness seen as the possessor of Fifine:

'Twixt fold and fold of tent, there looms he, dim-discerned,
The ogre, lord of all those lavish limbs have earned!
—Brute-beast-face,—ravage, scar, scowl and malignancy,—
O' the Strong Man, whom (no doubt, her husband) by and by
You shall behold do feats. (286-89)

The speaker is confident that Fifine prefers the Strong Man's
qualities to his own: "Oh, she prefers sheer strength to ineffective
grace, / Breeding and culture!" (292-93). But in a moment of in-
creased detachment, the speaker acknowledges that Fifine's prefer-

ence for the authentically physical is consonant with what we will
come to understand as the psychic quest underlying the progress of
the poem. She "seeks the essential in the case." The psychological
pattern of the moment is completed when the relationship of the
Strong Man to Fifine is imagined as abusive—the "squint / O' the
diabolic eye" and a "customary curse." The poet would seem to
have touched here upon an oedipal key to the psychological processes of the poem. That is not inconsistent with the fact that the
obstacle to Fifine is a male figure only here, and everywhere else a
spiritualized female image. The entire effort of the poem is to exorcize, and escape the influence of, a female modality associated with
the wife.

The poem turns now to its most elaborate effort in an artistic
strategy already begun, the strategy of the phantom wife. All the
women of the pageant are by implication "phantoms." Only for
Elvire is the conception of the phantom image important for the entire course of the poem. The purpose of the poet now is to elaborate
that duality. For this purpose the speaker recalls, and adapts, a
legend employed in the *Helen* of Euripides. It will be helpful to keep
in mind the parallels previously established between Helen and the
Saint. To Helen is now attributed a condition corresponding to that
of the Saint abiding in a realm of immortality. Helen and the legend
will be explicitly associated with the wife. According to the legend,
"Helen's self, never saw Troy at all" (XXVII, 309). The cause of the
Trojan war was an illusion:

> Jove had his fancy-fit, must needs take empty air,
> Fashion her likeness forth, and set the phantom there
> I' the midst for sport, to try conclusions with the blind
> And blundering race, the game create for Gods, mankind:
> Experiment on these,—establish who would yearn
> To give up life for her, who, other-minded, spurn
> The best her eyes could smile,—make half the world sublime,
> And half absurd, for just a phantom all the time! (310-17)

The legend as it appears in Euripides provides the true Helen with a
specific residence in this world; the place is Egypt. Browning's picture of the true Helen is quite significantly different:

> *Meanwhile true Helen's self sat, safe and far away,*
> *By a great river-side, beneath a purer day,*
> *With solitude around, tranquility within;*
> *Was able to lean forth, look, listen, through the din*
> *And stir; could estimate the worthlessness or worth*
> *Of Helen who inspired such passion to the earth,*
> *A phantom all the time!* (318-24)

The phrase "beneath a purer day" anticipates the light imagery later developed in the vision of a lost beloved in heaven (see LIX). More important, her being "able to lean forth" recalls the prologue: "What if a certain soul . . . thus look beneath?" Helen's being "able to lean forth" also recalls Rossetti's "blessed damozel."[11] Clearly Browning's true Helen abides in a condition modeled on the Christian traditions of heaven and the immortality of the soul. The application of the duality of the conception of Helen to the conception of the wife is articulated both at the beginning and at the end of the Helen legend. The speaker's recalling the legend, "a certain myth," is offered as explanation in answer to the rhetorical question, " 'What put it in my head to make yourself judge you?' " (304). This explanation is repeated at the end of the passage:

> *That put it in my head*
> *To make yourself judge you—the phantom-wife instead*
> *O' the tearful true Elvire!* (324-26)

It is essential to the artistic strategy developed here that there be imposed upon Elvire both a duality of identity and some ambiguity in the distinction between the two modes of identity. In the parallels established by the legend, "the tearful true Elvire" who walks beside the speaker corresponds to the Helen in heaven, but the other face of the parallel also argues the wife's insubstantiality. Elvire as "phantom wife" corresponds, obviously, to the Helen who is "a phantom all the time," who inhabits the worldly "din and stir" of the Trojan story. A major burden of the poem is to exorcize a modality of woman which exists only as a part of the memory and consciousness of the speaker and which, as a function of imagination, corresponds to the phantom wife. The Elvire beside the speaker embodies only the immediate restrictive element of the modality of woman which must be reinterpreted in the consciousness of the speaker. Eventually the immediate Elvire is absorbed in the image of the phantom wife who persists in the end and will not be exorcized.

The burden of the poem may at this point be stated more specifically. The phantom wife represents the psychological expression in the world and present time of an experience of woman belonging logically to the past and metaphysically to heaven. A goal of the poem is to consign this experience to the past and to memory and thus to end its domination of present consciousness. Heaven is the imaginative corollary of memory and the past. The initial need to be served by the poem is to exorcize the phantom wife, along with other restrictive modalities of the experience of woman, and to affirm the remote and benefic conditions of a heavenly wife—somehow to forget without violating the claim of loyalty that memory makes upon the present. The true wife, affirmed in heaven, can judge the phantom wife, can forgive the exorcism of the phantom wife and the affirmation of Fifine—or so the effort of the poem assumes. This end will be served by what will be called an elegiac motif which dominates a large part of the poem and of which the Helen legend is the foundation and the earliest expression.

In consonance with the heavenly image of Helen (Helen-wife), the arguments now offered in defense of the speaker's interest in Fifine are abstract and gentle. The wife will forgive him, "when I prove that bodies show me minds" (XXVIII, 335). Next there is an argument from the idea of plenary creation in accord with which, from the perfection of the whole, each part "gets glory all its own" (XXIX, 342). This dry argument, thoroughly consistent with Browning's habitual view of the world, now serves as the stem and branch of symbol, in a complex development. The psychological demands of the poem are for an intensified realization, no less of Fifine than of the wife of memory. Or to express it from another point of view, the need in both cases is for a purification of symbol. The spiritual reality of the heavenly wife must be rid of the detritus of the world. The physical reality of Fifine must be divested of cultural concretions. These concretions are represented in all the female figures of the pageant except Fifine. Thus represented, these concretions on the notion of the human female are now subjected to a process of reduction, a process emphasized in elaborate repetition developed once in small (XXX), then again in large (XXXI-XXXIII).

The first execution of the process of reduction, which is complementary and essential to the assimilation of Fifine, establishes one of the major motifs of the poem in the imagery of light. Fifine, "least sand-grain, she, of shadiest social state" (XXX, 357), is compared to Helen, Cleopatra, Saint, and wife. The unifying metaphorical device is a diversity of ways of mirroring and refracting light. This must be recalled when we come to the vision of heaven in part 2. The reductive process consists first in denying to Fifine the splendid and imperative meanings of the others: the polished "adamantine shield" of Helen, its glare "dazing the universe" (XXX, 358-60); the "Asian mirror" of Cleopatra, which can "fix sun fast and tame sun down," its beams, "rolled / About her, head to foot, turned slavish snakes of gold" (362-65); the Saint's "tinted pane of oriel sanctity" through which the sun of noon "pales, through thy lozenged blue, to meek benefic moon" (366, 370). (It should be noted here that Helen, Cleopatra, and Fifine are spoken of here in the third person, while the Saint and the wife are assimilated to each other by address in the second person.) For the wife the refraction of light involves class distinction in a reference to her clothes and jewels, "that satin-muffled mope, your sulky diamond" (375). In this line there occurs the radical turn of attitude usual in the ambivalent pattern. The previous tenderness toward the wife, associated with a female image in heaven, gives way to direct though brief affront. Then imagination moves toward the sexuality of Fifine which emerges in the following sections. The point made most emphatically is that Fifine's power of light must be conceived in a condition of debasement:

> What then? does that prevent each dunghill, we may pass
> Daily, from boasting too its bit of looking-glass,
> Its sherd which, sun-smit, shines, shoots arrowy fire beyond
> That satin-muffled mope, your sulky diamond?
>
> (372-75)

This reduction of Fifine in connection with the spiritual imagery of light is now to be translated into social terms in an extraordinary passage. The dramatic wife is now conspicuous as auditor; her attitude of class and superior morality are assumed and scorned in ironic conterpose. The imagery makes it clear that the issue intended as underlying the social distinction is sexuality:

> *And now, the mingled ray she shoots, I decompose.*
> *Her antecedents, take for execrable! Gloze*
> *No whit on your premiss: let be, there was no worst*
> *Of degradation spared Fifine: ordained from first*
> *To last, in body and soul, for one life-long debauch,*
> *The Pariah of the North, the European Nautch!*
> *This, far from seek to hide, she puts in evidence*
> *Calmly, displays the brand, bids pry without offence*
> *Your finger on the place. You comment, "Fancy us*
> *So operated on, maltreated, mangled thus!*
> *Such torture in our case, had we survived an hour?*
> *Some other sort of flesh and blood must be, with power*
> *Appropriate to the vile, unsensitive, tough-thonged,*
> *In lieu of our fine nerve! Be sure, she was not wronged*
> *Too much: you must not think she winced at prick as we!"*
> *Come, come, that's what you say, or would, were*
>   *thoughts but free.* (XXXI, 376-91)

The degradation of Fifine as "the Pariah of the North / The European Nautch" does not occur as fictional actuality; rather it is offered as an hypothesis and the stigmatic effect of the hypothesis is ironically diluted when it is followed by the prim scorn of the wife. The passage is part of a subtle process in the psychological progression of the poem. The validity of Fifine as a focus of value must be preserved, while the hypothesis of social degradation serves the symbolic purpose of removing her from a social perspective, a purpose that becomes more apparent when continuing developments of the poem remove her explicitly from all cultural contexts to establish a meaning that is both reductive and fundamental. Approaching now what amounts to a kind of epiphany, the speaker celebrates its value in anticipation: "So absolutely good is truth, truth never hurts / The teller, whose worst crime gets somehow grace, avowed" (XXXII, 395-96). The sincerity of this, the authentic joy of realization, will be clearer when it is recognized that the reduction to be achieved here in a human image in a dramatic context is the first full expression of a realization toward which the poem strives through its entire course and which has its ultimate expression in a symbolic treatment of history, culture, and metaphysics in part 5.

For many lines now to follow, the speaker's words are such as he imagines to be spoken by Fifine:

> *"Know all of me outside, the rest be emptiness*
> *For such as you! I call attention to my dress,*
> *Coiffure, outlandish features, lithe memorable limbs,*
> *Piquant entreaty, all that eye-glance over-skims.*
> *Does this give pleasure? Then, repay the pleasure, put*
> *Its price i' the tambourine! Do you seek further? Tut!*
> *I'm just my instrument,—sound hollow: mere smooth skin*
> *Stretched o'er gilt framework, I: rub-dub, naught else within—*
> *Always, for such as you!"* (398-406)

In the repetition of the phrase "for such as you" there is an important moralizing in favor of Fifine as victim. This also is designed to preserve Fifine as a focus of value. Yet unmistakably the meaning of Fifine arises from her existence as a physical organism and an object of sexual interest:

> *"—if I have use elsewhere,—*
> *If certain bells, now mute, can jingle, need you care?*
> *Be it enough, there's truth i' the pleading, which comports*
> *With no word spoken out in cottages or courts."* (406-9)

The word with which the pleading "comports" and which is not spoken out in "cottages or courts" is, of course, some vernacular variant of "sex." The reductive process continues, is reiterated and amplified, in specific rejection of other modalities of woman while affirming Fifine's meaning as simple, objective sexuality.

Again our understanding of what Browning is doing will be

strengthened by a reference to Jungian psychology. The four stages of the development of the anima corresponding to the four mythological figures previously mentioned are the stages of the process by which the anima wins its freedom from the archetype of the Great Mother. This, in Jungian terms, is the process which Freud describes as the resolution of the Oedipus complex. Discussing the process against the background of mythic archetypes, Erich Neumann comments as follows: "The transformation which the male undergoes in the course of the dragon fight includes a change in his relation to the female, symbolically expressed in the liberation of the captive from the dragon's power. In other words, the feminine image extricates itself from the grip of the Terrible Mother, a process known in analytical psychology as the crystallization of the anima from the mother archetype."[12]

In Jungian terms, Fifine is the anima. In another perspective she symbolizes the organic vitality which is revealed in part 5 as the substratum of psyche and culture in a vision of man unified and whole.

We now find the speaker imagining the words of Fifine who articulates imagined words of the other women of the pageant of women worthies—in quotation marks within quotation marks. The logic of this is that Fifine in a sense contains the claims of all the others and that she presents the claim of each in order to reject it, introducing each imagined speech with "Do I say, like . . ." Like "your wife," "your Helen," and so on. Soon, however, Fifine tends to disappear as in lengthy passages the various women seem to speak for themselves. Their utterances define the emotional demands that imprison the speaker. Indeed, in the eventual development of this episode, in a return to the pageant-of-women motif in part 2, the poem moves from its relatively discursive beginnings to the symbolic expression of an intense emotional stasis the full realization of which is necessary to the effort for freedom (see XXXVIII, 584-97). Such effort then begins anew, exposing deeply buried trammels of memory.

The first of the lengthy speeches is attributed to Helen. The speech begins with a demand that is the keynote of the restrictive element in the subjective condition projected:

" *'Yield yourself up, obey*
Implicitly, nor pause to question, to survey
Even the worshipful! prostrate you at my shrine!' " (XXXII, 416-18)

The word "shrine" provides another subtle association of Helen with the Saint. The idea of obedience without questioning the "worshipful" implies an identification of social opinion as a prohibitive power which is repeatedly recognized in the poem. In the continuation of Helen's speech this power of opinion is elevated as a claim of civilization, perhaps embodying also, at another level, a memory of Elizabeth as poet:

" *'Shall you dare controvert what the world counts divine?*
Array your private taste, own liking of the sense,
Own longing of the soul, against the impudence
Of history, the blare and bullying of verse?' " (419-22)

In the lines that follow we recognize the second instance of the ambivalent pattern. These lines continue the theme of social pressure. The passage will be obscure in immediate context unless it is seen as epitomizing an aspect of the basic movement of the poem. The logic is as follows: One does not take love in this world until the price is approved by social opinion. Even if he knows that the others would act as he wishes to act, disapproval is no less certain. He is

" *'Sure that particular gain implies a public loss,*
And that no smile he buys but proves a slash across
The face, a stab into the side of somebody—
Sure that, along with love's main-purchase, he will buy
Up the whole stock of earth's uncharitableness,
Envy and hatred.' " (428-33)

Envisioned here is not just general social disapproval but also a particular offense to particular people, and the poem offers no internal rationale for this. Certain of social and personal pressure, one acquiesces, and thus is anticipated the final acquiescence of the poem.

The next speaker whose words are imagined as being imagined by Fifine is Cleopatra: "Do I say, like your queen of Egypt?" The appeal of Cleopatra is antithetical to that of Helen. It is an invitation to sensual pleasure and is thus comparable to the appeal of Fifine, but with an important difference. Fifine is sensual health and gaiety, bright and clear; her image is the correlative of a longing for youth. The appeal of Cleopatra is that of a dark passion, frenzied lust under pressure. Her tone is of anger, and the combination of anger and the imagery of wine will be repeated significantly in section LXXIX:

> *"Do I say, like your Queen of Egypt? 'Who foregoes*
> *My cup of witchcraft—fault be on the fool! He knows*
> *Nothing of how I pack my wine-press, turn its winch*
> *Three-times-three, all the time to song and dance.' "* (436-39)

The end of this lascivious possibilty is ominous. She does not "flinch"

> *" 'From charming on and on, till at the last I squeeze*
> *Out the exhaustive drop that leaves behind mere lees*
> *And dregs, vapidity, thought essence heretofore!' "* (440-42)

The appeal of Cleopatra suggests also fear and despair. It is thus in a sense prohibitive of Fifine, for its basis is the harsh reality of the speaker's condition. Eventually his acquiescence, the failure of his quest, results from, or is at least rationalized by, the limits of time and age, which are here an appeal of urgency. Cleopatra's appeal is that of passion under the pressure of time—the theme of carpe diem at middle age:

> *" 'Sup of my sorcery, old pleasures please no more!*
> *Be great, be good, love, learn, have potency of hand*
> *Or heart or head,—what boots? You die, nor understand*
> *What bliss might be in life: you ate the grapes, but knew*
> *Never the taste of wine, such vintage as I brew!' "* (443-47)

Though the impulse of the speaker is for the graceful joy of Fifine and not the feverish passion of Cleopatra, the painful note of life's passion and joy missed, so common in Browning's poetry, will be heard again in this poem. Helen's demand of worship and Cleopatra's ominous challenge to passion are a counterpoise defining the speaker's condition in present time, escape from which is the experiential impulse of the poem. Underlying the present and integral with it, as we will come to understand, is a past of innocence radically in contrast with the dark and heated urgency of Cleopatra's appeal. From the untrammeled present the movement of the poem is now to memory and thence in memory's temporal process through narrative actuality again to the condition of the present. The Saint speaks next, followed by Elvire, and they represent different aspects and phases of a single narrative continuity.

When the Saint speaks now we need not be surprised to find that the sobriquet "Saint" is a metaphor and that she represents a modality of woman as wife. Her speech celebrates the ineffable tenderness of the spirituality of young love as it deepens to carnality:

> " *'when sanctity betrays*
> *First fear lest earth below seem real as heaven above,*
> *And holy worship, late, change soon to sinful love—*
> *Where is the plenitude of passion which endures*
> *Comparison with that, I ask of amateurs?'* " (457-61)

Among the images celebrating this realization is that of a brook:

> " *'What sound outwarbles brook, while, at the source, it wins*
> *That moss and stone dispart, allow its bubblings breathe?'* "
> (453-54)

This image will be repeated twice in other contexts in a progressive pattern uniting disparate elements of the poem and indicating their symbolic continuity (see XXXIX, 620-22; LXXIII, 1202-12).

In the next speech we hear the words of Elvire, in the imagined words of Fifine. Elvire as dramatic wife is constrained to hear the words of the phantom wife: "(Your husband holds you fast, / Will have you listen, learn your character at last!)" (XXXIII, 462-63).

Grim experience now is the unhappy sequel to early marriage—the tedium, the conflict, and constraints that grow in marriage with passing years. The continuity of this long passage with the expression of the "Saint" is reinforced in two ways. Elvire characterizes herself, in terms applied earlier to the Saint, as half in heaven, and her imagery of wind, rain, and storm is that which earlier linked the Saint with Helen:

> " 'Though dew-prime flee,—mature at noonday, love defied
> Chance, the wind, change, the rain: love strenuous all the more
> For storm, struck deeper root and choicer fruitage bore,
> Despite the rocking world.' " (473-76)

Though love may last into maturity, it does not avail for happiness: " 'Yet truth, struck root in vain: / While tenderness bears fruit, you praise, not taste again' " (476-77). The reason is that possession allays desire. The role of the husband then is submission to unhappiness:

> " 'Your part was to bow neck, bid fall decree of fate.
> Then, O the knotty point—white-night's work to revolve—
> What meant that smile, that sigh? Not Solon's self could solve.
> Then, O the deep surmise what one word might express,
> And if what seemed her "No" may not have meant her "Yes!"
> Then, such annoy, for cause—calm welcome, such acquist
> Of rapture if, refused her arm, hand touched her wrist!
> Now, what's a smile to you? Poor candle that lights up
> The decent household gloom which sends you out to sup.
> A tear? worse! warns that health requires you keep aloof
> From nuptial chamber, since rain penetrates the roof!' " (481-91)

In this passage, which is continuous with the speech of the Saint, we may perhaps see reflected some of the stresses which Betty Miller has observed in the Browning marriage in later years.[13]

The final lines of Elvire's speech, the tone deepening in anger of verbal chastisement, are compact with diverse effects:

" 'Give you the sun to keep, forthwith must fancy range:
A goodly lamp, no doubt,—yet might you catch her hair
And capture, as she frisks, the fen-fire dancing there!
What do I say? at least a meteor's half in heaven;
Provided filth but shine, my husband hankers even
After putridity that's phosphorescent, cribs
The rustic's tallow-rush, makes spoil of urchin's squibs,
In short, prefers to me—chaste, temperate, serene—
What sputters green and blue, this fizgig called Fifine!' "
(499-507)

In the words "chaste, temperate, serene" Elvire is linked with the original lily imagery symbolically uniting and contrasting Elvire and Fifine. The association of the word "phosphorescent" with Fifine is important because it is repeated at a later stage of the psychic quest, to link Fifine with a victory song filled with erotic imagery (see LXXVIII). This word, anticipated by "fen-fire," is part of the concentration of light imagery in the passage. Elvire is associated with the sun and with the "meteor half in heaven"; Fifine, with "tallow-rush" (a candle), "squibs" (firecrackers), and "fizgig" (a light woman and a form of fireworks). The sputtering of the fizgig as "green and blue" is echoed later in the poem when the idea of light, refracted on earth, is conceived as recombining in the white light of the vision of heaven in part 2. The association of Fifine, as well as Elvire, with that vision by repetition of light imagery will be important for interpretation of the passage in which it occurs.

In the sustained anger of Elvire's attack, the artistic device by which her words are being imagined by Fifine is forgotten, and Elvire becomes in effect the real speaker. Indeed, the speaker of the monologue is taken aback by her attack and startled into hapless defense in one of the few humorous passages of the poem:

So all your sex mistake! Strange that so plain a fact
Should raise such dire debate! Few families were racked
By torture self-supplied, did Nature grant but this—
That women comprehend mental analysis!
(XXXIV, 508-11)

It is as though the vigor and harshness of Elvire's attack have shocked the speaker back into his propensity for obedience and loyalty, while shifting the focus of the poem back to the dramatic level. This return to the dramatic level serves the progress of the poem as it takes a new direction.

5

The Elegiac Process

Part 1 has served to establish basic symbolism—the meaning of Fifine, a variety of images projecting modalities of the experience of woman, and a pattern of reference to images associated with the wife but treated as the distant content of memory. The quest consists in the making of the symbols. Next follows what must be called an elegiac process—a process of remembering in order to forget, in which forgetting must not betray a loyalty.

Part 2 begins with an assertion of loyalty to the dramatic wife. The speaker employs an allegory in which our awareness remains close to the dramatic level of the poem. Then he invokes the phantom wife and the poem generates a fluid and complex sequence of images reflecting symbolism from part 1 and informed consistently by the idea of a death and of the loss of a loved one in the past. Part 2 is the most personal part of the poem. The symbolism contains unmistakable references to Browning's life, and the symbolic development becomes intelligible only on the assumption that the phantom wife is for Browning an artistic means of dealing with the memory of Elizabeth. Symbolic movement alternates with philosophical speculation arising from urgent memories, and the entire development culminates in a vision of a reunion of lovers in heaven, the vision implying the reconciliation of a heavenly loyalty with earthly freedom. Then the vision is disrupted and the quest continues.

In the allegory with which part 2 begins, the wife corresponds to a painting of Raphael newly purchased. For a few weeks the speaker remains excited by the painting but with the passing of time he can "saunter past," even turn his back "perchance to overlook /

With relish, leaf by leaf, Doré's last picture book" (XXXV, 549-51). But, even though the speaker were "engaged / In Doré, elbow-deep, picture-books million paged" (XXXVI, 571), if a servant cried " 'Fire in the gallery,' " he would risk all to save the Raphael. The quality of sincerity in this avowal of loyalty at the explicit and dramatic level of the poem is suggested when the speaker turns back to the symbolic idiom to interpret loyalty as an imprisoning obsession and thus achieves the ultimate expression of the psychological condition of the speaker in present time. The movement (in section XXXVIII) from the dramatic to the symbolic level of realization is radical. The speaker abruptly returns to the pageant of women, and, explicitly to the conception of the phantom wife: "But no, play out your *rôle* / I' the pageant! 'T is not fit your phantom leave the stage" (XXXVIII, 579-80).

The poetry becomes again extremely intense as the conception of the phantom wife is developed under protean imagery. The phantom wife, "inviolate of life," inhabits the realm of death. She is "my new-created shape." Her very existence, that is to say, the imagery in which she has her chimerical being, has its origin in the subjectivity of the speaker. Acknowledgment of the subjective powers at work is important to self-realization as part of the psychic struggle for freedom. Equally important is the definition of the initial predicament in the next five words: "Fettered, I hold my flower." The holding is the fettering. The restraint entrammeling the speaker is an intentional power of his subjectivity. These five words may be taken as the key to the poem. Left to the powers external to the speaker, the phantom wife would dissolve into nothingness. A death would be complete. The internal tensions of the extremely compact and complex passage are the central tensions of the poem:

Fettered, I hold my flower, her own cup's weight would win
From off the tall slight stalk a-top of which she turns
And trembles, makes appeal to one who roughly earns
Her thanks instead of blame, (did lily only know),
By thus constraining length of lily, letting snow
Of cup-crown, that's her face, look from its guardian stake. (589-94)

By "lily" the phantom wife is associated with the central female image of the poem and with the initial Saint imagery, this latter association reinforced by "snow." The meaning and the power of the phrase "guardian stake" may not be fully appreciated without reference to a tendency seen often in Browning's work. In Browning's poetry the beloved is frequently asked by the speaker to adopt toward him an attitude that is motherly and protective. A speaker's passive and dependent relationship to the beloved is most fully expressed in the poem "The Guardian Angel." The frequency of the pattern suggests that it was deeply implicated in Browning's conception and experience of love.[1] In the very intense fusion of associations in the passage under consideration, the word "guardian" may be taken to reflect the recurrent pattern of feeling. The "guardian stake" supports a guardian. The stake has taken on the function of "I hold," without which the flower would collapse, disappear. The symbolism suggests recognition of the fact that the love upon which the speaker feels a dependency owes its own existence to a power within the subjectivity of the speaker. The fusion of ideas is parallel to that in "Fettered, I hold . . ."

In the passage just quoted the incipient lyric flow is inhibited by analysis and self-awareness. Only with the word "guardian" does the passage move toward unreserved expression of love and only in the light of this may one understand, in accord with the basic pattern of ambivalence, the hostility of the flower-insect imagery which follows. The flower face can look

> *Superb on all that crawls beneath, and mutely make*
> *Defiance, with the mouth's white movement of disdain,*
> *To all that stoops, retires and hovers round again!* (595-97)

The words of the last line must be emphasized. "Stoops" is the response to that demand projected on the figure of Helen: " 'Yield yourself up, obey / Implicitly' " (XXXII, 416-17). The word "retires" represents a corresponding withdrawal from the world, the world represented most significantly by Fifine, and "hovers round again" suggests an obsessive returning, pursuant to which there now emerges an image of adoration strangely flawed. The reader must be prepared for rapid transformations in which the head of a flower becomes the head of a person, the lily becomes a corpse, and the corpse awakens:

> How windingly the limbs delay to lead up, reach
> Where, crowned, the head waits calm: as if reluctant, each,
> That eye should traverse quick such lengths of loveliness,
> From feet, which just are found embedded in the dress
> Deep swathed about with folds and flowings virginal,
> Up to the pleated breasts, rebellious 'neath their pall,
> As if the vesture's snow were moulding sleep not death.
>   (XXXVIII, 598-604)

Association with the Saint persists in the image of snow and of the feet "swathed about" by folds of the garment. Snow takes on here a new dimension which should be kept in mind in later recurrences. Snow is here the agent of death. The words "death" and "pall" mark an extraordinary development of the poem. In the phrase "pleated breasts rebellious 'neath their pall" there is an intermingling of necrotic and sexual imagery. The total image of this passage is that of a female body in death, and we arrive at a primary depth of the elegiac theme. In overt elegy, traditional form provides release from the pressures of death. In this poem the pressures of death erupt within a form. Traditional elegy is ritualistic and communal. Elegy here is intensely personal with a pattern not that of ritual but of dream. As in funeral and elegiac ritual, however, the goal is reconciliation to death by realization of death. In this poem the goal is never won, for the ending passages and the epilogue are haunted by a ghost; but the effort is begun, the process put in motion, and the basic strategies of elegy arise. In the psychological substratum of the beginning of elegy there is an intermingling of life and death. As in dream, the lost one awakes from death. The snow

> Must melt and so release; whereat, from the fine sheath,
> The flower-cup-crown starts free, the face is unconcealed,
> And what shall now divert me, once the sweet face revealed,
> From all I loved so long, so lingeringly left? (605-8)

The last line is not coherent with the dramatic context. Rather it develops the symbolic theme of the phantom wife as a loved one lost through death. Its use of the past tense draws attention to the dramatic present before turning attention back to what has happened in the preceding lines. In those lines the imagination had gone back in time beyond an ambivalent present infused with hostility and back beyond the necrotic interlude to release from the more distant past the image which is the central meaning of the phantom wife. The psychological disposition of the speaker is now unflawed commitment, a condition which will remain now essentially undisturbed through an extensive progession of the poem. Despite the shift to direct dramatic address it is very clear in the lines following that the idea of death associated with the phantom wife is still on the speaker's mind:

> *Because indeed your face fits into just the cleft*
> *O' the heart of me, Elvire, makes right and whole once more*
> *All that was half itself without you. As before,*
> *My truant finds its place! Doubtlessly sea-shells yearn,*
> *If plundered by sad chance: would pray their pearls return,*
> *Let negligently slip away into the wave!* (XXXIX, 609-14)

It will be recalled that the final line of the phantom wife passage previously quoted was "From all I loved so long, so lingeringly left?" Nothing in the dramatic circumstance of the poem, or in the Don Juan tradition, for that matter, justifies the lingering departure. This line expresses an elegiac note. The image of the pearl lost in the sea connotes a finality equally irrelevant to dramatic circumstance. The image, as has been shown, comes from the Browning love letters where it signified an imagined loss of Elizabeth. The image in the poem is elegiac and marks a transposition of the idea of death from the phantom to the dramatic wife as part of the fusion of the two figures now being accomplished. The phantom wife who awoke under the power of imagination from death into life has become the dramatic wife. Now the movement from death to life is recapitulated as the flow of poetry around the image of the dramatic wife moves from elegy to sensual immediacy:

Never may eyes desist, those eyes so gray and grave,
From their slow sure supply of the effluent soul within!
And, would you humor me? I dare to ask, unpin
The web of that brown hair! O'erwash o' the sudden, but
As promptly, too, disclose, on either side, the jut
Of alabaster brow! So part rich rillets dyed
Deep by the woodland leaf, when down they pour, each side
O' the rock-top, pushed by Spring! (615-22)

This restoration of the dramatic wife momentarily to the heart and bosom of the speaker occurs at a special point in a chronological progression which is beginning to emerge and which is a function of memory and of the elegiac process. The rillet imagery occurred previously in association with the Saint and was expressive of the tenderness of young passion. The brook was imagined in the purity of its source (XXXII, 453-54). The brook now is "dyed / Deep by the woodland leaf." When the image occurs again it will recapitulate this progress and end in elegiac loss (see LXXIII). This is the second of a number of instances in which the poem registers a sequence representing stages in a life, the first being in the imagined words of the Saint (XXXII, 448-61). The wide separation of the parts of this sequence may alert us to the subtlety with which biographical elements are to be reflected.

At the present point of progress, the speaker has undergone a critical psychic experience. In effect the need that underlies the poem, its basic experiential impulse expressed in forward movement and the anticipation of joy, has been fulfilled from within by memory and imagination. An appetite has generated its own sustenance. Such a possibility must be a factor in the inhibition which is a basic condition of the experience the poem expresses. It accounts for the deep commitment to the dramatic wife now in effect. The speaker is fascinated by the experience and he will discourse on it through sixty-eight lines (XLI-XLIV). Indeed, the theme will recur thereafter, for the experience is the real concern of all the speaker's comment on subjectivity in art and life. The initial discourse on the subject comes in response to a question at the dramatic level from the wife:

> *"And where i' the world is all*
> *This wonder, you detail so trippingly, espied?*
> *My mirror would reflect a tall, thin, pale, deep-eyed*
> *Personage, pretty once, it may be, doubtless still*
> *Loving,—a certain grace yet lingers, if you will,—*
> *But all this wonder, where?"* (XL, 622-27)

Elizabeth had protested similarly: "You see in me what is not:— *that* I know: and you overlook in me what is unsuitable to you . . *that* I know, and have sometimes told you."[2] To the protesting question of the dramatic wife the speaker poses an answer which begins as follows:

> *Why, where but in the sense*
> *And soul of me, Art's judge? Art is my evidence*
> *That something was, is, might be; but no more thing itself,*
> *Than flame is fuel.* (XLI, 627-30)

The metaphysical theme here suggests the immortality of the soul and prefigures a later symbolic development of that idea. It is of some importance to observe that art is not the speaker's exclusive subject here and yet is introduced as something more than an analogy; art and life are essentially identified. Both are a product of "soul-proficiency" (L, 737).

The speaker continues as follows:

> *Once the verse-book laid on shelf,*
> *The picture turned to wall, the music fled from ear,—*
> *Each beauty, born of each, grows clearer and more clear,*
> *Mine henceforth, ever mine!* (XLI, 630-33)

A number of biographical associations seem to cluster in the theme of the discourse. The passage recalls a letter in which Browning imagined that Elizabeth might "take all yourself away." He wrote, "I have your memory, the knowledge of you, the idea of you printed into my heart and brain,—on that, I can live my life."[3] There may be, however, another biographical association of more importance. It may explain the extensive attention given to the theme of the discourse. In the Humanities Research Center of the University of Texas there is a Browning letter from which the name of the addressee has been carefully removed. It would seem clear, however, that the letter was written to Mrs. Story. It concerns the sculptor William Story and a plan, at some time after Elizabeth's death, to do a sculptured bust of her.

References to Elizabeth in her last years speak of a "pain worn face," a body "shattered by disease."[4] Browning is so impressed with the idea that Elizabeth's meaning for him came from her inner light and from his own subjectivity that he seems to be terrified at the possibility of confronting the physical facts of her countenance:

> And now—about the "Bust": I shall tell you my mind, because you deserve it,—and so does Story, who knows my belief in his genius and power to do whatever can be done: *can* this be done? In that face, which I shall not apply any epithet to, the inner light of the soul was used to fill up all deficiency, and—for me—transfigure all actually there: this light gone, what can replace it? A painter's skill, perhaps, who can give a few leading points and leave the rest to fancy—but a sculptor must make *all out*—and his facts will be the dead facts—Do you wish for these? I should turn away anxiously from such. I have been endeavoring to do this very thing, spite of my conviction of its impossibility—with every help from photographs, picture, and my memory and affectionate zeal—but it could not be, and I think never can. If you think otherwise, of course, I will send the photograph you mention—but I want you, in our common interest, to consider well before you begin what—I much fear—will only end disastrously. Story will do his utmost—as no one will—but! And then we shall all be sorry. Now decide—and understand that if I am wrong, it is a happy chance indeed.[5]

It would seem probable that in part 2 the preoccupation with the disparity between face and soul reflects a troubling conflict between different modes in which Browning remembered Elizabeth.

In the poem the speaker proceeds in his resolve to "test fancy in my brain / By fact which gave it birth" (XLII, 635-36). He finds that if he returns to the work of art he fails to discover there the subjective effect it has engendered:

> *I re-peruse in vain*
> *The verse, I fail to find that vision of delight*
> *I' the Bazzi's lost-profile, eye-edge so exquisite.* (XLII, 636-38)

Anticipating his explanation, the speaker shifts and broadens the question to which it will apply. He says, "I seem to understand the way heart chooses heart / By help of the outside form" (XLIII, 646-47); more specificially the question concerns the way in which one lover responds to an external deficiency in the other,

> *why each grows reconciled*
> *To what is absent, what superfluous in the mask*
> *Of flesh that's meant to yield,—did nature ply her task*
> *As artist should,—precise the features of the soul.* (648-51)

These questions lead to still another, one suggested by the suspicion here of nature's betrayal of the soul. Each soul is unique and so complete, the speaker argues. All souls are therefore, "types perfect everyone" (662). But if this is so, the failure of perfection in the outer form is "a mystery / Insoluble to man, a plaguy puzzle" (664). The speaker's explanation is that the subjectivity of the observer transcends the outward form observed and that eventually this may be objectively justified. The total process

> *yet succeeds the same: since, what is wanting to success,*
> *If somehow every face, no matter how deform,*
> *Evidence, to some one of hearts on earth, that, warm*
> *Beneath the veriest ash, there hides a spark of soul*
> *Which, quickened by love's breath, may yet pervade the whole*
> *O' the gray, and, free again, be fire?—of worth the same,*
> *Howe'er produced, for, great or little, flame is flame.* (671-77)

The speaker expands his explanation. Each soul "goes striving to combine / With what shall right the wrong" (XLIV, 681-82), not only to perceive the perfection but to be united with it, to "supplement unloveliness by love" (683). There is recognition of the idealism, however uncertain or inexact, which informs this part of the poem: "Ask Plato else" (684). Once again art and life are identified, for the work of love is also that of art, which the speaker defines as instinctive and a function of the soul, and which, he says,

> I may style the love of loving, rage
> Of knowing, seeing, feeling the absolute truth of things
> For truth's sake, whole and sole, not any good, truth brings
> The knower, seer, feeler, beside, —instinctive Art
> Must fumble for the whole, once fixing on a part
> However poor, surpass the fragment, and aspire
> To reconstruct thereby the ultimate entire. (685-91)

The speaker now undertakes to provide examples. He draws three faces in the sand and, apologizing for his lack of skill, says that they represent his "three prime types of beauty" (XLV, 700). Of the first the speaker says, "And who wants Horror, has it" (XLVII, 718). The second reminds him of Reynolds's portrait of Garrick between the muses of comedy and tragedy (XLVIII). The third is characterized as "the portrait of Elvire" (XLIX, 735).

The three drawings will seem irrelevant to the speaker's remarks on aesthetic theory until we realize that the remarks concern the imaginative power at work in this particular work of art entitled *Fifine at the Fair* and that the three drawings construct an "ultimate entire" which is organically related to the total substance of the poem. It should be kept in mind that there have already appeared in the poem progressions, subtly noted, corresponding to stages in a life.

The description of the first drawing is introduced by imagining the effect if the speaker had "Gérôme's force," referring to the nineteenth-century French painter (XLVII, 706), and then by suggesting that in fact the drawing proceeds "With Gérôme well at work" (709).[6] The description of the first drawing in the sand is as follows:

> *observe how brow recedes,*
> *Head shudders back on spine, as if one haled the hair,*
> *Would have the full-face front what pin-point eye's sharp stare*
> *Announces; mouth agape to drink the flowing fate,*
> *While chin protrudes to meet the burst o' the wave: elate*
> *Almost, spurred on to brave necessity, expend*
> *All life left, in one flash, as fire does at its end.* (709-15)

This is a highly particularized description of a woman at the moment of death.[7] Suggestions of a condition of immortality and of a remembered death have been repeatedly associated with female figures heretofore. Now the moment of death itself has been realized. The second description is as follows:

> *What does it give for germ, monadic mere intent*
> *Of mind in face, faint first of meanings ever meant?*
> *Why, possibly, a grin, that, strengthened, grows a laugh;*
> *That, softened, leaves a smile; that, tempered, bids you quaff*
> *At such a magic cup as English Reynolds once*
> *Compounded: for the witch pulls out of you response*
> *Like Garrick's to Thalia, however due may be*
> *Your homage claimed by that stiff-stoled Melpomene!*
>   (XLVIII, 720-27)

A progession occurs within the description. The condition from which it begins is marked by the words "faint first of meanings ever meant" which echo "that fine, that faint fugitive first of all" (XXXII, 450), descriptive of the deepening of the spirituality of young love into passion which is associated with the Saint and eventually with the wife. Then as we may imagine the speaker changing the lines in the sand, a progession occurs from grin, to smile, ending in a condition which must be ascribed to the speaker himself who is identified sympathetically with Garrick at the center of Reynolds's painting.

In Reynolds's painting, Thalia, or Comedy, decolleté and amply sensuous, has one hand on Garrick's upper arm, the other probably on the back of his shoulder. There is a definite tug suggested in the attitude of her arms and the force of her tug angles downward.

She is physical, voluptuous, and blonde. Her eyes are large and languorous and there is a faintly coy and whimsical look on her face. Her position is physically close to Garrick. Their hips must be touching. There is also a certain complacency in her look. Her direction is definitely earthward, her head considerably lower than Garrick's.

Melpomene, or Tragedy, on the other side of Garrick, to his left, is a very different figure. She is tall, her head higher than Garrick's, her body erect. She stands further from Garrick, one hand on his outstretched wrist, the other raised and pointing upward. There is a slight frown on her face. Her mouth is open and she speaks. What she says may be some noble thought appropriate to tragedy, but her expression could certainly be taken as rebuke and her utterance interpreted as remonstrance. She is a brunet; her breasts are ample but chastely covered. She is "stiff-stoled."

Garrick's attitude expresses dilemma in that his hands are spread in equal deference to each, and while the movement of his body is toward Comedy, his head is turned toward Tragedy and his eyes are on hers. The expression is somewhat ambiguous, but his attitude may be read as not quite ambivalent. His good-humored smile is in harmony with Comedy as are his raised and somewhat quizzical brows. The expression in his eyes is quite marvelous. In his attitude toward Tragedy there is a certain recognition, the suggestion of a sense of responsibility, almost as through he were asking permission to go with Comedy, and unquestionably there is laughter in his eyes. His hands are opened outward in a gesture of diffidence as though to say, "How can I resist this tug of Comedy?" The picture is finely attuned to the tensions of the poem.

The progression of Browning's description, then, is from an echo of first love to the condition of Garrick in the painting, which corresponds to the condition of the speaker torn between the attractions of Fifine and the restraints represented by Elvire. Now, as has occurred before in the poem, a female image emerges from nothingness or from death into life under the creative pressure of the speaker's subjectivity. The third drawing is described as follows:

And just this one face more! Pardon the bold pretence!
May there not lurk some hint, struggle toward evidence
In that compressed mouth, those strained nostrils, steadfast eyes
Of utter passion, absolute self-sacrifice,
Which—could I but subdue the wild grotesque, refine
That bulge of brow, make blunt that nose's aquiline,
And let, although compressed, a point of pulp appear
I' the mouth—would give at last the portrait of Elvire?

(XLIX, 728-35)

We may now consider the three drawings more curiously. The physical posture of the woman depicted at the moment of death in the first drawing must inevitably remind us that Elizabeth died in Browning's arms, as did her sister Arabel seven years later.[8] The association of "fire" with the "end" anticipates the culmination of the elegiac movement in the vision of heaven which is to come. The sequel to the first drawing is a progression beginning in the memory of first love, then proceeding from grin to laugh to smile and then the tempering of a smile to arrive in Reynolds's painting at symbolism that corresponds to the central predicament of the poem. The description of the second drawing encapsulates subliminally the progress of a lifetime. The eventual goal of the sequence of these drawings is the point in present time in which Elvire, identified with the phantom wife by third-person reference, is beloved, but represents the prohibitive power in the memory of Elizabeth. The earlier description of Elvire as a "tall, thin, pale, deep-eyed / Personage" (XL, 624-25) differentiates her from Elizabeth, but the third drawing in its specific details—"compressed mouth," "strained nostrils," "steadfast eyes," "point of pulp in the mouth"—is strikingly consistent with the painting of Elizabeth by Michele Gordigiani.[9]

The elegiac movement of the poem is now increasingly ascendant. The emergence of the beloved image into life incorporates memories which lie behind the image. Such memories will remain subliminal but they will be increasingly particularized. The speaker comments on his drawings, observing, in effect, the power of memory and imagination:

Shall any soul despair of setting free again
Trait after trait, until the type as wholly start
Forth, visible to sense, as that minutest part,
(Whate'er the chance) which first arresting eye, warned soul
That, under wrong enough and ravage, lay the whole
O' the loveliness it "loved"—I take the accepted phrase? (L, 741-46)

The problems of integrating the poem may be epitomized in connection with this passage. What is to be said of the following: the obscure suggestions revolving around the words "chance," "first," "warned"; the association of these words with "wrong" and "ravage"; the reservation in connection with the use of the word "loved"? The passage hardly gives rise to an image at all. Rather there is an abstract triangulation, so to speak, of an occasion. The occasion is a first viewing of the beloved. An element of chance is involved in the occasion. Despite "wrong enough and ravage" in the person of the beloved there is an indication of the "whole of loveliness," to which the observer responds. The indication of "loveliness," however, is ambivalent, a warning. So it must be assumed that the observer, through some tendency of nerves or habit, is in some sense both disposed and indisposed to love.

It would seem clear that in this passage memory arrives at the farthest remove from the present that is achieved in the poem. We may project from this passage a first meeting of the fictional persons Don Juan and Elvire in an occasion anterior to other experiences reflected in the poem. That fictional occasion, however, will bear remarkable resemblance to one that was historical.

Browning was thirty-three years old when he first stood beside the bed to which Elizabeth had been confined for nine years. The famous invalid was thirty-nine years old. The meeting was arranged by Elizabeth's cousin and benefactor, John Kenyon. An earlier plan for the meeting had fallen through. Browning, who had long ago consigned himself to permanent bachelorhood, referred in his first letter to her poetry, writing, "I do . . . love these books with all my heart—and I love you too."[10] A second letter must have carried rashness to an extreme, for Elizabeth returned it and insisted that he destroy it. It is the only letter of the courtship correspondence not extant.

The reservation expressed in " 'loved'—I take the accepted phrase" is an acknowledgment of that precipitant rashness, informed now by a more experienced conception of love. That, however, does not exhaust the meaning of the phrase. Symbol as memory intermingles here with symbol as part of poetic dynamics. The phrase also expresses an ambivalence related to the recoil in hostility which occurs throughout the poem. The recoil here, the momentary qualification, comes eight lines before the introduction of a new symbol the elaboration of which will achieve the poem's most spiritualized treatment of the wife and lead directly to the vision of heaven which is the culmination of the elegiac process. The new development parallels the Raphael passage, explicitly, as a testament of love. But while the Raphael painting represents the dramatic wife, the new development involves explicitly the phantom wife. While the Raphael passage was allegorical, the new development is symbolic and much more complex, elaborating the subjective nature of a spiritualized love. It introduces in the central symbol a temporal dimension which opens to biographical allusion and, terminating in apocalypse, provides the elegiac basis for escape from the love it attests. The speaker pontificates: "Let each, i' the world, amend his love, as I, o' the shore / My sketch" (LI, 751-52). The result will be "more beautiful than beauty's self, when lo / What was my Rafael turns my Michelagnolo!" (754-55). The speaker explains:

> *For, we two boast, beside our pearl, a diamond.*
> *I' the palace-gallery, the corridor beyond,*
> *Upheaves itself a marble, a magnitude man-shaped*
> *As snow might be. One hand,—the Master's,—smoothed*
> *   and scraped*
> *That mass, he hammered on and hewed at, till he hurled*
> *Life out of death, and left a challenge: for the world,*
> *Death still,—since who shall dare, close to the image, say*
> *If this be purposed Art, or mere mimetic play*
> *Of Nature?* (LII, 756-64)

A distinctive characteristic of the sculpture being described is that the figure emerges, as though still half-embedded, from the matrix stone out of which it is carved. From a point "close to the image" the figure seems to be lost in the matrix. The poem continues:

> Death therefore to the world. Step back a pace or two!
> And then, who dares dispute the gradual birth its due
> Of breathing life, or breathless immortality,
> Where out she stands, and yet stops short, half bold, half shy,
> Hesitates on the threshold of things, since partly blent
> With stuff she needs must quit, her native element
> I' the mind o' the Master,—what's the creature, dear-divine
> Yet earthly-awful too, so manly-feminine,
> Pretends this white advance? What startling brain-escape
> Of Michelagnolo takes elemental shape?
> I think he meant the daughter of the old man o' the sea,
> Emerging from her wave, goddess Eidotheé. (768-79)

The figure, as Browning describes it, is similar to Michelangelo's series of "Captives" now in the Academy of Florence. The figure called "Youthful Captive" corresponds essentially to Browning's description. This is probably intended as a male figure, as are the other sculptures of captives. However a striking characteristic of these figures is the symbolically amorphous treatment of the genitalia. Other aspects of the "Youthful Captive" easily admit of Browning's considering the figure as female—"so manly-feminine."[11]

The name of the goddess, Eidotheé, means "divine idea." She is associated with "breathless immortality" and in the words "startling brain-escape" the subjectivity of the divine idea is identified. The stone matrix is nature, and death, and the nothingness that precedes imagination. Eidotheé is the culminating product, save for one remaining image, of that effort announced by the speaker to "test fancy in my brain / By fact which give it birth" (XLII, 635-36). She is identified directly with the pageant of women and the phantom wife, "Shaming all other forms, seen as I see her here / I' the soul" (LIII, 803-4). By the close association of "snow" and "death" Eidotheé is made continuous with the Saint imagery (XX) and with imagery of life emerging from death (XXXVIII, 603-8). The words "dead" or "death" are used seven times in connection with Eidothee imagery, recalling inevitably that death in the first drawing in the sand. Within a few lines, a statement derived from the Eidotheé symbolism will employ the imagery of flame in an extended antici-pation of the vision of heaven soon to follow. Thus the symbolism of an extensive development is clustering around the Eidotheé sym-bolism.

In the poetry thus far examined, however, Eidotheé is emerging from death into life, and immediately after she is identified by name, there follows a passage based upon the Homeric source of the myth and employing, perhaps, echoes of Shelley and *The Tem-pest*. The passage might be taken as an unnecessary and playful di-gression if we did not remember that we are within thirty-four lines of a subliminal reference to the first meeting of Browning and Eliz-abeth:

> She who, in elvish sport, spite with benevolence
> Mixed Mab-wise up, must needs instruct the Hero whence
> Salvation dawns o'er that mad misery of his isle.
> Yes, she imparts to him, by what a pranksome wile
> He may surprise her sire, asleep beneath a rock,
> When he has told their tale, amid his web-foot flock
> Of sea-beasts, "fine fat seals with bitter breath!" laughs she
> At whom she likes to save, no less. (LII, 780-87)

This passage brings together the following suggestions: a promise of salvation for the hero (hero as artist insofar as he is associated with Prospero) and an end to his solitary misery; collaboration of the female lover in deceit of her father; and an attitude both amused and loving toward the father's "flock." This cluster corres-ponds to the sequel to the first interview: the hope and love of the lovers; the extraordinary deception of Mr. Barrett, including not only the elopement but also the fact that though Browning visited the house continually, Mr. Barrett died without Browning having ever met him; the strange Barrett family whom Elizabeth loved and lamented.

The biographical sequence that began with the first meeting of Robert and Elizabeth has moved to the next major event in their lives—the elopement and marriage—and memory will continue in the temporal path so established. For the moment, the words immediately following those last quoted above will be symbolically enriched by the reading just proposed:

> *Eidotheé,*
> *Whom you shall never face evolved, in earth, in air,*
> *In wave; but, manifest i' the soul's domain, why, there*
> *She ravishingly moves to meet you, all through aid*
> *O' the soul!* (787-91)

Within another three lines the imaginative focus of the poem moves to Italy, the goal of the flight of the newlyweds from the Barrett household, and we find the speaker buying an art work (the Michelangelo), far more valuable than the seller knows. Comparable purchases, or so he considered them, were a favorite pastime of Browning in the Italian years.[12] The passage is as follows:

> *I bought*
> *That work—(despite plain proof, whose hand it was had wrought*
> *I' the rough: I think we trace the tool of triple tooth,*
> *Here, there and everywhere)—bought dearly that uncouth*
> *Unwieldy bulk, for just ten dollars—"Bulk, would fetch—*
> *Converted into lime—some five pauls!" grinned a wretch,*
> *Who, bound on business, paused to hear the bargaining,*
> *And would have pitied me "but for the fun o' the thing!"* (794-801)

Read at the dramatic level such a passage is incidental, a casual, mildly egotistical memory of luck and expertise, the purchase and the condition of it having nothing to do with the course of the narrative. But read in the biographical context, it will be seen as coherent with the symbolic progress of the poem. Only thus will we understand that the text, at this point apparently narrational and

thin, bears an immense penumbra of imagination. A whole condition of life has been recalled from memory, a condition now filling
imagination, made real and palpable because invoked in the mode
of an immediate and specific episode. It was a condition of life per-
meated by love.

And yet suddenly the speaker turns viciously on the dramatic
wife:

> Shall such a wretch be—you? Must—while I show Elvire
> Shaming all other forms, seen as I see her here
> I' the soul,—this other-you perversely look outside,
> And ask me, "Where i' the world is charm to be descried
> I' the tall thin personage, with paled eye, pensive face,
> Any amount of love, and some remains of grace?"
> See yourself in my soul. (LIII, 802-8)

We may understand this if we keep in mind that the problem of
the poem is enslavement to memory and that anger is a periodic
means of extrication from memory, of distancing from the past.
The speaker's anger here, while integral with the symbolic movement, has also a pretext at the dramatic level. The dramatic wife
will not believe the speaker's argument. Her skepticism will be even
more conspicuous a short while later. Her resistance is an especially
effective point of convergence between the dramatic and symbolic
levels of the poem. Immediately after the speaker's angry outburst
in the passage quoted above, the poem moves in predominantly
discursive passages to the vision of heaven, which is potentially the
justification for which the poem quests. The speaker's freedom
would have been won. In effect the poem would be over with this
vision which is the culmination of part 2. The dramatic wife's refus-
al to be convinced is but another expression of the restrictive power
attributed to the phantom wife.

Movement to the vision of heaven develops the ideas, with increasing conviction, of the immortality of the soul and the existence
of God. Preparation for that vision (LV-LVIII) continues the biographical sequence in the sense that it treats the intellectual and religious concerns of Browning during the early Italian years. The

basis for the religious affirmations at this point is the idea of the subjective source of value, which has been the unifying theme in most of part 2 (from section XLI onward). The subjectivity of the individual is the sole source of value: "In the seeing soul, all worth lies" (LV, 824). The world as it can be known objectively is dead, meaningless, but it is objective existence from which the "soul" begins. The point of greatest importance for the eventual argument is that positively any aspect of objective existence will serve as the material with which the soul begins:

> ·And naught i' the world, which, save for soul that sees, inert
> Was, is, and would be ever, —stuff for transmuting, —null
> And void until man's breath evoke the beautiful—
> But, touched aright, prompt yields each particle its tongue
> Of elemental flame, —no matter whence flame sprung
> From gums and spice, or else from straw and rottenness,
> So long as soul has power to make them burn, express
> What lights and warms henceforth, leaves only ash behind.
>
> (LV, 825-32)

Here, as throughout the first movement, the spiritual product of the imaginative power of the soul is characterized as flame and light. The import of the vision of heaven will be made clearer by recognizing the associations here with the material from which the flame may spring. It is of this world and what it is makes no difference: either "gums and spice," or "straw and rottenness." Both spice and rottenness have been associated with Fifine (see XVII and XXXIII). Now the speaker describes two occasions for the spiritual achievement of the soul, and both have occurred heretofore (see L and LII). One involves a first viewing, the other a death; and both have been associated with the phantom wife. The passage continues as follows:

> Howe'er the chance: if soul be privileged to find
> Food so soon that, by first snatch of eye, suck of breath,
> It can absorb pure life: or, rather, meeting death
> I' the shape of ugliness, by fortunate recoil
> So put on its resource, it find therein a foil

> *For a new birth of life, the challenged soul's response*
> *To ugliness and death,—creation for the nonce.* (833-39)

The symbolic statement, then, is that both Fifine and the wife provide the grounds from which the "elemental flame" of spirit may be
evoked by the soul of the speaker. The sincerity of the statement is
made evident by the fact that it gives rise to the possibility of a
larger faith: "I gather heart through just such conquests of the soul"
(LVI, 840). Mounting enthusiasm leads, not at this point to a statement of faith, but to praise of such a statement, echoing the terms
in which it had been made by Browning's Rabbi Ben Ezra:

> *I praise the loyalty o' the scholar,—stung by taunt*
> *Of fools "Does this evince thy Master men so vaunt?*
> *Did he then perpetrate the plain abortion here?"*
> *Who cries, "His work am I! full fraught by him, I clear*
> *His fame from each result of accident and time,*
> *Myself restore his work to its fresh morning-prime,*
> *Not daring touch the mass of marble, fools deride,*
> *But putting my idea in plaster by its side,*
> *His, since mine; I, he made, vindicate who made me!"* (850-58)

Echoes of the pessimism of Fitzgerald's *Rubaiyat* have been
heard heretofore and will be heard again. Affirmation here, not of
the faith of "the scholar," but of his motivation—his "loyalty"—is a
mark of the transience of the heat of faith that warms this part of
the poem. For the moment, however, the mode of affirmation
strengthens as imagination focuses on the phantom wife under the
image of Eidotheé: "For, you must know, I too achieved Eidotheé, / In silence and by night" (LVII, 859-60). This clause seems to
echo "white-night's work" in the most unpleasant experience associated with the dramatic wife (XXXIII, 482-91). Characteristically a
negative memory is transformed into a memory of love. The
achievement of Eidotheé suggests to the speaker the reality of a
divine creator:

> *If she stood forth at last, the Master was to thank!*
> *Yet may there not have smiled approval in his eyes—*

That one at least was left who, born to recognize
Perfection in the piece imperfect, worked, that night,
In silence, such his faith, until the apposite
Design was out of him, truth palpable once more?
And then—for at one blow, its fragments strewed the floor—
Recalled the same to live within his soul as heretofore. (LVII, 863-70)

The idea expressed in the last two lines is that the spiritual product of the imagination survives, in memory and consciousness, the objective existence from which the imaginative work began. It applies to Eidotheé and so to the phantom wife with whom death has been repeatedly associated. The beloved no longer exists but there continues to exist an ideal and spiritualized conception which arose from the experience of her. This, being ideal, is permanent. The general notion has been previously expressed in connection both with the wife and with art used as illustration (see XLI), and in the courtship letters Browning had applied it hypothetically to Elizabeth. This idea is the direct basis for the religious affirmation which follows immediately. It is a matter of the greatest importance for interpretation of the poem and of the tendencies of Browning's mind that in this context the experience of woman is prior to and essential to the experience of God:

And, even as I hold and have Eidotheé,
I say, I cannot think that gain,—which would not be
Except a special soul had gained it,—that such gain
Can ever be estranged, do aught but appertain
Immortally, by right firm, indefeasible,
To who performed the feat, through God's grace and man's will.
(LVIII, 871-76)

The vision of heaven will now emerge, but one may not fully appreciate its status in the total experience of the poem without examining the metaphysical difficulties of the vision. We do not require that a poet be rigorously consistent—it suffices that the poetry of the vision is intense—but analysis of Browning's metaphysics, and its defects, will clarify his symbolism. The premise is that spiritual reality exists within a solipsistic idealism. The difficulty arises

in the adaptation of this premise to the conception of personal immortality in a traditional heaven, and the difficulty is compounded
when the heavenly consummation is conceived not as a union of
the individual with God but as the union of the spirts of lovers with
each other, this union giving rise to an image which may be considered to express a metaphysical equivalent of God. Man thus
creates God. The logic of this suggests that the vision of heaven is
tentative, valid only for the psychological needs effective at this
point in the symbolic development of the poem.

The heavenly condition of the vision is imagined as a yearning:

> *While, oh, how all the more will love become intense*
> *Hereafter, when "to love" means yearning to dispense,*
> *Each soul, its own amount of gain through its own mode*
> *Of practising with life, upon some soul which owed*
> *Its treasure, all diverse and yet in worth the same,*
> *To new work and changed way!* (LIX, 881-86)

While the wording here describes the complementarity of two
souls necessary to the heavenly consummation, the word "yearning" suggests the isolation of the departed beloved, and the "new
work and changed way" to which "some soul" owed "its treasure"
prefigures the conquest of soul to be achieved by the lover in his
new condition on earth following the departure of the beloved.
Suddenly the beloved is addressed directly:

> *Things furnish you rose-flame,*
> *Which burn up red, green, blue, nay, yellow more than needs,*
> *For me, I nowise doubt;* (886-88)

The "you" here is the beloved in heaven. The progression from
"rose-flame" to yellow, "nay" even to yellow "for me," is the departed beloved's spiritualized experience in heaven of the lover who
remains on earth. The realization of "yellow," as will be seen, is an
approach to the consummation to be symbolized by "white," which
will not be achieved in the absence of the lover, the speaker, who

remains on earth. The "I no wise doubt" carries an element of at least some doubt. Further, it must be read as a tribute to the spiritual superiority of the lost beloved to the speaker. Thus, as the sequel will make clear, affirmation of the brief scene of flame and color is semantically compromised, and it is with a measure of semantic instability that it serves as premise for projection of the remainder of the vision—"why doubt a time succeeds." The ultimate realization will come in the future with the union of the lovers in heaven and will be but a consummation of the complementarity they have experienced on earth in the past. The passage is also a consummation of the symbolism of flame and light so extensively developed heretofore:

> *why doubt a time succeeds*
> *When each one may impart, and each receive, both share*
> *The chemic secret, learn,—where I lit force, why there*
> *You drew forth lambent pity,—where I found only food*
> *For self-indulgence, you still blew a spark at brood*
> *I' the grayest ember, stopped not till self-sacrifice imbued*
> *Heaven's face with flame? What joy, when each may supplement*
> *The other, changing each, as changed, till, wholly blent,*
> *Our old things shall be new, and, what we both ignite,*
> *Fuse, lose the varicolor in achromatic white!*
> *Exemplifying law, apparent even now*
> *In the eternal process.* (888-99)

The elegiac theme, though it will be heard again, receives its climactic expression here in the imagery of "pure white light" which Robert had used in the love letters for the truth with which he would speak when he succeeded, as he and Elizabeth imagined, in transcending the dramatic monologue. The possibility of the knowledge of such truth will be treated differently later in the poem. Even here the possibility of such truth is one with the transiency of the vision, which now collapses and is replaced by something else, in a striking development. The vision, the speaker says, exemplifies "love's law" which he "thus would formulate":

> *each soul lives, longs and works*
> *For itself, by itself, —because a lodestar lurks,*
> *An other than itself, —in whatsoe'er the niche*
> *Of mistiest heaven it hide, whoe'er the Glumdalclich*
> *May grasp the Gulliver: or it, or he, or she.* (900-4)

Abruptly the lodestar, harmonious with the white light of the beatific vision, becomes something very different. Glumdalclich was,
of course, Gulliver's captor, and the relationship thus parallels the
relationship essential to the poem. This, however, does not exhaust
the symbolism, which in this poem is never fixed, is always moving
under the pressure of need. As the star, the white light, gives way
to a misty heaven enveloping the massive female form darkened by
the sounds of her name and carnalized by the erotic association of
her toying with Swift's Gulliver, the beatific vision undergoes, is replaced by, a startling materialization. This change involves the central dynamics of the poem. Its central impulse—male loneliness, the
need for woman—can be allayed only by a dual function: first the
elegiac, the dismissal of the dead by discharge of emotional debts,
then the legitimation and affirmation of interest in woman as flesh
in this world. So the vision of heaven achieves the elegiac function
(though in the nature of symbolic gratification of psychic needs the
function must be repeated), and immediately the imagination of the
poet moves back to the sensual need.

With this movement accomplished, the pivotal phrase of the
poem is first introduced in grammatical if not logical apposition to
the final "as it, or he, or she" quoted above:

> Theosutos e broteios eper kekramene, —
> *(For fun's sake, where the phrase has fastened, leave it fixed!*
> *So soft it says, —"God, man, or both together mixed"!)* (905-7)

The first point to be made concerning the phrase from *Prometheus Bound* is that, like any part of that play, it is redolent of the
love letters and of Elizabeth. Its use is a tribute to her, a private
tribute, its occult intention defined both by fear of self-revealment
and by the central ambivalence of the poem. The use of the phrase
is symbolic both of Elizabeth and of ambivalence. That the phrase

in context is not entirely clear Browning has, of course, acknowl-edged. He leaves it fixed "for fun's sake." The public import of the phrase is to suggest a question about man's hope for deliverance which is essential to the quest. Shall he look to a transcendent de-ity, to a human relationship in an otherwise meaningless world, or to immanent spirit redeeming human relationships?

Within the vision of heaven we have observed a movement to-ward an answer to that question. The vision is thus a remarkable manifestation of the interaction of intellectual and psychological elements. The heaven of achromatic white is the product of intellect in the service of psychological needs. The heaven of Glumdalclich is an expression of the persistence of those needs and of a massive, enthralling power of a modality of woman as an element of mem-ory and consciousness. The heaven of Glumdalclich marks the fail-ure of the effort of the poem to this point and anticipates the poem's further progress. The heaven of achromatic white is the faltering culmination of the elegiac movement. The purpose of this move-ment is to cope with a loss by reorientation of memory. The in-tellectual effort is to absorb a beloved memory in a generalized spirituality, to absolve a sense of personal disloyalty in a general loyalty. The need of personal loyalty is served by the idea of a per-sonal reunion; the need for oblivion is served by diffusion of all worldly particularities in the white light of ultimate being.

In another perspective, the need served is for realization of the condition of the lost beloved. She must, in some sense, be exor-cized. The speaker must realize that while he retains a fond and tender memory of her, she has disappeared. She retains no further personal claim or power over this world except insofar as she has been absorbed in a general spirituality. Loyalty to that spirituality is all there can reasonably be of loyalty to her. Reasonably—for the strategy is intellectual, the only recourse of a trammeled psyche and usually inadequate. Eventually the exercise of any kind of loyalty is an exercise of emotional energy that must run in old channels. Even in the end, the intellect does not prevail; the strug-gle is only partly successful; the freedom won is, like the tools of its achievement, intellectual, hardly personal at all. And yet, within the realm of art there is a sense of progress.

With the vision of heaven a certain kind of experience has been completed and left behind, and the elegiac movement comes to an end, though elegiac strains will recur. In the rest of the poem, and over half of it remains, there is no further reference to the subjective component of art or of love. When elegiac strains recur, they do not rise again to consolatory conceptions involving the immortality of the soul, heaven, or philosophical idealism. The focus of interest turns to this life.

Movement beyond the vision of heaven is accomplished by two lengthy transitional speeches—the first by the dramatic wife, the second by the speaker. The speech of the dramatic wife is of the greatest significance. It is, to begin with, a vigorous repudiation of the major statement of the poem thus far. The mordant sarcasm of the speech is an expression of the hostility that repeatedly emerges between the speaker and the dramatic wife. More than this, however, the speech is one of the points in the poem at which the dramatic and thematic elements are most thoroughly integrated. Browning maintains the monologue convention only by putting this long speech of the dramatic wife in quotation marks. Elvire, for the most part as shadowy as the phantom wife, becomes here vividly dramatic, expressing the fiery contempt of a wronged woman for what she considers the vapid rationalizations and excuses of a perfidious husband. However, it is in this most dramatic expression of the dramatic wife that she most fully embodies her relationship to the speaker. For what she repudiates is an elegy so conceived as to tend to liberate the man who has conceived it. Thus the dramatic wife represents the enthralling aspect of an experience of which the phantom wife is another aspect as an object of love. In her caustic tone and the deprecatory imagery of her speech, the dramatic wife speaks for the wronged wife and for no-nonsense Victorian morality, but unquestionably she expresses also the poet's own ambivalence and his dissatisfaction with the tenuous, idealized metaphysical structure he has thus far erected in the service of psychic freedom. Thus it is that the elegiac arguments developed so far symbolically are for the first time made explicit in ironic statement designed for their refutation. The wife's vituperation as the immediate sequel to the loving tones of the vision of heaven conforms to the pattern of ambivalence. Interestingly in this connection, the manuscript of the poem shows that the wife's first angry "you" was originally "I," as though Browning had forgotten for a moment that the anger at the dramatic level is not the speaker's.[13]

The speech of the dramatic wife begins as follows:

> *"you abdicate*
> *With boast yet on your lip, soul's empire, and accept*
> *The rule of sense; the Man, from monarch's throne has stept—*
> *Leapt, rather, at one bound, to base, and there lies, Brute."*
>
> (LX, 913-16)

The term "brute" appears first in association with the life of the "truants" of the carnival and next in association with a prohibition of the impulse toward Fifine. The eventual development of the poem will achieve a reconciliation to the "brute" realities of human nature. After her first angry outburst, the wife articulates in embarrassing literalism the metaphysical premise of the heavenly vision:

> *"You talk of soul,—how soul, in search of soul to suit,*
> *Must needs review the sex, the army, rank and file*
> *Of womankind, report no face nor form so vile*
> *But that a certain worth, by certain signs, may thence*
> *Evolve itself and stand confessed—to soul—by sense.*
> *Sense?"* (917-22)

The conception of reviewing "the army, rank and file of womankind" may have its source in the *Symposium* of Plato, to whom Browning has referred elsewhere in the poem. The conception is integral with the metaphysics of subjectivity and of freedom expressed in the speaker's argument that no face or form is "so vile" but as to serve the spiritual purposes of the beholder. The relationship of this authentically Platonic conception of love to the central argument is clearer as the wife continues:

> *"Oh, the loyal bee endeavours for the hive!*
> *Disinterested hunts the flower-field through, alive*
> *Not one mean moment, no,—suppose on flower he light,—*

To his peculiar drop, petal-dew perquisite,
Matter-of-course snatched snack: unless he taste, how try?
This, light on tongue-tip laid, allows him pack his thigh,
Transport all he counts prize, provision for the comb,
Food for the future day,—a banquet, but at home!" (922-29)

The passage refers in parody to the heavenly vision. Three years after the death of Elizabeth and seven years before *Fifine*, Browning, in a startling letter, expressed to Isabella Blagden the idea of a reunion in heaven with a departed loved one, that reunion to be enriched by the use on earth of the intervening years:

Yes, dearest Isa, it is three Christmasses ago—*fully* now: I sometimes see a light at the end of this dark tunnel of life, which was one blackness at the beginning. It won't last forever. In many ways I can see with my human eyes why this has been right and good for me—as I never doubted it was for Her—and if we do but re-join any day,—the break will be better than forgotten, remembered for its uses.[14]

In *Fifine*, the uses have become specific. The trouble, at least from a Victorian point of view, is that where a distinctively sensuous woman is concerned, the ultimate spiritual objective may be suspect. This suspicion informs the bitterness of the dramatic wife as she again restates ironically the metaphysical argument:

"Soul? Ere you reach Fifine's, some flesh may be to pass!
That bombéd brow, that eye, a kindling chrysopras,
Beneath its stiff black lash, inquisitive how speeds
Each functionary limb, how play of foot succeeds,
And how you let escape or duly sympathize
With gastroknemian grace,—true, your soul tastes and tries,
And trifles time with these, but, fear not, will arrive
At essence in the core, bring honey home to hive,
Brain-stock and heart-stuff both—to strike objectors dumb—
Since only soul affords the soul fit pabulum!
Be frank for charity! Who is it you deceive—
Yourself or me or God, with all this make-believe?" (930-41)

6

Affirmation of the World and the Flesh

The elegiac process is a negative function of the quest to the extent that its purpose is remembering in order to forget. But recognition of a death may mean acknowledgment of death in a way that is generative of meaning and coherent with the affirmation of life and this world which is the purpose of part 3. When the heavenly vision has been disrupted by the emergence of Glumdalclich and when its implications have been discredited by the bitter attack of the dramatic wife, the speaker does not at first respond directly to or deny the wife's charges. Rather, his long speech, poetically diffuse, serves as a prologue to the rest of the poem, and one may have the feeling that the writer here began the poem anew. It is consistent with this suggestion that there appears here for the first time a theme that will be heard again. There is a passing wish for escape from the struggle which the poem embodies: "I would our souls were found without / The pale, above the dense and dim which breeds the doubt!" (LXI, 958-59). After the speaker expresses a wish for the aid of music, he again suggests that the effort is toilsome, "since to weary words recourse again must be" (961). The wording at one point may remind us of the death that lies behind the poem; more important, it asserts that the world left dead by the solipsistic subjectivism of part 2 is now to be endowed with life by another kind of knowledge. Music, says the speaker, can "win a passage through the lid / Of earthly sepulchre" (949-50). For the moment, however, the speaker despairs of the aid of music: "But Music,

dumb for you, withdraws her help from me" (960). We may be re-
minded that Elizabeth did not share Browning's love of music.[1]
Eventually music will, in a sense, be achieved, attending the climactic movement of the quest in part 5. The movement now is toward
a quiet but vital knowledge and toward a metaphysical orientation
new to the poem.

"Once fairly on the wing," says the speaker, "let me flap far and
wide" (965-66). But after the discursive and somewhat fatuous prologue to a new beginning, there follow passages of intense poetry
which lie close to the elegiac heart of the poem and are vibrant with
knowledge of life. Heretofore, the symbolic motif has been a pattern in which the knowledge of death has given rise to a memory of
life which emerges as a reality, enthralling consciousness. Now
there is a profound change, a turning to the objectivity of nature
and the recognition of a vitality in nature's intermingling of life and
death. The turn from transcendence to nature, to the witness of
earth, is decisive for the course of the poem. Speaker and wife at
the end of day walk to a point where the village gives way to the
countryside, and here they experience a mood in which all things
"clash forth life's common chord" (LXII, 968). The wife's question
had been, "Who is it you deceive— / Yourself or me or God, with
all this make-believe?" Here at sunset the speaker says:

> How fail
> To find or, better, lose your question, in this quick
> Reply which nature yields, ample and catholic? (971-73)

Now speaker and wife progress together in the sunset toward a
moment of knowledge. Cautiously they undertake a perilous descent to a scene in which are commingled three images of death: the
margin of beach and bay, the Island of the Dark Convent (Île Noirmoutier) which lies off the the coast, and the rushing waters of the
sea toward that island. Yet these images of death have implications
of life. The waters "freshen as they haste," and in the dusk a
"breadth of blue retains its self-possession still":

> Thither the waters tend; they freshen as they haste,
> At feel o' the night-wind, though, by cliff and cliff embraced,

This breadth of blue retains its self-possession still;
As you and I intend to do, who take our fill
Of sights and sounds. (LXIII, 988-92)

Then as speaker and wife turn back from the sea to the countryside and into the stir, the warmth and scurry, of insect and animal
life, there enters a symbol of death; yet its meaning as death does
not prevail, for here life is being engendered from death. The

soft sound, the countless hum and skip
Of insects we disturb, and that good fellowship
Of rabbits our foot-fall sends huddling, each to hide
He best knows how and where; and what whirred past,
    wings wide?
That was an owl, their young may justlier apprehend. (992-96)

The owl, which is a symbol of death, is also a bird, as ironic reference to its predatory habits indicate, and in context a bird is a
symbol of life. It is to be understood that here again we experience
the elegiac strain of the poem, now in its restorative phase tending
back to life. The sequel is a lengthy development (LXIV-LXVIII) of
the metaphor used also in the prologue, the image of the swimmer
in the bay, the water representing the "wash o' the world," the air
above representing spirit. Within the dualistic scheme of the metaphor occurs a marked modification of the dualism that has pre-
vailed in the poem hitherto. Each experience "proves / Air—the
essential good, not sea," (LXV, 1053-54) says the speaker, "And yet
our business with the sea / Is not with air, but just o' the water,
watery" (1057-58). We must abjure metaphysics and "only swim
the water, that's native to a fish" (LXIV, 1033). In connection with
the image of the swimmer in the water, the realm of matter and the
world, there arises a new meaning of truth, "one truth more true
for me than any truth beside— / To-wit, that I am I, who have the
power to swim" (LXVI, 1064-65), truth as a sense of ontological certainty.

This eruption of self-awareness is of the greatest significance.
The solipsistic tendency of mind in part 2, creating and transform-

ing the world, is a much less assertive principle than it is made to seem. In that tendency of mind, the individual contains the world and is identical with it. He has no existence separate from the world. His consciousness is consciousness of the world into which he has disappeared. This is the condition of consciousness which produces the dramatic monologue as Browning practiced it. In a consciousness deficient in *self*-consciousness and a sense of onto-logical certainty, there is no center, no point of view, no focus of value to structure the world. The psychic struggle underlying the poem is in one respect a struggle for a different mode of conscious-ness. It is a struggle for liberation of ego and will, a struggle for the assertive powers of self. This struggle is implicit in the impulse for sensuality, which is an impulse for sensual existence. Self-con-sciousness is based upon a consciousness of physical separateness and is related to an affirmation of the body. Underlying the strug-gle is an awareness, perhaps not entirely conscious, that, as Scho-penhauer said, the sexual organ is the organ of the will. Thus we may understand the coherent unity of the eventual developments of the poem in which affirmation of Fifine is eventually an opinion about the world. Affirmation of Fifine will be implicit in all that follows. First will come the achievement of an opinion about the world, the metaphysical perspective reducing it to nullity having been abandoned. Linked to the achievement of this opinion is an abandonment of the habit of consciousness essential to the dra-matic monologue. While the decisive achievement is the affirma-tion of a perspective, the gain so won is consolidated by the content of the opinion providing the perspective—recognition of the sexual basis of the world. This, however, is to anticipate.

The swimmer has achieved a new sense of mastery in which equanimity survives excesses both of sea and air:

> *Meantime I buoy myself: no whit my senses reel*
> *When over me there breaks a billow; nor, elate*
> *Too much by some brief taste, I quaff intemperate*
> *The air, o'ertop breast-high the wave-environment.* (1078-81)

With a sense of strengthened control over the tensions which inform the poem, the poet turns again to its elegiac burden, with an

image of the experience in which one soul gains and then loses
another:

> *So with this wash o' the world, wherein life-long we drift;*
> *We push and paddle through the foam by making shift*
> *To breath above at whiles when, after deepest duck*
> *Down underneath the show, we put forth hand and pluck*
> *At what seems somehow like reality—a soul.*
> *I catch at this and that, to capture and control,*
> *Presume I hold a prize, discover that my pains*
> *Are run to nought: my hands are balked, my head regains*
> *The surface where I breathe and I look about, a space.*
> *The soul that helped me mount?* (LXVII, 1089-98)

The answer comes in a recurrence once again to the metaphor
for death which appears first in the epilogue to *Dramatis Personae*,
to which there is added a significant echo:

> *Swallowed up in the race*
> *O' the tide, come who knows whence, gone gaily*
> *who knows where!* (1098-99)

The words "come who knows whence, gone gaily who knows
where" echo Fitzgerald's *Rubaiyat*: "What, without asking, hither
hurried *Whence*? / And, without asking, *Whither* hurried hence."[2]
The fact that Browning can echo these deeply cynical lines in such a
context, capturing even something of Fitzgerald's ironic mood in
the word "gaily," is another measure of the relative detachment
achieved in elaboration of the swimmer metaphor. When Browning, having echoed Fitzgerald's skepticism, turns almost immediately to castigate Byron for his skepticism in *Childe Harold*, it would
seem fairly clear that Browning is covering his own tracks for the
benefit of the Victorian public and pious friends. In connection
with the digression on Byron (the only digression in the poem, inci-
dentally, and a late addition to the manuscript) Browning emphasized to his friend Domett his pride in this rejection of Byron's lack
of faith.[3]

In the development of the swimmer metaphor a pretext is found
for a discussion in which the speaker explains elaborately why he
needs "woman" rather than "man." It is soon apparent that the
comparison is not symmetrical. The comparison is between a public relationship with men—a collectivity—and a personal relationship with a single woman. The relationship to men is described at
first as that of leadership or "ruling them" (LXXI, 1166), but it is
soon clear that the leadership envisioned is that of Shelley's unacknowledged legislators of mankind. Each man

> *for his own sake*
> *Accepts you as his guide, avails him of what worth*
> *He apprehends in you to sublimate his earth*
> *With fire.* (1166-69)

The speaker's power over men is that of utterance: "and if I have
the knack / Of fitting thoughts to words, you peradventure lack"
(LXXVI, 1263-64). Furthermore, the speaker's complaint against men
is really against that necessity of dissimulation which we have recognized as characteristic of Victorian poets since E. D. H. Johnson's
The Alien Vision of Victorian Poetry:[4]

> *To make, you must be marred,—*
> *To raise your race, must stoop,—to teach them aught, must learn*
> *Ignorance, meet half-way what most you hope to spurn*
> *I' the sequel. Change yourself, dissimulate the thought*
> *And vulgarize the word, and see the deed be brought*
> *To look like nothing done with any such intent*
> *As teach men—though perchance it teach, by accident!*
> (LXXV, 1222-28)

The thought of the contrasting values of "woman" leads to a
final recurrence of the elegiac motif in an image of water, a configuration marked by movement, and final oblivion; the image is the
"rillet" that "goes headlong to her death in the sea" (LXXIV, 1215-
16). Here the elegiac theme evolves a quiet, plaintive grief in one of
the most exquisite passages of the poem:

But take the rill which ends a race o'er yonder ledge
O' the fissured cliff, to find its fate in smoke below!
Disengage that, and ask—what news of life, you know
It led, that long lone way, through pasture, plain and waste?
All's gone to give the sea! no touch of earth, no taste
Of air, reserved to tell how rushes used to bring
The butterfly and bee, and fisher-bird that's king[5]
O' the purple kind, about the snow-soft silver-sweet
Infant of mist and dew; only these atoms fleet,
Embittered evermore, to make the sea one drop
More big thereby—if thought keep count where sense must stop.

(LXXIII, 1202-12)

The snow image connects the passage with the elegiac theme as it appears in various guises. Furthermore, the rillet image echoes its two previous occurrences in the poem, both earlier instances associated with the wife. The first instance is that in which the phantom wife as the Saint represents the exquisite, earliest deepening of spiritual to physical love (XXXII). In the second instance the rillet, or brook, is the culminating image in the complex elegiac process in which the imagination begins with the beloved in death and after transmutations, ends with her restored to life, her presence fused with that of the dramatic wife, who becomes for a moment an object of love (XXXVIII-XXXIX). The three instances of rillet imagery are widely dispersed in the poem, the first two separated by six sections, the third instance thirty-three sections beyond the second, but they are a unifying element. The rillet represents a remembered love in its fondest and tenderest moods, and its three instances constitute a life sequence. Remotely and serenely remembered, there is a first beginning of human love; then there is a culmination, the object of mature love evolving as though out of a miasma of death into fleshly existence and living immediacy. Then a life and a death take on reality in the firm distinctness of the past as the rillet makes its inland traverse under sunlight to disappear in the sea.

This is the final funereal note of the elegiac process. Heretofore, memory of a death entailed memory of a life, and elegy brought a resurrection that made emotional claims upon the poet. Here the elegiac process is complete in that death is imagined as finality. The struggle which is the experiential content of the poem has succeeded. It will issue soon in a transformation and a song of victory, but for the moment it is important to observe the intellectual matrix of the emotional regeneration now occurring.

The penultimate chapter of this study will demonstrate that in the part of *Fifine* dealing with "men" and "women" Browning is reversing an old pattern in his poetry, a pattern repressive, or at least evasive, of love. The reversal serves the quest. The world of men, meaning the realm of the collectivity and the world of affairs into which Browning's early lovers escaped from love, is now recognized as a realm inimical to love, and its specific Victorian character is identified. That an effort for psychic freedom should become social commentary and protest is not coincidental. One of the ways of defining the basic tension of the work is to say that the poetic function as formed by the public expectation which it has been able to accommodate is in conflict with the tendency of the private consciousness, which struggles to liberate itself in this poem. The goal is a new unity in which the private consciousness may flourish in poetry. The prohibition to be overcome is here conceived as socially imposed, and the struggle, by implication, indicts a culture. What the speaker rejects is presented as a statement of subservience to the collectivity:

> *"What though I seem to go before? 't is you that lead!*
> *I follow what I see so plain—the general mind*
> *Projected pillar-wise, flame kindled by the kind,*
> *Which dwarfs the unit—me—to insignificance!*
> *Halt you, I stop forthwith, —proceed, I too advance!"*
>   (LXXVI, 1272-76)

The idea of the artist's capturing his public by falsifying his individuality is developed under the metaphor of the primitive hunting stratagem of the American Indian who disguised himself in the skin and antlers of the animal hunted. In evaluating the prize thus captured, the speaker comments on the objective of the hunt and thus further defines that against which he wishes to revolt, making specific the character of the artist's conformity:

Well, there's your prize i' the pound—much joy may it afford
My Indian! Make survey and tell me,—was it worth
You acted part so well, went all-fours upon earth
The live-long day, brayed, belled, and all to bring to pass
That stags should deign eat hay when winter stints them grass?
(LXXV, 1242-46)

"Winter" in the passage above is the prohibitive puritanism of Victorian public opinion. The private impulse is, eventually, an impulse for poetic freedom and insistence upon an integrity uniting the private and public consciousness. The private consciousness requires the celebration of a sexual relationship. It is of the greatest significance, however, that in the statement of this need, we must read "Victorian public" for "men" and "a woman" for "womankind":

So much for men, and how disguise may make them mind
Their master. But you have to deal with womankind?
Abandon stratagem for strategy! Cast quite
The vile disguise away, try truth clean-opposite
Such creep-and-crawl, stand forth all man and, might it chance,
Somewhat of angel too!—whate'er inheritance,
Actual on earth, in heaven prospective, be your boast,
Lay claim to! Your best self revealed at uttermost,—
That's the wise way o' the strong! (LXXVI, 1247-55)

In the passage that follows, a part of which has already been quoted, there is recognition of a danger that frank sensuality may breed licentiousness, but there is also a positive claim for sensuality. This claim is not now for the "white light" of eschatological spirituality, but for a more limited ennoblement and for health, linked with a suggestion that inhibition has already resulted in sickness and it would be better to mimic health by frankness. This passage is totally unintelligible unless we read consistently the vocabulary Browning has gone to so much trouble to establish; to read "falsehood" here as "mimesis" plays havoc with the context; "falsehood" means "the false" which means the material condition of existence; it means Fifine and the flesh; as will become clear later in the poem, the word "lie" means "art":

And e'en should falsehood tempt
The weaker sort to swerve,—at least the lie's exempt
From slur, that's loathlier still, of aiming to debase
Rather than elevate its object. Mimic grace,
Not make deformity your mask! Be sick by stealth,
Nor traffic with disease—malingering in health!
No more of: "Countrymen, I boast me one like you—
My lot, the common strength, the common weakness too!"
(LXXVI, 1255-62)

This is a protest against the censorial powers of Victorianism which forbade frank artistic treatment of man as a physical being and which basic strategies of the poem were designed to elude. In part these prohibitive powers were subjectivized, enforced by psychic inhibitions, and self-imposed. For a moment now prohibitions of freedom, in being experienced, have been overcome, and the result is the freedom gained in a sensual love song bringing to climactic fulfillment the central movement of the poem as the speaker celebrates the meaning to him of "woman" (LXXVIII).

In that love song we observe the second of two decisive images for woman. The first of these was the final note in the elegiac theme in which the rillet after its long traverse of land goes to oblivion in the sea. The image that emerges now is one of solidity, grace, and a vitality congenial with the sea. It rises in response to song and will love the poet and save him, and it should be kept in mind that Fifine is later "the sea-Fifine" (CXXV, 2223). The new image is the dolphin. The speaker employs the legend of Arion, the poet of Lesbos of the seventh century B.C. who was befriended by Periander, tyrant of Corinth. According to the legend, Arion sang aboard ship to delay his death at the hands of sailors who had seized his treasure, then leapt into the sea where he was borne up by a dolphin and carried to Taenarus. Arion made his way from Taenarus back to Corinth where the miracle was confirmed by investigations of Periander, and the sailors punished.

The sight of dolphins in the bay brings to the speaker's mind the meaning of woman. What I have called a love song is a song of triumph filled with sexual imagery:

> *Art fain the fish to captivate?*
> *Gather thy greatness round, Arion! Stand in state,*
> *As when the banqueting thrilled conscious—like a rose*
> *Throughout its hundred leaves at that approach it knows*
> *Of music in the bird—while Corinth grew one breast*
> *A-throb for song and thee.* (LXXVIII, 1293-98)[6]

The erotic image of the rose will presently recur significantly transformed. The import of the song will be more fully appreciated if it is realized that in similar architectural imagery later in the poem the collapse of edifice symbolizes the insubstantiality of human institutions, and that the Arion epiphany here prefigures a symbolic analysis of the energy from which human culture derives. Here the import of the sensual song is to imperil the banquet hall representing the state and the society it houses:

> *The pillar nods,*
> *Rocks roof, and trembles door, gigantic, post and jamb,*
> *As harp and voice rend air—the shattering dithyramb!* (1301-3)

The sequel to the narrative and poetic treatment of the triumphant song is a passage in which the concentration of sexual imagery must be taken as a symbolic identification of poetic and sexual power:

> *then leap from music's lofty throne,*
> *Into the lowest surge, make fearlessly thy launch!*
> *Whatever storm may threat, some dolphin will be staunch!*
> *Whatever roughness rage, some exquisite sea-thing*
> *Will surely rise to save, will bear—palpitating—*
> *One proud humility of love beneath its load—*
> *Stem tide, part wave, till both roll on, thy jewell'd road*
> *Of triumph, and the grim o' the gulph grow wonder-white*
> *I' the phosphorescent wake; and still the exquisite*
> *Sea-thing stems on, saves still, palpitatingly thus,*
> *Lands safe at length its load of love at Taenarus,*
> *True woman-creature!* (1309-20)

Thus, the impulse to sexual freedom which is the motive force of the poem comes to its fullest expression; the poem as the experiential component of imagination arrives at climactic development. Here, that need expressed in the phrase "frenetic to be free" comes most nearly to fulfillment. Nothing in the poem will prepare us for what now follows. The pattern of ambivalence, though it has occurred before, does not prepare us for the magnitude of its climactic expression. This pattern, it should be recalled, is interpreted as reflecting the fact that the poet may participate in the quest of the poem but that achievement of the quest within the realm of imagination will be followed by a record of frustration in experience external to the poem. The sequel to the poetic triumph is an eruption of bitterness which makes abundantly explicit the origin of this bitterness in the frustration of love. Though this much is clear, the passage is the most difficult in the poem; a precise reading is nearly impossible. Its intensity as an expression of frustration, anger, and bitterness is disproportionate to the dramatic components (that is, the persons or personifications imagined in conflict) by which the expression is achieved. Repeatedly there is an oppressor and an oppressed, but these opposing persons or elements are not clearly distinguished from each other. The oppressive relationships seem to undergo a reversal, and at one point the two are merged in a single image. Such confusion, however, will be seen as consistent with the theme when one realizes that the conflict treated is that previously developed between "man" (for which read "public opinion," "Victorian readers," and especially, "Victorian critics") and freedom of sensuality as an element of love in the creative passion of the poet. "Man's" repression falsifies and vitiates the poet, and the dissimulation required of him has as its purpose "that stags should deign eat hay when winter stints them grass" (LXXV, 1246). The obscurity results from anguished concentration. The speaker as poet, himself repressed, seems to cooperate as the agent of a repressive society. A single theme emerges consistently. Expressed in anger, the theme (first articulated in *Paracelsus*) is the value of anger as self-expression. Here the idea is dramatized, and hatred is clearly a response to repression and an affirmation of sensuality emerging as angry defiance. Some lines will not yield a specific reading, but examination of the entire passage part by part will be helpful.

> *Man? Ah, would you prove what power*
> *Marks man, —what fruit his tree may yield, beyond the sour*
> *And stinted crab, he calls love-apple, which remains*
> *After you toil and moil your utmost, —all, love gains*
> *By lavishing manure? —try quite the other plan!*
> *And, to obtain the strong true product of a man,*
> *Set him to hate a little!* (LXXIX, 1320-26)

The phrase "lavishing manure" represents as linguistic violence the anger inspiring the writing and must be taken to correspond to the poetic dissimulation which has been rejected in section LXXVI:

> *Leave cherishing his root,*
> *And rather prune his branch, nip off the pettiest shoot*
> *Superfluous on his bough! I promise, you shall learn*
> *By what grace came the goat, of all beasts else, to earn*
> *Such favor with the god o' the grape: 't was only he*
> *Who, browsing on its tops, first stung fertility*
> *Into the stock's heart, stayed much growth of tendril-twine,*
> *Some faintish flower, perhaps, but gained the indignant wine,*
> *Wrath of the red press!* (1326-34)

The phrase "pettiest shoot" corresponds to the sensual object of love which is symbolized by Fifine. With the transformation of the tree into the vine Browning establishes an image that he employs with powerful sexual overtones later in the poem. The key to the most difficult aspects of the entire passage may be found in the treatment of the goat whose symbolism involves a strange inversion. A symbolic agent of action takes action contrary to its symbolic nature, and the result of this discordant action is in some sense deformed, distorted. The goat, symbolic of sexuality and fertility, impairs and limits the fruit of fertility, the grape vine closely associated with the goat in Dionysian symbolism; the result is fertility ominously invigorated, "the indignant wine, / Wrath of the red press"—this corresponding to "the strong true product of a man" when you "set him to hate a little." Immediately following is a new symbol, a special case of "man." This is a "man-animalcule." It is in accord with the entire treatment of "man" and "woman" as described above that the man-animalcule should represent literary critics and more specifically the critic Alfred Austin, whose diminutive size was later exploited in Browning's bitter satire in *Pacchiarotto*.[7] The passage in *Fifine* is also brutal:

> Catch the puniest of the kind—
> Man-animalcule, starved body, stunted mind,
> And, as you nip the blotch 'twixt thumb and finger-nail,
> Admire how heaven above and earth below avail
> No jot to soothe the mite, sore at God's prime offence
> In making mites at all,—coax from its impotence
> One virile drop of thought, or word, or deed, by strain
> To propagate for once—which nature rendered vain,
> Who lets first failure stay, yet cares not to record
> Mistake that seems to cast opprobrium on the Lord!
> Such were the gain from love's best pains! (1334-44)

Here, in rapid, even violent, movement of imagery, the man-animalcule becomes a blotch, or imperfection, pinched between the fingers as one may crush an insect and then becomes a mite resentful of its own existence. By punitive treatment paralleling the goat's nipping of the vine, the mite's impotence is coaxed to propagate and the result of that propagation is nothing, for nature though tolerant of first failures, will make no record of a "mistake that seems to cast opprobrium on the Lord." Such treatment of the mite and such result is the best that even love produces. As the passage continues it is suggested that this wholly abortive fertility is better than the result of the anger of the mite, now become an elf, and later an ant, when he confronts the boldness of a real man:

> But let the elf
> Be touched with hate, because some real man bears himself
> Manlike in body and soul, and, since he lives, must thwart
> And furify and set a-fizz this counterpart
> O' the pismire that's surprised to effervescence, if,
> By chance, black bottle come in contact with chalk cliff,
> Acid with alkali! Then thrice the bulk, out blows
> Our insect, does its kind, and cuckoo-spits some rose! (1344-51)

The breaking of the black bottle against the chalk cliff is first a visual image and then a chemical image. The black bottle is first ink, then acid. As ink it is consistent with the disguised discussion of the experience of the poet between "man" and "woman." The image of black on white reflects the act of the writer. The scale of the image reflects the boldness of the act and the conversion of ink into acid reflects its anger, the effect of his being "set to hate a little." Though the "insect" is sterile, its anger is deadly. The rose it blights is the quivering symbol of sexuality at the center of the song which is the climactic development of the movement.

The final image here—"and cuckoo-spits some rose"—in conjunction with the general massive outpouring of bitterness as the immediate sequel to the sensual love song suggests that the triumph celebrated in the epiphany of the union of artistic and sexual power has been attended by a failure. The conjunction of the image of the pernicious goat and the allusion to Alfred Austin is a symbolic corollary in failure of the synthesis of poetic and sexual power in the celebration of the triumph of Arion. As has been pointed out, the source of this failure is not to be found in the poem. The outburst of bitterness would seem to have served an emotional need and to have issued in a new serenity as the speaker reaffirms the importance of woman. The personal relationship with woman, whether Elvire or Fifine, is a source of "truth" amidst pervasive "falsity," the source of a sense of ontological certainty in a general condition of delusory flux. Elvire and Fifine "convince unreasonable me / That I am, anyhow, a truth, though all else seem / And be not" (LXXX, 1357-59). The difference between the spiritual imports of Elvire and Fifine is recognized but deemed unimportant to the basic proposition—" 't is they / Convince,—if little, much, no matter!—one degree / The more, at least" (1355-57). The sense of ontological certainty resulting from the relationship to woman reassures the speaker of the value of which he speaks in the past tense:

> *I waged*
> *No foolish warfare, then, with shades, myself a shade,*
> *Here in the world—may hope my pains will be repaid!* (1365-67)

The passage derives its meaning from controlling conceptions of the poem. The terms "shades" and "foolish warfare" reflect the conception of the phantom wife and the tensions involved in the speaker's fidelity to her. The hope that "pains will be repaid" reflects the eschatological symbolism of an ultimate value to which tends the knowledge of both Elvire and Fifine. It also anticipates the intellectual achievement which will be the eventual reward of the quest. The failure of experience will give rise to a triumph of thought.

7

Translation of the Quest into Mind

Part 4 has its definition chiefly by its position between two parts of the poem that are themselves well defined. The image of slack tide, introduced at the beginning, characterizes this part of the poem. It is diverse though brief, and its symbolic developments are transitory and occur in close communication with the dramatic surface. Part 4 is transitional. It marks a translation of the quest into the realm of intellect. Up to this point the development has been an imaginative process, intensely personal and concerned with a transformation of affect and attitude. Part 5 will bring something new into the world. Quite impersonal, it begins in a moment of profound intuition from which there grows an intellectual process, the results of which are conceptions of great magnitude. Hitherto the poem has involved a measure of wish fulfillment. Part 5 will pose a frightful revolutionary challenge, one to which the poet's temperament eventually proves unequal. Part 4 is therefore slack tide, moving with some uncertainty toward a new beginning, but giving portentous expression to a moment of weariness, a passing sense of regret, in renewal of the quest.

As the poem continues, its basic contention of an ultimate loyalty consistent with sensual experience in the here and now is elaborated under the imagery of two vessels—one a large ship that is being fitted out in port, the other a " 'merest willow-leaf of boat,' " the two equated with Elvire and Fifine. The new imagery, like the earlier, related imagery of the " 'loyal bee,' " is introduced under quotation marks abruptly indicating the speech of the dramatic wife. The tone, however, is very different, with nothing of the fiery bitterness of the earlier passage. The irony is restrained, the argument quiet as the wife recalls a recent experience

> *"When we two watched the rounds*
> *The boatman made, 'twixt shoal and sandbank, yesterday,*
> *As, at the dead slack of tide, he chose to push his way,*
> *With oar and pole."* (LXXXI, 1377-80)

The image suggests both the psychological condition from which the quest begins and a proposal for time and life remaining. It also defines the mood of the poem at this point. The speaker's reply to the wife expresses a weariness that will eventually control the course of the poem:

> *I would there were one voyage, and then no more to do*
> *But tread the firmland, tempt the uncertain sea no more.*
> *I would we might dispense with change of shore for shore*
> *To evidence our skill, demonstrate—in no dream*
> *It was, we tided o'er the trouble of the stream.*
> *I would the steady voyage, and not the fitful trip,—*
> *Elvire, and not Fifine,—might test our seamanship.*
>   (LXXXII, 1399-1405)

There follows within a few lines a passage that may provide some insight into the failure of the quest. A man managing a small boat, to which Fifine is compared, is seen as representing

> *Mind, paramount*
> *Throughout the adventure: ay, howe'er you make account,*
> *'T is mind that navigates,—skips over, twists between*
> *The bales i' the boat,—now gives importance to the mean,*
> *And now abates the pride of life, accepts all fact,*
> *Discards all fiction.* (1412-17)

Within the complex interfusions and the overlying of theme and theme which characterize the poem, the imagined effort of managing Fifine, of navigating, is equivalent to the effort to win through social and psychological obstacles to her. When one attempts to free himself of deep inhibitions, he has only mind to pose against psychic and somatic forces, and there is the danger that he will conceive the problem as intellectual and that the struggle will be confined to the realm of intellect. For the moment the impulse for transferring from the larger to the smaller craft is conceived as response to a challenge. Fifine, the embodiment of flesh, of matter, and of this life is "so bad, and yet so delicate a brown!" (1418). She would "rob" him—perhaps of a higher spirituality associated with Elvire—and yet "do men blame a squirrel, lithe and sly, / For pilfering the nut she adds to hoard? Nor I" (1420-21). Of Elvire, "true, as truth," says the speaker, and "too safe the ship" (1421-22). Of Fifine, he says,

> How can I but suspect, the true feat were to slip
> Down side, transfer myself to cockle-shell from ship,
> And try if, trusting to sea-tracklessness, I class
> With those around whose breast grew oak and triple brass:
> Who dreaded no degree of death, but, with dry eyes,
> Surveyed the turgid main and its monstrosities—
> And rendered futile so, the prudent Power's decree
> Of separate earth and disassociating sea;
> Since, how is it observed, if impious vessels leap
> Across, and tempt a thing they should not touch—the deep?
> (See Horace to the boat, wherein, for Athens bound,
> When Virgil must embark—Jove keep him safe and sound!—
> The poet bade his friend start on the watery road,
> Much re-assured by this so comfortable ode.) (1428-41)

In anticipation of part 5 there is prefigured an act of courage overcoming a "prudent Power" to bridge the dualism of earth and sea, of matter and spirit. Most of the imagery in this passage is from Horace's Ode 1.3, referred to in parenthesis. Here we observe an example of the subtle associations providing the subterranean elements of unity in the poem. More than half of Horace's ode is devoted to the Promethean movement in which men usurp divine authority and violate divine commands as symbolized most conspicuously by Prometheus in the ode but also by Daedalus and Hercules. Thus the passage links with imagery and allusion which are

the most obvious unifying devices of the poem and which provide
unquestionable evidence of the poem's biographical significance.

   The reference to Horace's bon voyage to Virgil is another instance in which, in context, there is special relevance to the poets—
to Browning and to the Elizabeth of the past—and none, on the
dramatic level, to Don Juan and Elvire. In the passage that follows,
allusion is explicit to the departure and bon voyage which is the occasion of Horace's ode, and the biographical association is
strengthened when the speaker addressing his wife refers to himself
as "Your Virgil of a spouse" and the image for Fifine is developed as
that of a "rakish craft" that carries the Virgil of a spouse to Athens.
This voyage is seen as ending in truth, and, abruptly, the speaker is
again with Elvire. The rationale of the experience and its goal is
that of the vision of heaven in part 2 translated from Christian to
pagan imagery. Both the abrupt transition and the stateliness of the
verse are made understandable by those symbolic conceptions in
accord with which Fifine as fleshly and sensual woman provides intimations of the "truth" in which Elvire as departed and phantom
wife has been absorbed:

> *So, off we push from beach*
> *Of Pornic town, and lo, ere eye can wink, we reach*
> *The Long Walls, and I prove that Athens is no dream,*
> *For there the temples rise! they are, they nowise seem!*
> *Earth is not all one lie, this truth attests me true!*
> *Thanks therefore to Fifine! Elvire, I'm back with you!*
> *Share in the memories!* (LXXXIII, 1452-58)

   The goal, ennobled by historical and personal associations, is
ontological—a sense of the reality of the world that affirms the
world as no "dream," no "lie." The dualism of part 2 is explicitly rejected with this access of ontological certainty. Fifine can provide
this as has Elvire (Elizabeth) in the past. So with renewal of the
world, which was once before renewed, one may share in the memories, remain thus both "true" and loyal. There follows quickly a
merging of the conceptions of the phantom and dramatic wives as

anticipation of death and its sequel, conceived as a condition re-
warding poets, enters the poem at the dramatic level:

> *Embark I trust we shall*
> *Together some fine day, and so, for good and all,*
> *Bid Pornic Town adieu,—then, just the strait to cross,*
> *And we reach harbor, safe, in Iostephanos!* (1458-61)

Anticipation of death, a note consonant with the weakening of
the forward movement of the poem at this point, is deepened by the
symbolism of nightfall, and death is also associated with that tendency of the world to ontological vacuity the psychological resistance to which is the meaning of Fifine and, for this moment of
calm empathy at dusk, of the dramatic wife:

> *How quickly night comes! Lo, already 't is the land*
> *Turns sea-like; overcrept by grey, the plains expand,*
> *Assume significance; while ocean dwindles, shrinks*
> *Into a pettier bound: its plash and plaint, methinks,*
> *Six steps away, how both retire, as if their part*
> *Were played, another force were free to prove her art,*
> *Protagonist in turn! Are you unterrified?*
> *All false, all fleeting too! And nowhere things abide,*
> *And everywhere we strain that things should stay,—the one*
> *Truth, that ourselves are true!* (LXXXIV, 1462-71)

"Are you unterrified?" Perhaps for a fearful moment the meaning of "truth" wavers to mean only loyalty to a memory. And the
fear is complex. The poem is moving toward a horrendous "fancy
which turned a fear" and which for Browning in afterthought
"brought dark night before his eyes." That fancy, however, is also
to be experienced otherwise, in the exhilaration of new knowledge,
exulting in the "truth" of the way things are.

"A word, and I have done," the speaker says, and though his
monologue will continue for 884 lines, the movement of the poem
comprised by parts 3 and 4 is in fact drawing to a close. In anticipation of the climactic intellectual effort of the poem the speaker now

undertakes a disposition of the question of the nature of truth. The topic is undertaken with the elaboration of a new metaphor. "Fifine and all her tribe," seen in the beginning as varied performers at a village fair—gymnast, aerialist, strong man, and so forth—are also actors. The dissemblance of the stage is compared on the ontological frailty of the world. The artistic truth of dramatic dissemblance is identified with the untruth which is the "truth" that may be known in the world as expressed in the gnomic statement: "The histrionic truth is in the natural lie" (LXXXV, 1492).

There follows the anticipatory celebration of truth shot through with the paradox of truth's limitations (LXXXVI), which has been previously noted. When the song to truth has ended on the despairing counterpoint of "Wait threescore years and ten," the speaker turns to a more particular and more personal abnegation—a discursive parallel to and comment upon the subjective outpouring of rage which followed the epiphany of the union of artistic and sexual power in the Arion passage (LXXVIII):

> *Therefore I prize stage-play, the honest cheating; thence*
> *The impulse pricked, when fife and drum bade Fair commence,*
> *To bid you trip and skip, link arm in arm with me,*
> *Like husband and like wife, and so together see*
> *The tumbling-troop arrayed, the strollers on their stage*
> *Drawn up and under arms, and ready to engage.*
> *And if I started thence upon abstruser themes . . .*
> *Well, 't was a dream, pricked too!* (LXXXVII, 1517-24)

The "abstruser themes" and the "dream, pricked too" refer to the central development of the poem culminating in the Arion epiphany. In the developmental process, inhibitions were overcome and freedom achieved. The writer as poet achieved emotional freedom. Now, however, the poet makes it clear that his freedom exists only within poetry and stops at its border. The translation into personal freedom does not occur. To signal this default the writer, in effect, poses a dichotomization of personality symbolized in a contrast between the "poet" and "prose-folk." The real distinction here, however, is not between poetry and prose. It is the distinction between art and experience, and the passage recognizes the inadequacies of art to the immediate urgencies of life.[1] The poet is free; the man as "prose-folk" remains entrammeled:

> *A poet never dreams:*
> *We prose-folk always do: we miss the proper duct*
> *For thoughts on things unseen, which stagnate and obstruct*
> *The system, therefore; mind, sound in a body sane,*
> *Keeps thoughts apart from facts, and to one flowing vein*
> *Confines its sense of that which is not, but might be,*
> *And leaves the rest alone. What ghosts do poets see?*
> *What dæmons fear? what man or thing misapprehend?*
> *Unchoked, the channel's flush, the fancy's free to spend*
> *Its special self aright in manner, time and place.*
> *Never believe that who create the busy race*
> *O' the brain, bring poetry to birth, such act performed,*
> *Feel trouble them, the same, such residue as warmed*
> *My prosy blood, this morn,—intrusive fancies, meant*
> *For outbreak and escape by quite another vent!*
> *Whence follows that, asleep, my dreamings oft exceed*
> *The bound. But you shall hear.* (LXXXVIII, 1524-40)

The success of the poet, the freedom he wins, depends on his keeping "thoughts apart from facts." In the realm of experience fancies are "intrusive"; they warm the "prosy blood" but have not achieved "outbreak and escape." And so they emerge in dreams. One of the difficulties of reading *Fifine* is simply that of believing that Browning has said what the words do say. The words here mark the divergence of imagination and experience which is central to the eventual development of the poem. Furthermore, this divergence is explained in a way that assumes a dynamic conception of the unconscious which was not recognized until the present century. In addition, in the light of the nature of the freedom which has been won in the realm of the imagination as symbolized in the Arion epiphany, the analysis presented in the poem must be taken to assume a thoroughly Freudian conception of the relationship of sexuality to the unconscious. If this seems improbable, as it must inevitably, it will seem much less so when we examine the thesis symbolically developed in part 5.

At the present point in the poem, the experience of faltering energy is not without recompense, for it issues in a new realization and a renewal in another mode of the impulse of hope. Up to this point the poem has been concerned with metaphysical and personal relationships and with the individual as artist. The perspective has been essentially personal. Now psychic tension is resolved, for the time being, in a new intellectual awarenes. Effort and failure of the individual are succeeded by a general conception the perspective of which is one of human society and "the state of mankind" (CVIII, 1858).

8
The Cultural Vision

The poem now achieves its culminating realization in a breathtaking transformation of Victorian vision. Though the new vision is eventually betrayed, its validity is not denied. It has been implicit from the beginning—in the image of Fifine as physical and sensual vitality untouched by, and rejecting, the forces of cultural configuration, and in a moment sensing unity with animal nature in awareness that the boundaries of life are generation and death. Fifine has served as an objective symbol of sexuality throughout the poem, a fleeting, tantalizing image, perhaps pruriently beheld. Now in a moment of intuitive realization sexuality moves serenely to the center of consciousness. Fifine is epiphanized as sexuality and as a symbol of generative vitality uniting man. The intuition and the epiphany have their sequel in an allegorical-symbolic structure at the center of which are a dream vision of Venice at carnival and a "Druid" monument referred to twice as a single image but actually experienced as two related but diverse configurations in stone. Meaning arises first of all from a general transformation of imagery from the beginning of this part of the poem. Imagery of densified materiality, predominantly an imagery of stone, expresses a new response to the human condition. The allegorical-symbolic structure gives expression to a number of closely related conceptions which would await the twentieth century to effect a revolution in Western culture.

Most of part 5 is devoted to the last major movement of the poem, a dream-vision (XCIV-CXX) which is more properly a dream than the "dream, pricked too." A quality suggestive of actual dreams pervades the somewhat elaborate introduction.

The opening passage, while providing reiterative links with the progress of the poem up to that point, is also an imagistic statement of the central theme of part 5. This is one of the most extraordinary passages in the poem. The preceding passage had suggested the recounting of a dream. Part 5 begins as follows:

> *I smoked. The webs o' the weed,*
> *With many a break i' the mesh, were floating to re-form*
> *Cupola-wise above: chased thither by soft warm*
> *Inflow of air without; since I—of mind to muse, to clench*
> *The gain of soul and body, got by their noon-day drench*
> *In sun and sea,—had flung both frames o' the window wide,*
> *To soak my body still and let soul soar beside.* (LXXXIX, 1540-46)

Here, and in subsequent lines, there are echoes not only of the swimmer theme of part 3 and the prologue, but of the first fourteen lines of the poem. Of special interest are the following: an awareness of vegetation in tobacco imagined as weed, the suggestion of a parterre, an awareness of sun and sea ("sun and air" in section II), and of the out-of-doors, as will be seen. The general imagery of section II is of barrenness from which flowers have suddenly bloomed. Totally visual in section II, the imagery is deepened now by touch and smell. It is as though the scene of section II has been transformed by dream and deeply sensualized:

> *In came the country sounds and sights and smells—that fine*
> *Sharp needle in the nose from our fermenting wine!* (1547-48)

This echoes an earlier imagery of wine. The wine here is no longer "the indignant wine, / Wrath of the red press" (LXXIX, 1333-34), but wine fermenting quietly. In what follows immediately we may see another echo from section II and from the prologue, one in which a butterfly image his been strangely deepened in materiality and one in which, perhaps, the wine's indignation has been stilled and objectified:

> *In came a dragon-fly with whir and stir, then out,*
> *Off and away:* (LXXXIX, 1549-50)

Then, dreamlike, something else comes into the room in which again there is a fusion of earlier imagery. The anger of section LXXIX "stayed much growth of tendril-twine." Within twenty lines of the flower imagery of section II Fifine was called "queen-tulip of the Fair." Now vegetation imagery is animated and given the coquetry always associated with Fifine, this being immediately linked with more specifically sexual imagery:

> *in came, —kept coming, rather, —pout*
> *Succeeding smile, and take-away still close on give, —*
> *One loose long creeper-branch, tremblingly sensitive*
> *To risks, which blooms and leaves, —each leaf tongue-broad,*
> *   each bloom*
> *Mid-finger-deep, —must run by prying in the room.* (1550-54)

The fusion of imagery from the beginning of the poem and from the immediate angry sequel to the Arion passage occurs when the poem is beginning anew but doing so in a way that is organically connected with what has gone before. The line following these epitomizes in four verbs the total development of the poem. The room into which the flower-bearing creeper-branch comes is that "of one who loves and grasps and spoils and speculates" (1555). The effect of the spoiling has been observed in reiterated notes of hostility succeeding expressions of love and most conspicuously in the sustained anger following the Arion passage. The speculation is embodied in the final movement of the poem which is now beginning. It is speculation anticipated now in intuition, in passionate realization transcending objective formulation:

> *All so far plain enough to sight and sense: but, weights,*
> *Measures and numbers, —ah, could one apply such test*
> *To other visitants that came at no request*
> *Of who kept open house, —to fancies manifold*
> *From this four-cornered world, the memories new and old,*

> *The antenatal prime experience—what know I?—*
> *The initiatory love preparing us to die—*
> *Such were a crowd to count, a sight to see, a prize*
> *To turn to profit, were but fleshly ears and eyes*
> *Able to cope with those o' the spirit!* (1556-65)

The passage is difficult and very important. The speaker turns from that which is rationally comprehensible to "other visitants." Of these "memories" and "fancies" only one is characterized, but that in extraordinary words: "The antenatal prime experience— what know I?— / The initiatory love preparing us to die—." One may be tempted to read here the God of Plotinus, adjusting the neoplatonic act of creation in reconciliation with a phrase Browning earlier associated with the idea of a first cause. His phrase in "The Pope" is "the initiatory spasm." One may be encouraged in the neoplatonic reading by the echo in "this four-cornered world" of John Donne's "Holy Sonnet, Number Seven." The poem will not sustain neoplatonic myth or metaphysics, however, and temperament will explain sufficiently the aura of spirituality which persists as the poem turns decisively now away from final things to beginnings and finds those beginnings in the material basis of life and the somatic basis of human existence. Here, as at other points, the poem achieves a deeply intuitive moment of mythic realization. The lines quoted above represent the central experience of the poem, an experience that will be elaborated later in part 5. Within that symbolically elaborated experience it will be found that the "fancies manifold" correspond to human consciousness embodied in human culture and that underlying these is "the antenatal prime experience" and the "initiatory love preparing us to die." The realization here is intuitive and subtle. It is, as the speaker says later, "a certitude I yet may hardly keep" (XC, 1581).

Both as a matter of temperament and as a strategy of conceal-ment the poem in its essential development proceeds henceforth by symbol and suggestion. Accordingly the speaker now invokes mu-sic, in order to express "truth that escapes prose,—nay puts poetry to shame" (1572). It is indicative of the developmental progress of the poem that the speaker had previously forgone the aid of music in deference to the wife's relative lack of interest in it. It is also significant that from this point until the ending of the poem in part 6 the wife is essentially forgotten and the dramatic situation is almost entirely absorbed in the progession of symbol and narrative. The wife who restrained the impulse of joy and hope does not obstruct the subtle realization which is the by-product of the frustration of that impulse. The speaker addresses a musician now "dead and gone away":

> *"With me, must knowledge melt*
> *Into surmise and doubt and disbelief, unless*
> *Thy music reassure—I gave no idle guess,*
> *But gained a certitude I yet may hardly keep!*
> *What care? since round is piled a monumental heap*
> *Of music that conserves the assurance, thou as well*
> *Wast certain of the same!"* (1578-84)

The phrase "since round is piled a monumental heap" anticipates an image basic to subsequent development and enforces an identification of the particular music invoked with the palpability of the imagery now prevailing. This music, the speaker says, is Schumann's *Carnaval* (XCI, 1588). With the music established, the speaker returns again to the scene of the beginning of the poem as he recalls the arrival of the gypsy caravan on the evening before the fair. Here, when her meaning may be generalized in its significance for mankind, the meaning of Fifine for the speaker is made explicit:

> *I heard across the dusk*
> *Creak a slow caravan, and saw arrive the husk*
> *O' the spice-nut, which peeled off this morning, and displayed,*
> *'Twixt tree and tree, a tent whence the red pennon made*
> *Its vivid reach for home and ocean-idleness—*
> *And where, my heart surmised, at that same moment,—yes,—*
> *Tugging her tricot on,—yet tenderly, lest stitch*
> *Announce the crack of doom, reveal disaster which*
> *Our Pornic's modest stock of merceries in vain*
> *Were ransacked to retrieve,—there, cautiously a-strain*
> *(My heart surmised) must crouch in that tent's corner, curved*

Like Spring-month's russet moon, some girl by fate reserved
To give me once again the electric snap and spark
Which prove, when finger finds out finger in the dark
O' the world, there's fire and life and truth there, link but hands
And pass the secret on. Lo, link by link, expands
The circle, lengthens out the chain, till one embrace
Of high with low is found uniting the whole race,
Not simply you and me and our Fifine, but all
The world: the Fair expands into the Carnival,
And Carnival again to . . . ah, but that's my dream! (1591-1611)

It will eventually be seen that the symbolic sequence—initiatory
love, monumental heap, Fifine, carnival—is entirely unitary. The
reclustering of basic images in the passage above—the red pennon,
the sea, Fifine—revives the sanguine energy, that hope of joy
which, as will be seen at the end, is never entirely absent from the
poem. The truth proved by the fingers finding out each other in the
dark is the truth of "fire and life"—the sense of ontological certainty, that single stable meaning of the truth throughout the poem, a
meaning consistently associated with a human relationship specifically sexual. In the last two lines of the passage, the speaker
broaches, but then interrupts, expression of the meaning which the
movement now beginning will eventually elaborate. The carnival
into which the fair "expands" symbolizes the condition of man in
civilization, and that to which the carnival turns "again" symbolizes the idea that the forms of civilization are a sublimation of the
energies of which Fifine, or woman as sensuality, is the object. "I
somehow played the piece" (XCII, 1612), says the speaker, who then
discourses for some forty lines on the thesis that just as human
emotions are the same from age to age so the essential values of art
are constant though outward forms continuously change. The central metaphor here is "the banquet-room o' the world" (1617), and
the discourse is warm and heavy with imagery of food and of eating, the tastes, and, repeatedly, even the sounds. In the new age
gums may be "obtuse to gust and smack" of the "meat o' the meal"
relished some fifty years before. And yet "another age, by due /
Rotation, pries, sniffs, smacks, discovers old is new" (1645-46).

Thus Schumann's suite becomes new again as the speaker plays it, music lending itself to such renewal most easily "of all the arts, since change is there / The law, and not the lapse" (1649-50).

The themes of permanence and change are obviously integral with the entire poem, but the heavy emphasis on eating may seem at first irrelevant. In the perspective of the entire poem, however, the vigorous imagery of sensual gusto is fundamental.[1]

The speaker "somehow-nohow played / The whole o' the pretty piece" (XCIII, 1669-70) and is soon "gone off in company with Music" (1683). Then the dream-vision begins (XCV). The speaker finds himself in Venice. Venice as the city of the sea recalls the water imagery pervading the poem and symbolizing the emergence of life in matter. Venice "was by instinct found / Carnival-country proper" (XCIV, 1684-85). The speaker realized that "Venice was the world; its Carnival—the state / Of mankind" (CVIII, 1858-59).

The speaker is at the square of Saint Mark's. From a position of great elevation, atop the campanile "opposite Mark's church," he observes below "a prodigious Fair." The first point he observes about the concourse of people is that they are all masked. Most of the masks represent animal life—"beast or bird, / Nay, fish and reptile even." Others represent "the infinitude / Of passions, loves and hates, man pampers till his mood / Becomes himself." There is affirmed here a thesis previously expressed as possibility (XLIII, 659-60): the face is "an evidence / O' the soul at work inside; and, all the more intense, / So much the more grotesque" (XCVI, 1719-21).

The speaker, his confidence growing in his ability to understand, "pitched into the square— / A groundling like the rest" (XCIX, 1737-38). Then a change occurs. In the masks of carnival, symbolizing faces, the speaker

> *found brutality encroach*
> *Less on the human, lie the lightlier as I looked*
> *The nearlier on these faces.* (1742-44)

The observed change is attended by a subtle but most significant change of conception. The faces "seemed but now so crook'd / And clawed away from God's prime purpose" (1744-45). Now, however, they "rather urged to pity than disgust" and what the speaker sees in them is "The certain sign and mark,—say hint, say, trick of lip / Or twist of nose,—that proved a fault in workmanship" (1751-52). The difference is, of course, enormous. In the first conception there is a responsibility external to God's, a source of failure and guilt violating the divine purpose. In the second conception man is united with his defects as victim of a God conceived as an erring workman. The movement is from dualism to a monism in which God is a rhetorical hypothesis. It will be remembered that the problem was confronted earlier in the poem. The solution earlier was that imagination restored perfection in a dualistic, even a solipsistic, universe. The resolution now employs a different strategy. Human defect is no longer relegated to the realm of illusion, "the false." It is now affirmed as reality and reinterpreted.

The defect of the "workmanship" is that it "checked the man and let the beast appear" (1754). The progression to be accomplished is toward reconciliation with what has previously offended. "Ugliness" and "repugnance" now "perished off." An evolutionary process is intimated in explanation. Ugliness and repugnance suggest a "wrong" which "Might linger yet i' the make of man" (CI, 1768). But this suggestion does not issue in a vision of man ultimately free of the "wrong." Rather this "wrong" is found essential to life:

> brute-beast touch was turned
> Into mankind's safeguard! Force, guile, were arms which earned
> My praise, not blame at all: for we must learn to live,
> Case-hardened at all points, not bare and sensitive,
> But plated for defence, nay, furnished for attack,
> With spikes at the due place, that neither front nor back
> May suffer in that squeeze with nature, we find—life.
> Are we not here to learn the good of peace through strife,
> Of love through hate, and reach knowledge by ignorance?
> Why, those are helps thereto, which late we eyed askance,
> And nicknamed unaware! (1775-85)

The nickname was "brute-beast touch." In the sequel to this passage the process of renaming and reconceiving will continue. If here the conception of man's material nature as protective does not seem entirely reconcilable with the doctrine of opposites, the more important point is that both conceptions affirm and justify man's material nature. A monistic tendency to make all things coherent and consistent is now dominant in the poem. The masks at carnival symbolize faces. The masked carnival throng is a "brute-pageant"; the exterior semblance is a "brute-beast touch" (CI, 1775); it lets "the beast appear" (XCIX, 1754). The point of the first part of the dream vision is that the speaker overcomes his "late disgust / At the brute-pageant" and is reconciled to "the brute-beast touch" in man. He comes to "do justice to the drift of nature" (CVIII, 1873), to see a unity in face and soul, and, indeed, to "explain the glories by the shames / Mixed up in man, one stuff miscalled by different names" (1874-75).

Two considerations must influence our interpretation of the first part of the dream-vision. The first is that the word "brute" has been associated in the early part of the poem with the performers at the Pornic fair who symbolize the goal of the quest and that the word "brute" in Browning's work may nearly always be taken as referring to man's sexuality. The second consideration is the strange pattern in most of Browning's early work in which the imminence of erotic love has as its immediate sequel an act of social love. (see discussion below, chap. 10). The individual is integrated in one way or another with a social collectivity, usually in a position of leadership. In "The Flight of the Duchess" the act of social love is seen as coincident with erotic consummation, but usually the movement to social union seens to be an evasive substitute and is eventually unsatisfactory.

After Sordello has collapsed in a condition of ontological diffusion, he resolves to wake

> *From out his lethargy and nobly shake*
> *Off timid habits of denial, mix*
> *With men, enjoy like men.* (II, 704-6)

As it turns out, however, Sordello cannot become one with and be like men. He can become part of the social entity only in a special relationship, serving as "Soul to their body" (III, 557). This aspiration fails and Sordello dies. The pattern is rejected in Browning's later poetry, most conspicuously in *The Ring and the Book*, where love and the social collectivity are seen as antithetical. In part 2 of *Fifine at the Fair* we have seen a rejection precisely of that version of the pattern in which the protagonist becomes "Soul to their body." In part 5 the speaker's descent into the square, recalling Arion's leap into the sea, is an act of union, abandoning "pride of place" and a "pinnacled pre-eminence" (CVIII, 1864, 1866) and accepting oneness with mankind to be "a groundling like the rest," and the condition for this is affirmation of the "brute" nature of man, thus reconciling "face" and "soul." The "brute-pageant" introduction of the dream-vision symbolizes a psychological integration the intellectual corollary of which will be elaborated in the remainder of the dream-vision explaining "the glories by the shames / Mixed up in man, one stuff miscalled by different names" (1874-75).

The speaker now introduces a major image first anticipated in the characterization of music as "a monumental heap." The image is that of a prehistoric stone monument of the sort confidently associated in the nineteenth century with Druids. A bit later in the poem a subtle shift of reference will introduce another kind of stone monument and a different shape, but at first the term "Druid temple" (CII-CXXI) seems to refer either to Stonehenge or to comparable ruins in Normandy and Brittany.

The imagery now elaborated is a striking example of the material densification of imagery in this climactic movement of the poem and of the application of such imagery in realms previously conceived as ethereally spiritual. In parts 2 and 3 the luminous images for soul or spirit were light, then air; water was a constant image for the material condition of life. Now a drop of water represents the soul. This drop of water is hermetically sealed in an "orb" or crystal. Perhaps the enclosing material is partly stone; at any rate it is directly associated with the stone monument. Stone or crystal now represents the material or surface aspects of life and the appetites with which they are related:

> I found, one must abate
> One's scorn of the soul's casing, distinct from the soul's self—
> Which is the centre-drop: whereas the pride in pelf,
> The lust to seem the thing it cannot be, the greed
> For praise, and all the rest seen outside,—these indeed
> Are the hard polished cold crystal environment
> Of those strange orbs unearthed i' the Druid temple, meant
> For divination (so the learned please to think)
> Wherein you may admire one dew-drop roll and wink,
> All unaffected by—quite alien to—what sealed
> And saved it long ago. (CII, 1788-98)

The conception of the drop of dew as "centre-drop" conditions in some measure the symbolism of stone in later passages, modifying cold and hardness with intimations of life. Here, too, the stone is an active principle: it "sealed" and "saved," though, as will be seen, its action is due to the vitality of the "centre-drop." The passage that follows is remarkable for two reasons. It denies any knowledge of the ultimate relationship of spirit and matter; in effect it renounces all unifying metaphysics. It also sees the duration of the soul as intimately associated with its material conditon. Of the center-drop the speaker says,

> though how it got congealed
> I shall not give a guess, nor how, by power occult,
> The solid surface-shield was outcome and result
> Of simple dew at work to save itself amid
> The unwatery force around; protected thus, dew slid
> Safe through all opposites, impatient to absorb
> Its spot of life, and last forever in the orb
> We, now, from hand to hand pass with impunity. (1798-1805)

The development of densely material imagery continues. The delight of the speaker as he observes the crowd of the carnival is that of the "chemist" as he discovers the unity of life and matter. In this image, unquestionably, Browning characterizes the reductionist nature of the realization soon to be elaborated. The speaker is like the chemist who,

> *tracing each effect back to its cause, elate,*
> *Constructs in fancy, from the fewest primitives,*
> *The complex and complete, all diverse life, that lives*
> *Not only in beast, bird, fish, reptile, insect, but*
> *The very plants and earths and ores.* (CIII, 1810-14)

Then for the first time the search for underlying principles, compared here with the scientific process, is related to the search for
ontological certainty which was so conspicuous in parts 2 and 3.
Renewal of this theme makes all the more significant the conception
of the human body as representative of the soul:

> *Just so I glut*
> *My hunger both to be and know the thing I am,*
> *By contrast with the thing I am not; so, through sham*
> *And outside, I arrive at inmost real, probe*
> *And prove how the nude form obtained the checkered robe.*
>   (1814-18)

The remarkable image with its allusion to Harlequin, who appears in connection with Schumann's *Carnaval* (XCII, 1659-68),
brings to a close the first phase of the dream-vision of the Venetian
carnival. As the poem continues, the process of reductive realization is extended to all the forms of civilization. In the second phase
of the dream-vision, imagery, while retaining the fluidity of symbolism, takes on allegorical dimensions as a means of achieving the
central statement of the poem.

The speaker becomes aware of a change in the surroundings of
the carnival (CV). The change is compared to that in an "edifice of
cloud" glorified by sunset. Description of the diminishing brilliance
of the cloud as its parts form and re-form is touched by a sense of
regret and loss expressive of an aspect of the speaker's response to
the other changes to be witnessed in the dream-vision (CVI). We
have here a clue as to why in the prologue the "fancy turned a
fear." A change like that in the cloud now occurs in Saint Mark's
Church and in all the other edifices of the square (CVII, 1843-56).
The speaker is aware that the change results from the working of an

internal principle: "A subtle something had its way within the heart / Of each and every house I watched" (1847-48). The result of the change is an edifice which has "grown—new is scarce the phrase / Since older, in a sense" (1851-52). The change is toward a condition, or a principle, common in all the houses of the world. This common condition strikes the speaker with a sense of recognition: "In all the maze, no single tenement / I saw, but I could claim acquaintance with" (1855-56). At this point the speaker recalls his original position of "pinnacled pre-eminence" and "pride of place" above Saint Mark's square. He had then "pitched into the square" (XCIX, 1737). Now, as may occur in dreams, the action is repeated and changed. The speaker tells us that he "slid sagaciously betimes / Down heaven's baluster-rope." The image is integral with the symbolic shift of values from heaven to earth which begins after the elegiac movement of part 2; "the baluster rope," if suspending earth from heaven is also a support from earth of heaven. He descended to realize that "the proper goal for wisdom was the ground / And not the sky" (CVIII, 1867-68). His wisdom is a reconciliation to the world as it is:

> And—consequent upon the learning how from strife
> Grew peace—from evil, good—came knowledge that, to get
> Acquaintance with the way o' the world, we must not fret
> Nor fume, on altitudes of self-sufficiency,
> But bid a frank farewell to what—we think—should be,
> And, with as good a grace, welcome what is—we find.
>
> (CIX, 1879-84)

Having observed a radical and pervasive change occurring in the forms of the buildings in the square (CX-CXVI), the speaker now designates symbolic meanings for the separate buildings. The buildings represent the major intellectual and cultural institutions and activities affecting the consciousness of man—categories of human effort and achievement so broadly defined as to embrace, in effect, the totality of human culture: religion, science, philosophy, history, morality, and art (painting, music, and poetry). They are represented by "architecture" which "we, walled up within the cirque / O' the world, consider fixed as fate" (CX, 1888-89). These edifices "tremblingly grew blank" (1890); proceeded "to decay, evanishment in dust" (CXVII, 2007); they "subdivide, collapse" (CXI, 1913).[2] They will also "tower again, transformed" (1914), but the emphasis at first is on the forms that disappear, the loss that is ultimately felt with deep weariness and regret (CXVII, CXIX). The reaction here is quite impersonal and may be taken as an instance of what Morse Peckham calls "the dilemma of culture transcendence."[3]

The change is first observed in buildings recognized as "temples, sure," one of them distinguished as "a stately fane" (CX, 1897). The symbolism here is of faith itself rather than of specific creeds or sects. Later, "Religion" is seen as standing "at least in the temple-type" (CXII, 1928), the meaning of "temple" shifting here to refer either to religion as an organized activity or to Browning's own Evangelical sect, customarily associated with temples as distinguished from churches. It is clear, however, that the speaker's own religious faith does not stand intact although he has no greater faith in the modern thought which has undermined religion (CXII).

The change in the edifices is described in images related to the basic themes of part 5, and, as will be seen more clearly later, to its ultimate symbolic statement. The buildings are transformed because

> liquid change through artery and vein
> O' the very marble wound its way! And first a stain
> Would startle and offend amid the glory; next,
> Spot swift succeeded spot, but found me less perplexed
> By portents; then, as 't were, a sleepiness soft stole
> Over the stately fane, and shadow sucked the whole
> Façade into itself, made uniformly earth
> What was a piece of heaven; till, lo, a second birth,
> And the veil broke away because of something new
> Inside, that pushed to gain an outlet. (CX, 1892-1901)

The agent of change as liquid moving through "artery and vein" of stone recalls the earlier materialization of the soul imaged as dew enclosed in stone, an image which associates the conception of soul with the poem's primary symbol of life—water in its powers of fertility and mortality. The idea that the agent of change, of destruction, is an active inward principle, eventually creative, is an advance in the process of realization being achieved by the poem, for otherwise the conception of outward form and inward substance corresponds exactly to that of the speaker's discovery earlier of the "meat o' the meal" underlying the garnishes of Schumann's *Carnaval.*

Introduction again of the words "stain" and "glory" reanimates the connotation of a moralistic reaction to the kind of change that is occurring. But the context negates this moral overtone, both because the words "stain" and "glory" have been neutralized, and because the "spot" found the speaker "less perplexed." With the process of change thus imagined as it works in the fundamental element of faith, the dream vision turns to learning, science, and philosophy, and the speaker concludes that "these fare worst of all" (CXI, 1920). The speaker is especially emphatic in his rejection of the presumptuous certainty of modern knowledge dominated by science which seems to say "men thought they knew; we know" (CXIII, 1956). The speaker replies:

> *Do you, my generation? Well, let the blocks prove mist*
> *I' the main enclosure,—church and college, if they list,*
> *Be something for a time, and everything anon,*
> *And anything awhile, as fit is off or on,*
> *Till they grow nothing, soon to reappear no less*
> *As something,—shape re-shaped, till out of shapelessness*
> *Come shape again as sure!* (CXIV, 1957-63)

Having observed the transiency of religion, philosophy, and science, the speaker turns to other categories essential and yet inferior to these:

> *Leave watching change at work i' the greater scale, on these*
> *The main supports, and turn to their interstices*
> *Filled up by fabrics too, less costly and less rare,*
> *Yet of importance, yet essential to the Fair*
> *They help to circumscribe, instruct, and regulate!* (CXV, 1969-73)

The lesser categories are imagined as booths clustered below the larger architecture of the fair.[4] The treatment of these categories (CXVI) lends justification to Browning's claim that *Fifine* was "the boldest . . . since Sordello." It is of interest that history, with which the speaker obviously associates the higher criticism, should be made inferior to science. The pretense of history, however, is similar to that of science: " 'Man, hold truth evermore. Forget the early lies' " (CXVI, 1978). It is of greater interest in the light of the author's mid-Victorian background that the inferior categories should include "Morality." The relationship to the higher categories will be made clearer later. At this point the treatment is quite abstract except for two decisive points identifying morality as Victorian sexual morality. Morality is characterized twice within six lines as "demure"; the dictates of morality pretend to be fatally imperative, and the suggestion that they are a matter of life and death is essentially a way of associating morality with the depth of the central struggle of the poem as an effort for freedom and vitality:

> *There sits Morality, demure behind her stall,*
> *Dealing out life and death: "This is the thing to call*
> *Right, and this other, wrong; thus think, thus do, thus say,*
> *Thus joy, thus suffer!—not to-day as yesterday—*
> *Yesterday's doctrine dead, this only shall endure.*
> *Obey its voice and live!"—enjoins the dame demure.* (1979-84)

The reader may hesitate over the words, "not to-day as yesterday— / Yesterday's doctrine dead." We may ask what that morality is which Victorian prudery would acknowledge as its not remote predecessor, valid, by implication, for an earlier day. Within a few lines the speaker will delineate symbolically an older morality, a historical source of vitality the vindication and realization of which has been the goal of the poem from the beginning.

Next among the inferior categories is "Art" and its subdivisions: painting, music, and poetry:

> *Art gives flag to breeze, bids drum beat, trumpet blow,*
> *Inviting eye and ear to yonder raree-show.*
> *Up goes the canvas, hauled to height of pole.* (1985-87)

By the metaphor of flag and tent, "Art" is associated with the opening scene of *Fifine* and affirmed as integral with the experience of the poem. The passing denigration of that experience in the designation of fair and carnival as "raree-show" marks the beginning of a mood which within a few lines will be developed and explained. In connection with painting, Browning takes occasion for ironic expression of an issue of much concern to him—the defense of the nude, which was also a defense of the predilection of his son Pen as a painter:

> *We know the way—long lost, late learned—to paint! A wink*
> *Of eye, and lo, the pose! the statue on its plinth!*
> *How could we moderns miss the heart o' the labyrinth*
> *Perversely all these years, permit the Greek seclude*
> *His secret till to-day?* (1988-92)

The claim of music to finality is given ironic expression, and then in a moment dramatizing the protean adaptability of the essential form of the poem, Browning steps outside its margin:

> *But is the bard to be*
> *Behindhand? Here's his book, and now perhaps you see*
> *At length what poetry can do!* (1995-97)

What now occurs would seem to reflect a sense not only of seriousness but of certainty in what the poem is saying. It is here that the speaker, while acknowledging a permanence underlying change, for the first time expresses sorrow for the passing of the configurations of an older civilization:

> *Why, that's stability*
> *Itself, that change on change we sorrowfully saw*
> *Creep o'er the prouder piles!* (CXVII, 1997-99)

There follows recognition that morality—and, in effect, Victorian morality—has outlived the "Knowledge" on which it depended. Here "Knowledge" must be taken as religious certainty:

> *We acquiesced in law*
> *When the fine gold grew dim i' the temple, when the brass*
> *Which pillared that so brave abode where Knowledge was,*
> *Bowed and resigned the trust.* (1999-2002)

The passage continues with recognition of the fact that the claim of art as the source of truth is qualified by its status as successor and substitute for the knowledge by which it was previously vitalized. One must read here too a moment of revulsion for the discoveries artistically revealed in this poem as its experiential component takes a decided turn. The words "caprice" and "Harlequinade" and "tinsel-flag" stand here for the art of *Fifine at the Fair*, and though the words "glories" and "shames" have been semantically qualified they serve here a mood a deep regret. The speaker refers to

> *all this caprice,*
> *Harlequinade where swift to birth succeeds decease*
> *Of hue at every turn o' the tinsel-flag which flames*
> *While Art holds booth in Fair? Such glories chased by shames*
> *Like these, distract beyond the solemn and august*
> *Procedure to decay, evanishment in dust,*
> *Of those marmoreal domes, —above vicissitude,*
> *We used to hope!* (2002-9)

The passages depicting the deliquescence and vanishing of the forms in Saint Mark's are a witnessing of the dissolution of Western culture and a reluctant recognition that from that dissolution art emerges as the only form of knowledge. Art separated from its moorings in ideational certainty becomes a "poetry of experience" as Robert Langbaum has defined that term, but poetry of experience cannot serve a need for certainty.[5] The note of sorrow at the passing of the old, the regret of the usurpation of the new—these are part of the impulse of the movement now toward a new reduction of experience with its implications for a new ordering of life. The new reduction will be unstable because the energy and hope engendering it are unstable, because it is a reduction which cannot be frankly confronted by, or assimilated to, dominant cultural modes, and because in the last analysis, the means by which it is achieved is a quintessential example of the poetry of experience.

The poem now moves back to the larger perspective of the dream-vision with a deferential apology for what has been or will be revealed: "For, understand, I ought / To simply say—'I saw,' each thing I say 'I thought' " (CXVIII, 2012-13). Then the mood is touched by despair:

> *So, what did I see next but,—much as when the vault*
> *I' the west,—wherein we watch the vapoury manifold*
> *Transfiguration,—tired turns blaze to black,—behold,*
> *Peak reconciled to base, dark ending feud with bright,*
> *The multiform subsides, becomes the definite.*
> *Contrasting life and strife, where battle they i' the blank*
> *Severity of peace in death . . . ?* (CXIX, 2017-23)

The "blank severity of peace in death" and the "tired" that "turns blaze to black" are continuous with a sadness at the collapse of old values, old "glories," but they are also part of a weariness and resignation informed by deathly intimations that attend a sense of the failure of the hope of joy—a sense which recurs with increasing frequency as the poem draws to an end. The psychological corollary of this mood in the earlier parts of the poem is the recurrence of anger and hostility. However, the despair is perhaps never quite complete and the resignation never quite final. In the passage quoted above, "the blank severity of peace in death" is charged inwardly by the battle of "dark" with "bright," and when the phrase is repeated in the following section, as the imagery of the cloud is applied again to the architecture in the square, the note of despair is followed by anticipation of discovery. Distinctions are blurred, says the speaker, as

> *edifice . . . shall I say,*
> *Died into edifice? I find no simpler way*
> *Of saying how, without or dash or shock or trace*

Of violence, I found unity in the place
Of temple, tower, —nay, hall and house and hut, —one blank
Severity of peace in death; to which they sank
Resigned enough, till . . . ah, conjecture, I beseech,
What special blank did they agree to, all and each?
What common shape was that wherein they mutely merged
Likes and dislikes of form, so plain before? (CXX, 2032-41)

The answer to these questions, the definition of "the special blank" which the forms agreed to and the "common shape" wherein they merged, achieves the culminating realization of the dream-vision and the final result, symbolically expressed, of the intellectual process of the poem. Before examining this symbolic statement it will be helpful to consider briefly an essential aspect of the thought of the poem and the basic imagery related to it.

Throughout most of the poem distinctions have been articulated between inner and outer reality which correspond, roughly, to such philosophical distinctions as those between substance and accident, noumena and phenomena, will and idea. Browning was unquestionably influenced in this poem by the philosophical heritage, but the philosophical distinction as established by Kant merges, as it usually did in the romantic tradition, with the kind of distinction that may be made within the realm of time and space—distinctions between origins and ends, causes and effects, materials and products. Philosophy pervasively enriches Browning's imagery in *Fifine*, but the eventual question of part 5 is not really philosophical. The question concerns the phenomenal realms of biology and culture and is eventually psychological. From what materials are the forms of human culture elaborated? What is the basic and perennial energy underlying human activity? The question may best be formulated from the answers about to be elaborated symbolically.

The basic image of part 2 is light. Though the image of water recurs throughout the poem it is most important in part 3 where water in conjunction with air above the sea or at other times with the shore and inland provides a generalized symbolic structure corresponding to the dualistic orientation of parts 2 and 3. Human existence is seen as experience within the tensions between these elements of the structure. The symbolic structure is inherently dramatic.

In part 5 stone is omnipresent, both explicitly and in the architecture so conspicuous in the dream-vision, and it is the chief manifestation of the strong tendency to the dense and heavy materialization of imagery in this part. Stone is, in a sense, implicit in all the imagery of part 5. It is much to the point that stone is symbolic of reality. "The hierophany of a stone," says Mircea Eliade, "is preeminently an ontophany; above all, the stone *is*, it always remains itself, it does not change—and it *strikes* man by what it possesses of irreducibility and absoluteness and, in doing so, reveals to him by analogy the irreducibility and absoluteness of being."[6] Only somewhat later in the poem may we come to understand the sense of ontological vigor which adhered for Browning to the climactic vision of the poem.

Stone as symbolic of the monistic world obviously cannot easily serve as part of a dramatic structure. It is for this reason that there emerges in part 5 an important duality of symbolism—as it were, a symbolism of substance and a symbolism of form. Stone exists as though formless, without limit or definition. As such, it is symbolic, not only of the monistic materialism implicit in part 5, but also of the psychological impasse reached at the end of part 3 and registered in inexplicable fury following the Arion epiphany. Stone is therefore related to the personal component of the poem as it exists in part 5, symbolizing both a psychic stasis and the reality which revolt from that stasis asserts. In part 5 the original motive force of the poem is at impasse in a stasis of hope. Its energy is diverted to an intellectual effort involved in a rediscovery of the world and the dissolution of the cultural forms that are factors in the impasse. While stone itself is symbolically related to the experiential component of the poem, the forms contoured in, or imposed on, stone are symbolic counters in the intellectual effort. One of the tensions of part 5 is between symbol as substance and symbol as form.

Awareness of the general aspects of Browning's use of symbolism will greatly facilitate the reading of his eventual answer to the fundamental question of the poem: Is there a truth about the nature of things that will bring freedom and joy by justifying the fulfillment of desire? The answer is in the meaning emerging chiefly from two images. The first is a "Druid monument," reminiscent of Stonehenge though Browning probably has in mind one of the comparable dolmens common in Normandy and the area of Pornic. The second image is another primeval monument, "a huge stone pillar." These two images are eventually identified with each other verbally in such a way as to be treated as a single thing or two things closely unified. Intervening between these images, and directly associated with them, is the image of mushrooms, part of them strung together on a rope, part of them in a basket. Mushrooms, which are a sexual symbol, add the value of flesh to stone as reality. When the symbolic statement is complete, its meaning is made more explicit by a return to the Promethean theme, this being fused, as though in montage, with the re-emerging dramatic situation as the poem moves to its conclusion.

In introducing the dolmen, the speaker uses a past tense separating the scene in time and space and then a mixture of tenses dissolving time and space:

> *I urged*
> *Your step this way, prolonged our path of enterprise*
> *To where we stand at last, in order that your eyes*
> *Might see the very thing, and save my tongue describe*
> *The Druid monument which fronts you. Could I bribe*
> *Nature to come in aid, illustrate what I mean,*
> *What wants there she should lend to solemnize the scene?*
> (CXXI, 2041-47)

Then the anonymous enormity looms in view:

> *How does it strike you, this construction gaunt and grey—*
> *Sole object, these piled stones, that gleam unground-away*
> *By twilight's hungry jaw, which champs fine all beside*
> *I' the solitary waste we grope through?* (CXXII, 2048-51)

The word "grope" evokes darkness in "the solitary waste" and

contrasts the uncertain efforts of human bodies with giant dimensions which now occupy the imagination. The huge stones that
"gleam unground-away" are more forbidding for their immunity to
the menacing orifice of "twilight's hungry jaw," and shortly the
monument will be experienced as jawlike. Now man and wife move
closer to the stones. They "grope" but they also know the way:

> *Oh, no guide*
> *Need we to grope our way and reach the monstrous door*
> *Of granite!* (2051-53)

The emphasis on the word "granite" is ambiguous, suggesting
that the door is impenetrably closed, though it is not:

> *Take my word, the deeper you explore*
> *The caverned passage, filled with fancies to the brim,*
> *The less will you approve the adventure!* (2053-55)

In these lines the "you" replaces the "we" of the immediately
preceding lines and the reference tends to become rhetorical, uni-
versalizing and therefore defeminizing the experience of entering.
The imagination advances some further inward, but there are intimations of prohibition and of fear. There now follows the passage
which is crucial to the symbolism:

> *Such a grim*
> *Bar-sinister soon blocks abrupt your path, and ends*
> *All with a cold dread shape,—shape whereon Learning spends*
> *Labour, and leaves the text obscurer for the gloss,*
> *While Ignorance reads right—recoiling from that Cross!*[7] (2055-59)

In this passage three terms refer to an obstruction as prohibition. The term "bar-sinister" is a common though erroneous term
of heraldry used in place of "bend-sinister" or "baton-sinister." It is
highly probable that Browning understood the error. Whether he
did or not, one of the components of the term has clearly been reduced, in one of its implications, to its generic sense. The "bar" here

is not so much a coded decoration as an obstruction: it "soon blocks abrupt your path." The other part of the term—"sinister"— is affected by the suggestion of fear in the preceding line and by the modifier "grim" and thus the derivative sense of evil emerges. Partly for reasons which will become clear later, "sinister" must also be taken in its heraldic association with the female. The effects of "bar-sinister" inform the phrase "a cold dread shape" without dispelling its essential ambiguity. This ambiguity must be referred to the central thesis of the present reading which posits an inhibition of which Browning was intensely aware but for which the nineteenth century did not provide an analytic vocabulary. The immediate sequel to "cold dread shape" is syntactically double-handed and consistent with the verbal duplicity of the passage as a whole. The obfuscation of Learning as contrasted with the rightness of Ignorance provides a pattern that will also emerge in connection with the other prehistoric shape soon to be introduced, but in addition it expresses Browning's basic position on Christianity and the higher criticism, thus reinforcing the meaning of the third term in the passage for obstruction or prohibition, "that Cross." The "Cross," capitalized for emphasis, and however abruptly introduced, is as always a symbol for Christianity. In passages now to follow (CXXIII) Christianity will be explicitly identified as the cultural factor prohibitive of sexuality. The same point is symbolically involved in the passage under consideration, though a psychological component of the poem is also effective here. The terms "bar-sinister," "cold dread shape," and "that Cross" are intimately associated, thus assembling intimations of an ambiguous inhibition—a fear associated with the female source and linked with Christianity as a cultural prohibition. Another symbolic meaning is inescapable, though not all the arguments for this reading will be clear until the treatment of the "huge stone pillar" has been examined. The "caverned passage, filled with fancies to the brim" is intended as symbolic of female sexuality.[8] This reading is supported when immediately following the phrase "that Cross," the speaker elaborates on the failure of knowledge concerning the stone structure and then turns in a simile to imagery of sea and shell related in part 3 to sexual love:

Whence came the mass and mass, strange quality of stone
Unquarried anywhere i' the region round? Unknown!
Just as unknown, how such enormity could be
Conveyed by land, or else transported over sea,
And laid in order, so, precisely each on each,
As you and I would build a grotto where the beach
Sheds shell—to last an hour: this building lasts from age
To age the same. But why? (2060-67)

The response to the question follows in the longest single section of the poem (CXXIII). The symbolism to be evolved is integral
with the "caverned passage" symbolism and configures the culminating intellectual realization of the poem. The entire section except
for three and a half lines at the beginning and two and half at the
end is in quotation marks. It will be remembered that in a kind of
coda to part 2 the dramatic wife, though speaking in tones of deep
irony, makes explicit for the first time the argument justifying the
speaker's interest in Fifine (LX). So in what are essentially the two
terminal parts of the poem, parts 2 and 5, the basic conceptions are
spoken by characters other than the primary speaker. This circumstance suggests one of the grounds for caution against discrediting
the significance of the poem by attributing it to the speaker interpreted as a cynical casuist. The implications of the use of quotation
marks are quite to the contrary. Both in part 2 and in part 5 the
basic conceptual formulations simply bring to intellectual fruition
the symbolism of which the poem is fundamentally constituted.
The intellectual factors of the poem are the expressions of various
voices but they are undeniably integral with the dominant symbolic
developments of the poem and thus the various voices become one.
Indeed, the use of various voices serves the dissimulative strategy
of the poem, and to acknowledge this is to suggest the poet's awareness of the tendency of his own voice to subsume that of the primary speaker. The question was, "But why?" The answer begins as
follows:

Ask Learning! I engage
You get a prosy wherefore, shall help you to advance

> *In knowledge just as much as helps you Ignorance*
> *Surmising, in the mouth of peasant-lad or lass.* (CXXIII, 2067-70)

In these lines learning and ignorance, in contrast with their relationship in the statement quoted from the preceding section, are
given equal reliability. The reason for the change is artistic, not
philosophical. The poet is preparing the reader for the fact that ignorance will quote learning in a statement which would be out of
character for the youthful peasant who is the speaker but which is
essential to the entire argument of part 5.

The speaker is at first only diffidently particularized—as "peas-
ant-lad or lass"—in harmony with the notion that it is the personification of ignorance who is heard. In eventual effect, however, the
young peasant, referred to after his speech as "he," is highly particularized. The voice heard is the most distinctive in the poem. It
speaks with the beguiling simplicity of Pippa in *Pippa Passes* and
there emerges a comparable intimation of the poet's commitment to
the speaker. The speech begins as follows:

> *"I heard my father say he understood it was*
> *A building, people built as soon as earth was made*
> *Almost, because they might forget (they were afraid)*
> *Earth did not make itself, but came of Somebody.*
> *They labored that their work might last, and show thereby*
> *He stays, while we and earth, and all things come and go."*
>
> (2071-76)

Thus far there is affirmed a faintly anthropomorphic, but
thoroughly anonymous, principle of being which is associated with
the origin of things. The peasant lad interprets a primitive act of a
prehistoric people, but it becomes increasingly clear as the speech
continues that he conceives his voice as theirs, and that his conceptions are the speculative and partisan echo of their profound
though theologically ambiguous faith. The anonymous God,
though somehow an origin or source, is more important as a locus
of ontological stability. Stone as stone is the perfect symbol of such
stability. While the idea of the individual's participation in being as

permanence of being, as immortality, is dominant in part 2, it is effectively supplanted in parts 3 through 5 by another ontological mode, a sense of ontological certainty that arises from exertion of effort, from gaining perspective and intellectual mastery. The idea of immortality does not become important again until the motive force of part 5 has spent itself and the intellectual quest has, in part 6, been abandoned in a failure of temperament and in deep regret.

In accord with the ontological mode prevailing in parts 3 through 5, the speculative affirmation of the passage quoted immediately above is followed by a passage of vigorous agnosticism. The passage begins with a third and final echo in this poem of the Fitzgerald conundrum:

> *"Come whence? Go whither? That, when come and gone, we know*
> *Perhaps, but not while earth and all things need our best*
> *Attention: we must wait and die to know the rest."* (2077-79)

If we know essentially nothing in this life about origins and ends and if while we are here earth and things need our best attention, then why a religion at all? The question is raised in the following passage. The answer is essentially pragmatic, a matter of values and of morale. A kind of metaphysical conception, harmonious with the naïveté of the peasant lad emerges after all, but it is only a "hope," a "best chance," projecting and recapitulating a certainty of mundane value:

> *"Ask, if that's true, what use in setting up the pile?*
> *To make one fear and hope: remind us, all the while*
> *We come and go, outside there's Somebody that stays;*
> *A circumstance which ought to make us mind our ways,*
> *Because,—whatever end we answer by this life,—*
> *Next time, best chance must be for who, with toil and strife,*
> *Manages now live most like what he was meant*
> *Become: since who succeeds so far, 't is evident,*
> *Stands foremost in the file; who fails, has less to hope*
> *For new promotion."* (2080-89)

The peasant lad now illustrates the point in another striking example of what has been heretofore characterized as the materialization of imagery in part 5. This passage is rich with reverberation from earlier parts of the poem:

> *"That's the rule—with even a rope*
> *Of mushrooms, like this rope I dangle! those that grew*
> *Greatest and roundest, all in life they had to do,*
> *Gain a reward, a grace they never dreamed, I think;*
> *Since, outside white as milk and inside black as ink,*
> *They go to the Great House to make a dainty dish*
> *For Don and Donna; while this basket-load, I wish*
> *Well off my arm, it breaks,—no starveling of the heap*
> *But had his share of dew, his proper length of sleep*
> *I' the sunshine: yet, of all, the outcome is—this queer*
> *Cribbed quantity of dwarfs which burden basket here*
> *Till I reach home; 'tis there that, having run their rigs,*
> *They end their earthly race, are flung as food for pigs.*
> *Any more use I see?"* (2089-102)

The words "outside white as milk and inside black as ink" echo the earlier imagery of black bottle and white chalk cliff in the passage of smoldering fury at the end of part 3. Here as in the earlier passage, the color image is linked with a dwarf image and the affective contexts also correspond. The image of black and white is associated in the earlier passage with an act of strength and defiant assertion, here with health and a kind of fulfillment. In both instances the dwarf image represents a closely linked antithetical mode of failure and distortion, redolent in the earlier passage with the rage of frustration and touched here by a residual overtone of anger. The unifying power within the poem is never more intense than here. The emphasis of the earlier passage was on failure; the emphasis here is on fulfillment. The interest is in use, and if the abrupt question " 'Any more use I see?' " seems uncertain in its reference, that is because its reference is complex. The question concerns the use, the meaning, of the stone monument with its caverned passage, but it also concerns the fulfillment of the element of life that the monument symbolizes. The answer to the question develops the image of another prehistoric monument, of a different shape. The two structures are treated as one in their symbolic relationship to the deliquescing architecture of the dream-vision. Differentiation between the two stone configurations emphasizes a relationship between them and a special symbolic value in each. Again Browning's symbolism is most complex. The stone monuments in their relationship to the architecture of the dream-vision figure forth an intellectual statement, while as stone monuments in their relationship to each other and in their particularity, they are symbols associated with an experience of frustration. The peasant lad describes the second stone shape as follows:

> "Well, you must know, there lies
> Something, the Curé says, that points to mysteries
> Above our grasp: a huge stone pillar, once upright,
> Now laid at length, half-lost—discreetly shunning sight
> I' the bush and brier, because of stories in the air—
> Hints what it signified, and why was stationed there,
> Once on a time." (2102-8)

The precise definition of the major symbol here, especially when considered in its differentiation from and relation to the caverned passage symbolism, is conscious and deliberate. Evidence accumulates as the passage progresses that the "huge stone pillar" is conceived as a phallic symbol and a deliberate complement of the female symbolism associated with the earlier stone structure. There is no doubt about Browning's understanding of the symbol. Writing in a stance of sophistication touched by conventional propriety to Baron Seymour Kirkup, in 1867, Browning described a trip to the French coast:

I returned to London—we then went to France for the autumn,—not to Pornic, as before, but to a delicious place in Brittany, Le Croisic—glorified to me long ago by the Beatrix of Balzac, which I used to devour as it came out in feuilletons in the "Siècle" of those days. Croisic is the old head-seat of

Druidism in France, probably mentioned by Strabo: the people were still Pagan a couple of hundred years ago, despite the
priest's teaching and preaching, and the women used to dance.
round the phallic stone still upright there with obscene circumstances enough,—till the general civilization got too
strong for this.[9]

And surely in the symbolistic power of Browning's imagination
he understood that in early religions, as Mircea Eliade says, "if the
galleries of mines and the mouths of rivers were likened to the
vagina of the Earth-Mother, the same symbolism applied *a fortiori*
to grottoes and caverns."[10] The condition of the pillar "now laid at
length, half lost" represents the psychological corollary of the prohibition associated with the female symbol. These configurations,
each independently, and the two in conjunction, give symbolic expression to the inhibition that has been posited as essential to the
poem. The tension between inhibition and impulse to freedom is
the unifying element of the poem, controlling in every crucial instance. Momentarily now energy and joy will flourish again, the
imagination celebrating freedom, health, and vigor to issue in fundamental knowledge before coming to final and decisive frustration, but in the immediate sequel to the passage last quoted the
poem deals with the cultural component of the inhibition. That
component as in the female imagery is Christianity, personified
here in the parish priest:

> "In vain the Curé tasked his lungs—
> Showed, in a preachment, how, at bottom of the rungs
> O' the ladder, Jacob saw, where heavenly angels stept
> Up and down, lay a stone which served him, while he slept,
> For pillow; when he woke, he set the same upright
> As pillar, and a-top poured oil: things requisite
> To instruct posterity, there mounts from floor to roof,
> A staircase, earth to heaven." (2108-15)

Thus the curé remythologized and sublimated the "huge stone
pillar," but he spoke "in vain," and, as will be seen, the peasant lad

speaks for those who are unpersuaded. The curé's doctrine would transform the stone and also turn consciousness away from it altogether. He preached that the stone pillar, become Jacob's ladder,

> *"also put in proof,*
> *When we have scaled the sky, we well may let alone*
> *What raised us from the ground, and,—paying to the stone*
> *Proper respect, of course,—take staff and go our way,*
> *Leaving the Pagan night for Christian break of day."* (2115-19)

Then the peasant lad quotes the curé directly, making especially specific an essential point of doctrine that, as he indicates later, is unconvincing:

> " 'For,' *preached he, 'what they dreamed, these Pagans, wide*
>   *awake*
> *We Christians may behold. How strange, then, were mistake*
> *Did anybody style the stone,—because of drop*
> *Remaining there from oil which Jacob poured a-top,—*
> *Itself the Gate of Heaven, itself the end, and not*
> *The means thereto!* ' " (2120-25)

For the people and for the peasant lad who speaks for them, there is no mistake and the stone pillar, with its drop of spiritual oil a-top, is indeed an end and not a means:[11]

> *"Thus preached the Curé, and no jot*
> *The more persuaded people but that, what once a thing*
> *Meant and had right to mean, it still must mean."* (2125-27)

The loyalty of the people to the original meaning of the pillar arises from a vigorously instinctive knowledge and stubbornly resists the rarefication of reality by Christianity:

> *"So cling*
> *Folk somehow to the prime authoritative speech,*
> *And so distrust report, it seems as they could reach*
> *Far better the arch-word, whereon their fate depends,*

Through rude charactery, than all the grace it lends,
That lettering of your scribes! who flourish pen apace
And ornament the text, they say—we say, efface." (2127-33)

This passage will seem at first obscure, but it contains associations with preceding and succeeding passages which establish its meaning. Identification of their knowledge with "speech" and "word" is explained more fully within a few lines, suggesting here the sense of certainty which they experience and pointing a relationship with the word "truth" as it will be used in the next section (CXXIV). The word "prime," in "prime authoritative speech" provides an association with the intuitive awareness of the phrase "antenatal prime experience" (LXXXIX) and contrasts the strength of realization at this point in the poem with the subtle anticipation of the beginning of part 5. The characterization of "word" as "arch-word" and as an objective which the people can "reach" intimates the first stone structure with its "monstrous door of granite" and its "caverned passage." And though to make the point is to move from the collective to the personal, from the realm of fertility religion to the realm of concrete eroticism, and from a terminology of faith to a scatological vocabulary, the "arch-word" is consonant with that meaning of Fifine's "which comports / With no word spoken out in cottages or courts" (XXXII, 408-9).[12] Specific sexuality must be emphasized. To ignore the significance of the genital shapes would be to obscure a crucial aspect of the symbolism which has not yet been examined. But it is clear that Browning deeply intuited and gloried in something which enveloped and was larger than sexuality. Eliade explains it as follows in connection with a discussion of the Christianization of Europe: "On the other hand, the peasants, because of their own mode of existing in the Cosmos, were not attracted by a 'historical' and moral Christianity. The religious experience peculiar to the rural populations was nourished by what could be called a 'cosmic Christianity.' . . . Mystical empathy with the cosmic rhythms, which was violently attacked by the Old Testament prophets and barely tolerated by the Church, is central to the religions of rural populations, especially in Southeastern Europe."[13]

The poem reaches now its culmination bringing into convergence its major symbols and liberating, as it were, its essential value of joy in sexuality and fertility:

"Hence, when the earth began its life afresh in May,
And fruit-trees bloomed, and waves would wanton, and the bay
Ruffle its wealth of weed, and stranger-birds arrive,
And beasts take each a mate,—folk, too, found sensitive,
Surmised the old gray stone upright there, through such tracts
Of solitariness and silence, kept the facts
Entrusted it, could deal out doctrine, did it please:
No fresh and frothy draught, but liquor on the lees,
Strong, savage and sincere: first bleedings from a vine
Whereof the product now do Curés so refine
To insipidity, that, when heart sinks, we strive
And strike from the old stone the old restorative." (2134-45)

Fleetingly, long before, in *Paracelsus*, Browning had a glimpse of this: "savage creatures seek / Their loves in wood and plain— and God renews / His ancient rapture" (V, 679-81).

Within the vision of spring and its stirring of vitality with the mating of beasts and "folk, too, found sensitive," there converge the poem's major symbols of sensual reality—water, sea, and stone. In close relation to the water imagery (the waves that "wanton"), the "stranger-birds arrive" recalling the bird imagery characterizing Fifine in the early sections of the poem.

The idea that "the old gray stone upright there" could "deal out doctrine, did it please," sustains directly the conjunction of sexuality and a primitive mode of religion. In addition, doctrine in its identity with liquor "strong, savage and sincere: first bleedings from a vine" recalls the words "indignant wine, / Wrath of the red press" which, in section LXXIX, symbolize virility under pressure of defiance and anger, and something of this anger is alive in "we strive and strike." There is an echo also of Cleopatra's "wine-press" and "such vintage as I brew" (XXXII, 438, 441). The basic tensions of the poem are epitomized when after the sinking of the heart under

Christian repression the people "strive and strike from the old stone the old restorative." And surely "the old restorative" is that longed for when the speaker imagined curved

> *Like Spring-month's russet moon, some girl by fate reserved*
> *To give me once again the electric snap and spark*
> *Which prove, when finger finds out finger in the dark*
> *O' the world, there's fire and life and truth there, link but hands*
> *And pass the secret on. Lo, link by link, expands*
> *The circle, lengthens out the chain, till one embrace*
> *Of high with low is found uniting the whole race.* (XCI, 1602-8)

In the dream of spring the poem achieves for the second and last time a moment of fulfillment, of freedom and gratification. The first such moment is the Arion epiphany in part 3. There the sexual impulse is associated with poetry; in the dream of spring it is associated with religion. In the first instance the sexual impulse is associated with the poetic act; sexual and poetic power are symbolically identical, and in the dramatization of a symbolically unified act the poetic voice is imagined as actor, immediately involved. In the second instance the sexual impulse, now associated with religion, has become the subject of poetry. It has, furthermore, been exhaustively objectified in symbols; neither the speaker of the dramatic monologue nor a poet whom he imagines, such as Arion, is involved. The peasant lad as speaker, in a second remove from the poet Browning, is himself a symbol, a representative of a community— "*we* strive and strike"—and ultimately, as will be seen, of man.

In the progression from part 3 to part 5 individual experience is diffused in collective and cultural experience and in symbolic objectification. The original impulse is ultimately obscured in, and therefore partially frustrated by, an intellectual achievement. To this point what the poem does is what it says, or will momentarily say. Following part 5 the poem will do and say something different. What follows now is fundamental to the intellectual realization of the poem. The passage begins with a rhetorical question as to the meaning of "the old stone" and "the old restorative":

" 'Which is?'—why, go and ask our grandames how they used
To dance around it, till the Curé disabused
Their ignorance, and bade the parish in a band
Lay flat the obtrusive thing that cumbered so the land!"
(CXXIII, 2146-49)

The significance of the pillar is emphasized by the fact that it is unquestionably a symbol for the curé and the people. Its meaning is that communicated by its physical characteristics and its varying condition under the influence of the clergy. The sexual meaning is clear to all, and Christianity is seen as a force suppressive of instinctual vitality for the entire collectivity, a universal cultural debilitation. However, Browning's realization is not yet complete. The peasant lad says of the stone pillar:

"And there, accordingly, in bush and brier it—'bides
Its time to rise again!' (so somebody derides,
That's pert from Paris)." (2150-52)

The conception of instinctual vitality as perennial and its resurgence as inevitable is essential to this movement of the poem. The "somebody" from Paris is derisive and "pert" from the perspective of the rural community, but the peasant lad does not by such terms reject the urban opinion, which is rigorously coherent with the context. The somebody "pert from Paris" continues:

" 'since, yon spire, you keep erect
Yonder, and pray beneath, is nothing, I suspect,
But just the symbol's self, expressed in slate for rock,
Art's smooth for Nature's rough, new chip from the old block!' "
(2152-55)

After a century we may now read Browning's *Fifine* clearly, but because of the course of intellectual history since Browning's time, we read with surprise and recognition his contemporaries could not have known, however shocked they might have been if they had understood the poem.

While Browning's celebration of sexual freedom and of a vitality embodied in primitive, cosmic religion is quite clear, we have yet to examine closely the larger terms of the culminating symbolic statement. That complex symbolic statement begins in an architectural image the forms of which deliquesce and disappear as the result of "liquid change through artery and vein / O' the very marble" (CX, 1892-93). Then "because of something new / Inside, that pushed to gain an outlet" (1900-1901) new forms arise to replace the old. Then varied buildings of the square are seen as representing human institutions which constitute symbolically the totality of human culture. These buildings also change and subside into new forms. There follows the question: "What common shape was that wherein they mutely merged / Likes and dislikes of form so plain before?" (CXX, 2040-41). The point of crucial importance for the interpretation of part 5 is that the question concerns *shape*, external configuration. The rest of the symbolic statement is elaborated in answer to this question.[14] The next image is that of a Druid monument, whose "caverned passage" is its most conspicuous aspect within the poem. After the mushroom passage that follows (the mushroom being also a sexual symbol) the phallic symbol of the huge stone pillar is introduced. The vaginal symbol and the phallic symbol will be treated as one by a verbal reference which does not distinguish them—"this same primeval monument" (CXXIV, 2160). The two images represent human sexuality and constitute the form into which the buildings collapse and from which then achieve new forms. The implication is of such magnitude as to offend credulity and yet it is unmistakable: sexuality underlies all human culture and is the force from which its varied and successive forms are elaborated. It is thus that Browning can "explain the glories by the shames / Mixed up in man, one stuff miscalled by different names."

The general shapes of the "caverned passage" and "the huge stone pillar" may conveniently be referred to as the outer symbolism. The symbolism developed in connection with each of these images separately may be referred to as the inner symbolism. The ominous and prohibitive cross within the caverned passage identifies Christianity as a force repressive of sexuality. The sinister atmosphere and the "fancies" filling the passage "to the brim" symbolize the psychological components of repression and should make it clear that the repressive role of Christianity represented in the inner symbolism of the huge stone pillar is not only a matter of historical policy. The prone condition in which we first see the huge stone pillar represents a sexual debilitation existing in the present as the effect of the repressive effort of Christianity "to lay flat the obtrusive thing." The images of spring and of joyous mating in man and beast associated with the pillar erect reinforce the sexual symbolism of the pillar. The conception of the pillar as "the old restorative" affirms the importance of sexual vitality to human welfare, a conception which cannot really be separated from the pan-sexual cultural reduction. The religious associations with the pillar erect envision a condition of pagan religion sustaining human vitality as Christianity represses it. The idea that the pillar "bides its time to rise again" implies both expectation of cultural renewal and a cyclical conception of history. In the identification of the pillar with the church spire, the inner symbolism reiterates the outer symbolism. The symbolic statement as a whole implies both a diagnosis and an elaborate theory of culture awesome in its anticipation of the twentieth century.

The closing lines of the episode with the peasant lad demonstrate Browning's awareness of the way successive forms of religion—different and even essentially incompatible forms of religion—are historically interfused, as the peasant lad, historian and partisan of the ancient sexual faith, blesses the speaker in the name of a Christian saint:

> *"There, sir, my say is said! Thanks, and Saint Gille increase*
> *The wealth bestowed so well!"—wherewith he pockets piece,*
> *Doffs cap, and takes the road. I leave in Learning's clutch*
> *More money for his book, but scarcely gain as much.*
> (CXXIII, 2156-59)

The poet's recognition of the intellectual achievement of part 5 is expressed in a long passage containing the best-known lines of *Fifine*—those on "the happy moment" of truth. The passage rises to a paean of discovery and a celebration of intellectual fulfillment.

The opening lines restate in another dimension the relationship enunciated by the somebody "pert from Paris," and, as has been mentioned, they treat the "great stone pillar" and the dolmen with its "caverned passage" as one, the pronoun of the first line referring to the stone pillar, while the description that follows is of the dolmen:

> *To this it was, this same primaeval monument,*
> *That, in my dream, I saw building with building blent*
> *Fall: each on each they fast and founderingly went*
> *Confusion-ward; but thence again subsided fast,*
> *Became the mound you see. Magnificently massed*
> *Indeed, those mammoth-stones, piled by the Protoplast*
> *Temple-wise in my dream! beyond compare with fanes*
> *Which, solid-looking late, had left no least remains*
> *I' the bald and blank, now sole usurper of the plains*
> *Of heaven, diversified and beautiful before.* (CXXIV, 2160-69)

In the words "those mammoth-stones, piled by the Protoplast / Temple-wise in my dream" one may observe, perhaps, the suggestion of a collective memory.[15] Whatever is to be said of this suggestion, the intent of the words is to characterize the realization that has been symbolically articulated. The effect is to portray a subjective experience of extreme subtlety. The nature of the realization was prefigured in that basic expression at the beginning of part 5: "The ante-natal prime experience—what know I?— / The initiatory love preparing us to die" (LXXXIX, 1561-62). Sexual realization transforms religious awareness, but in the final effect the two are not distinguished. Sex is not conceived as a Freudian cause which negates the authenticity of its religious effect. The next lines in fact stress the identity of sexual and religious realization. In these lines the word "simplicity" stands for the stone monuments and "compound" for the "fanes" that were "solid-looking late." The word "core" is associated with the stone monuments and the word "crust" with the "fanes," and "word" echoes "the arch-word" of the stone-pillar passage and represents the meaning which has been symbolically realized, its content of religious feeling intimated by a suggestion of the Hebraic translation of the sacred word that is not uttered:

> *And yet simplicity appeared to speak no more*
> *Nor less to me than spoke the compound. At the core,*
> *One and no other word, as in the crust of late,*
> *Whispered, which, audible through the transition-state,*
> *Was no loud utterance in even the ultimate*
> *Disposure.* (CXXIV, 2170-75)

The content of the "no loud utterance" is "the certitude I yet may hardly keep" (XC, 1581), these words having announced quietly at the beginning of part 5 the subtle, indeed, the secet knowledge to be symbolically elaborated. And in the cryptic passage just cited, the knowledge of the peasant lad and the somebody "pert from Paris" is affirmed as the knowledge of the speaker. Now the knowledge symbolically achieved will be compared to music, and, in order to clarify a word—"commonplace"—it is necessary to return briefly to the treatment of music with which part 5 began.

The characteristics of Schumann's music are referred to as "Schumann's victories over the commonplace" (XCII, 652-53). His victory over the commonplace, the effacing of the old, does not occur

> *without a struggle, a pang. The commonplace*
> *Still clung about his heart, long after all the rest*
> *O' the natural man, at eye and ear, was caught, confessed*
> *The charm of change.* (1638-41)

In such passages "commonplace" refers to both inner, unchanging substance and to older forms with which this substance has been identified. The commonplace, we must assume, is valued because it is the substance of the "food o' the soul" and as such it must be associated with the "fire and life and truth" of the world, for which Fifine's sexual vitality is the symbol. Within a few lines beyond those thus far examined in part 5 the stone monuments will be identified with the commonplace, and Fifine and the stone monuments are the poem's symbols for sexuality.

The knowledge symbolized in the stone monuments is next characterized as having the quality of music. The passage of twenty-eight lines which then follows is laden with possibilities for crucial misunderstanding which the poet may have intended. All of the passage except the first line is within quotation marks. The words represent the voice of music which the speaker seems now to hear, and the meaning is that of the symbolism of the stone monuments which has just been identified with music. The passage imitates music as in chromatic movement thought flows into thought, one sentence running for sixteen lines. Vocabulary and allusion are complex. The elation at the momentous intellectual discovery that has been symbolically formulated continues. However, the imaginative power underlying the discovery is betrayed by public timidity and perhaps by an inability to achieve the fundamental change in affective orientation which the discovery implies. So the discovery must be both affirmed and denied. To this end recourse is taken to philosophical relativism based on an evolutionary conception of thought. In *Fifine*, as in *Sordello*, one becomes especially aware that relativism in Browning is not so much a matter of intellectual reservation as a means of accommodating a lust for incompatible absolutes. In other words, it serves psychological needs. Here relativism is expressed in a vocabulary subversive of meaning. As a further complexity, the passage must be described as a kind of paean to truth, a celebration of discovery. The words are those of music personified, the poetry filled with lyric surge; and relative truth is antithetical to lyricism. The lyricism is the voice of an affirming mode of temperament, and relativism is the voice of fear. That the discovery of part 5 does have decisive issue intellectually is acknowledged in the opening lines of the passage imagined as the voice of music:

—*Grave note whence—list aloft!—harmonics sound, that mean:*
"*Truth inside, and outside, truth also; and between*
Each, falsehood that is change, as truth is permanence."

                                        (CXXIV, 2181-83)

Thus the monistic implications of the stone-monument symbolism are affirmed as the terms of the dualism of parts 2 and 3 are negated. Yet the repetition of earlier lines, which follows, might lead one to believe that the position now achieved is no different from that of part 2. The pivotal motto "God, man or both together mixed" (2188) occurs again as part of seven lines (2184-90) repeating almost verbatim lines related to the vision of heaven (LIX, 900-909). The special point to note, however, is that these lines in their first occurrence are related to the emergence of Glumdalclich, who was a fleshly darkening of the light-filled vision and a prefiguration of the sexual symbolism of the "mammoth stones." Accordingly there follows a celebration of "truth" in the "happy moment" passage (CXXIV, 2193-200), which ends with the line "Then do we understand the value of a lie."

Both "truth" and "lie" refer unquestionably to the implications of the symbolic realization of part 5, for now in rapid succession Browning executes three distinct strategies for affirming this realization while exempting the discoverer of it from full commitment to it.

First, the truth of part 5, though a lie, is the basis for poetic truth, for the poetry of experience:

> *"Its purpose served, its truth once safe deposited,*
> *Each lie, superfluous now, leaves, in the singer's stead,*
> *The indubitable song." (2201-3)*

Second, the truth though somehow separated from the person who has formulated it, is representative of the time in which he lives:

> *"the historic personage*
> *Put by, leaves prominent the impulse of his age," (2203-4)*

But third, with the separation of the singer and the song in the first step of a remarkable defection of temperament from intellect which will soon develop, the validity of the intellectual development of the poem in part 5 must be asserted and its elemental simplicity affirmed:

> *"Truth sets aside speech, act, time, place, indeed, but brings*
> *Nakedly forward now the principle of things*
> *Highest and least."* (2205-7)

So ends the voice of music, music being the medium of truth. The words that follow are "Wherewith change ends" (CXXV, 2207). These words mark a momentous turning in the development of the poem. The "change" that ends here is the movement of the psychic quest that has compelled symbolic exploration and exulted in its fruition before faltering at its implications. Though the impulse to joy will recur fitfully before the poem ends, the quest has been abandoned. What follows is not intelligible except by awareness of the poet who is personally involved in the poem. The passage proposes that the source of "comfort" which has been the pursuit of the entire poem is a "nymph." In context the meaning of "nymph" is precisely the meaning of Fifine. Heretofore, however, the dramatic situation has usually represented a polarity with the emotional tendencies associated with the loss of Elizabeth and the quest for freedom. Now the element of the dramatic situation which emerges is the isolated image of Fifine, and she is introduced with the poem's most extended allusion to *Prometheus Bound*, which is intimately associated with Elizabeth. In this passage, the phrases in quotation marks which follow the repeated Promethean motto are translations of phrases from the speech of the sea nymphs to Prometheus, and the phrases in parentheses, except the last, draw a parallel with Fifine and the company of carnival performers. The final phrase in quotation marks is drawn from a later passage in *Prometheus Bound*:

> *As I mean, did he mean,*
> *The poet whose bird-phrase sits, singing in my ear*
> *A mystery not unlike? What through the dark and drear*
> *Brought comfort to the Titan? Emerging from the lymph,*
> *"God, man, or mixture" proved only to be a nymph:*
> *"From whom the clink on clink of metal" (money, judged*
> *Abundant in my purse) "struck" (bumped at, till it budged)*
> *"The modesty, her soul's habitual resident"*

(Where late the sisterhood were lively in their tent)
"As out of wingèd car" (that caravan on wheels)
"Impulsively she rushed, no slippers to her heels,"
And "Fear not, friends we flock!" soft smiled the sea-Fifine—
Primitive of the veils (if he meant what I mean)
The poet's Titan learned to lift, ere "Three-formed Fate,
Moirai Trimorphoi" stood unmasked the Ultimate. (2212-26)

A veil has been lifted and truth revealed but it is not enough.
The failure, which will be later rationalized again, is attributed to
fate. The immediate sequel marks with finality the end of the
dream-vision. It employs the words "poetry" and "prose," the
meaning of which was established at the end of part 4: poetry is art;
prose is life continuous with reality external to the poem. In the
dull light of day the "commonplace," once the substance of music
and symbolically parallel with Fifine and the mammoth stones, has
declined to prose, has taken on the generally evadable tawdriness
of the brute fact of sex as acknowledged in the perspective of com-
fortable propriety:

Enough o' the dream! You see how poetry turns prose.
Announcing wonder-work, I dwindle at the close
Down to mere commonplace old facts which everybody knows.
So dreaming disappoints! (CXXVI, 2227-30)

With renunciation the dream is dissipated in the light of Victorian common sense. In effect now one is aware that the primeval
monument, "sole usurper / Of the plains of heaven," is attended
with "obscene circumstances enough." But lest there be any confusion about the meaning of the dream, the succeeding lines make
clear that it was an exciting hope of freedom and life and that the
symbolism of the primeval monument was at its center:

The fresh and strange at first,
Soon wears to trite and tame, nor warrants the outburst
Of heart with which we hail those heights, at very brink
Of heaven, whereto one least of lifts would lead, we think,

But wherefrom quick decline conducts our step, we find,
To homely earth, old facts familiar left behind.
Did not this monument, for instance, long ago
Say all it had to say, show all it had to show,
Nor promise to do duty more in dream? (2230-38)

The remainder of the poem, the 116 lines of part 6 and the epilogue, embodies the process of resignation, which in turn, however, also fails, the impulse to joy awakening repeatedly, in regret, in anguished plea, then turning back upon itself in savage anger. The end will be despair.

9

Abandonment of the Quest

In part 6 and the epilogue the quest is abandoned, not in a denial of
the validity of the cultural vision of part 5, but in a tortured and
unstable turning away from its implications. It was this vision that
Browning had in mind when he recorded the Greek quotations on
the manuscript (see above, p. 2). It was the "new words," yet "this
doubtful word." The abandonment of the quest registers in the
poem Browning's personal response to the light that brought "dark
night before his eyes." Psychologically it is a corollary of that
strange defaulting in Browning's proposals to Elizabeth and Lady
Ashburton—his being "no more than one of your brothers—'no
more,' " and his explanation that his heart was buried in Florence.
In another perspective the abandonment of the quest dramatizes
the fact that Browning's intellect had illuminated a realm which his
temperament would not permit him to deny but which it could not
assimilate.

Perhaps the most important fact for the interpretation of part 6
is that this final movement of the poem is erratic and becomes increasingly so, as may be seen in a summary. After making it clear
at the beginning that the quest has been abandoned (CXXVII), the
speaker attempts to extract from this fact a general principle to justify it (CXXVIII, 2245-61). The argument, uncertainly developed, is
that the default, although a renunciation, is also a part of "Truth."
The implication is that whatever has happened is "Truth." The
reasoning here is tortuous and the attention given to a contrary
evolutionary argument supporting the quest tends to make that argument dominant (2261-73). The evolutionary argument is inter-

rupted by an explanation of the quest's abandonment—old age and the approach of death—which has nothing to do with general principle and leaves unquestioned the validity of the quest (2273-76). The general thesis is resumed and there follows an affirmation of the speaker's constancy to Elvire (CXXIX, 2282-86). Again an effort is made to derive a general principle from the fact (2287-99). Then the speaker expresses wonder at his having been unfaithful to Elvire (2299-305).Blame is attributed to the person who provoked the quest, presumably Fifine at the dramatic level, though she is not present, and the idea emerges that the guilty person has deliberately been a cause of pain. There is no dramatic justification for this and the reference at the personal level would seem clearly to be to Lady Ashburton. As speaker and wife arrive at their door, the wife takes on ghostly lineaments in which are merged the conceptions of the phantom and dramatic wives (CXXX, 2306-12). The wife is conceived as belonging to the past while needed in the present, over which she exerts influence. The speaker then expresses satisfaction in reconciliation with the wife (CXXXI, 2312-21), but no sooner has he done so than he abandons discursive argument for the first time in part 6. Returning to the level of symbolic statement in which the quest has moved throughout the poem, he gives expression in the imagery of a tower and the sea, to plangent regret of a loss in abandonment of the quest, which retains its power to attract him (2321-5). This is followed by a tender expression of resignation in love for the wife (2326-38), which turns abruptly into harsh demand (2338-40). Suddenly the speaker reveals a pretext for returning to the fair to seek out Fifine again, and his manner of addressing the wife as he departs is obscene in its harshness (CXXXII). Thus the poem ends. The note of anger recurrent in the quest is the note in which the renunciation ends. Anger is sustained in the epilogue, which gives expression successively to love, a wish that the impulse of the quest may last the speaker's life, followed by frustration, impatience with life itself, and final, reluctant resignation. The erratic movement of the last part of the poem implies instability and a tension which is never entirely resolved. The renunciation is both necessary and impossible. This will become clearer as the text is examined in more detail.

At the beginning of part 6 speaker and wife "awaking so" from the dream are "homeward-bound" (CXXVII, 2238-39). The speaker, in something of the weariness that has occurred before, affirms the finality with which he has renounced the dream:

> *We end where we began: that consequence is clear.*
> *All peace and some fatigue, wherever we were nursed*
> *To life, we bosom us on death, find last is first*
> *And thenceforth final too.* (CXXVII, 2242-45)

We may understand that the impossibility of this renunciation resides in its life-quenching depth: "We bosom us on death." The renunciation is insistently associated with death: "We live and die henceforth" (CXXIX, 2305), says the speaker, and increasingly the wife is identified as a ghostly and not a living woman.

The wife is clearly the dramatic, presumably living wife, only at the beginning and at the end of part 6. At the beginning we hear her voice challenging the speaker's credibility:

> *"Why final? Why the more*
> *Worth credence now than when such truth proved false before?"*
> (CXXVIII, 2245-46)

The speaker's reply is of crucial importance:

> *Because a novel point impresses now: each lie*
> *Redounded to the praise of man, was victory*
> *Man's nature had both right to get, and might to gain,*
> *And by no means implied submission to the reign*
> *Of other quite as real a nature, that saw fit*
> *To have its way with man, not man his way with it.*
> *This time, acknowledgment and acquiescence quell*
> *Their contrary in man; promotion proves as well*
> *Defeat.* (2247-55)

The duplicity of part of the vocabulary here has been established. The "lie" which is a "victory" is the intellectual realization of part 5. Man's nature has "the right to get" it and the "might to gain" it. The wording echoes the description of the stone pillar to the effect that "what once a thing / Meant and had right to mean, it still must mean" (CXXIII, 2126-27). What man had right to get "redounded to the praise of man." The renunciation is not a rejection of the knowledge gained in the quest. This is the crucial point. Renunciation has simply occurred in spite of that knowledge.

To deal with the remainder of the passage is to understand what Morse Peckham means when he says, "Reading the mature and more demanding Browning is like having one's brain squeezed by a gigantic hand. . . . Browning is truly one of the toughest of poets."[1] It is probable that no single reading of lines 2250-55 can be completely satisfactory. By considering two quite different readings we may come to understand the nature of the complexity here and identify some of its components. I would like to consider first what might seem a more or less obvious interpretation, exploring some of the difficulties it confronts.

Let us take "other quite as real a nature" to mean man's sexual nature. So sex "saw fit / To have its way with man." And the "victory" (2249) did not imply "submission to the reign" of sex, and by implication, man has had "his way with it," an act of self-control, of mastery and will. But in the next line we find "acknowledgment and acquiescence." Acknowledgment of what? That it is wrong for sex to "have its way with man"? Of course, but the poem does not explicitly say so. And that other nature is not here a violent, unruly force; rather, it simply "saw fit." Let us assume for the moment that we are not sure what is being acknowledged. In any event "acknowledgment" is linked with "acquiescence" in an effect of passivity. Yet we must imagine that they "quell" something. An overpowering is accomplished by passivity. A quelling occurs, but we may hardly think of it as a moral act or as a positive act of any kind. The *OED* definition of acquiesce is "to agree tacitly to, to concur in; to accept (the conclusions or arrangements of others)." The definition suggests that we should ask, Which others? But before trying to answer that, we must look at other difficulties.

It is quite clear that "Man's nature" is in tension with, somehow in opposition to, the "other quite as real a nature." So man's nature

opposes his sexual nature? Well, at least an aspect of his nature—
his moral nature—opposes his sexual nature. The poem does not
say that, just "Man's nature," and if this means morality, it must
mean a morality inherent in man's nature. That idea is not expressed anywhere else in Browning; rather, morality is everywhere
relative. And opposition between "Man's nature" and his sexual nature is extremely difficult to reconcile with the thoroughgoing monism of conceptions appearing elsewhere in the poem as well as in
the part we are now discussing. Within a few lines "nature" will be
closely identified, not only with "Sense," but also with "ourself"—
"nature, that's ourself" (2264-73). Browning will shortly offer yet
another explanation of the renunciation with which all of part 6 is
concerned, an explanation which has nothing to do with morality
(2264-77). This passage makes it clear, for one thing, that if "Man's
nature" is moral and opposed to man's sexual nature in a way that
leads to acquiescence, then it cannot have anything to do with
"Soul," a principle which aspires to mastery. The passage will also
throw light on the "other quite as real a nature." It begins by imagining a Lamarckian evolution of the senses (2264-69) which are
eventually implicated in "Soul." The principle of aspiration bringing about physical evolution is communicated to "Soul"—"would
stimulate Soul sweetly, I suppose" (2270)—and prompts "to recognize soul's self Soul's only master here" (2272). Elsewhere, however,
we are told that "Soul finds no triumph, here" (2259). So we might
imagine that "Man's nature," interpreted as moral, defeats "Soul,"
and we might be inclined to rest with another rather awkward Victorian compromise. But now we are given a very different reason
for the renunciation, for the speaker's failure "to recognize soul's
self Soul's only master here"; this reason is personal; it has nothing
to do with either metaphysics or morality and in no way affects the
conceptions developed in part 5. It is quite simply old age:

> But, if time's pressure, light's
> Or rather, dark's approach, wrest thoroughly the rights
> Of rule away, and bid the soul submissive bear
> Another soul than it play master everywhere
> In great and small . . . (2273-77)

Inescapably, the power represented in "another soul" is the power of the memory of the phantom wife, of Elizabeth in memory and imagination. It is this power to which the speaker has submitted, this control in which he has acquiesced. Old age is, indeed, a rationalization, but it is clear and not incredible. Furthermore, in this explanation of the renunciation there are no conceptions inconsistent with Browning's work in general. Let us return to lines 2247-55. It would seem probable that here Browning was attempting to make rational, both for himself and for his readers, a failure which he did not fully understand and did not wish to accept. He did not hesitate to look to a moral explanation. He was pleased enough if this explanation placated his reading public and concealed aspects of his true experience, and yet he could not adopt such an explanation if it falsified fundamentally his feeling about an experience he was passionately concerned to realize. Surely we must look for such a conflict of motives to explain the opacity of these lines.

I wish now to propose a reading of these lines which is radical, but not more so than the transformation by which a "victory" becomes a "lie" that "redounds to the praise of man." It is not in conflict with fundamental conceptions of the poem and meets no more resistance from the immediate text than does the moralistic interpretation. This second reading is the more fundamental of the two. The key is the "other quite as real a nature." It is not sex. It is not God and has nothing to do with religion except insofar as the renunciatory element in Browning's feeling for the memory of Elizabeth is harmonious with the renunciatory element in religious feeling. It is the imperative and inexplicable power in "man's nature" which will not grant freedom from the phantom wife and Elizabeth. In the old age passage, it is that power which "bids the soul submissive bear / Another soul than it play master everywhere / In great and small." Here it "saw fit / To have its way with man, not man his way with it." The "victory / Man's nature had both right to get, and might to gain," the knowledge achieved in part 5, "by no means implied submission to" the inexplicable control. A failure has simply occurred in spite of the knowledge and the victory. It happened for no reason, just "this time." "Acknowledgment and acquiescence quell" not sex, but "their contrary in man," or what has somehow been quelled is the poem's resistance to the dark power and a joyous exertion of the will. And "promotion," the victory and the liberation achieved in the realm of poetry, "proves as well defeat" when the new-won sense of freedom fades at the border of poetry.

Of course, if all this is to seem rational then the speaker's "I" must be generalized in "man." If the speaker may be seen as a casuist anywhere in the poem it is in this passage where Browning generalizes as the experience of "man" a purely contingent and personal experience, suggesting an interpretation of it which violates a conception of life elaborately developed through the entire course of the poem, an experience for which another rationalization will in its turn be renounced by the febrile vacillations in the remainder of the poem. The only possible excuse for this pretense is that it tends to disguise the intensely personal nature of the poet's experience. Duplicity will give way to diffidence as the argument proceeds and the wording of its conclusions becomes reserved and cautionary: "I fancy, there must lurk some cogency i' the claim" (2257); "I fancy none disputes / There's something in the fact" (2277-78).

After old age has been given as the cause of the defeat, there is little left for the metaphysical mill to grind, only "something in the fact." The speaker gives no further reason for the defeat, but reasons from the fact that it has happened:

> . . . *this time, I fancy, none disputes*
> *There's something in the fact that such conclusion suits*
> *Nowise the pride of man, nor yet chimes in with attributes*
> *Conspicuous in the lord of nature.* (2277-80)

Now the renunciation is described in terms that are ostensibly religious: "He receives / And not demands—not first likes faith and then believes" (2280-81). The context makes it clear that "faith" means constancy in relationship to the wife: "Inconstancy means raw; 't is faith alone means ripe" (CXXIX, 2283). Furthermore, the idea that "he receives / And not demands" and that "belief" precedes the need of it is entirely in accord with the element of compulsion which must be assumed to characterize the renunciation, while the idea is the reverse of the relationship between faith and the need of it which prevails throughout Browning's poetry.

The speaker acknowledges that the new direction of his imagination confronts an emptiness. Renunciation of the quest is not followed by an alternative reward, and the hope of such involves an impossibility—a memory and a longing:

> *The wanderer brings home no profit from his quest*
> *Beyond the sad surmise that keeping house were best*
> *Could life begin anew.* (2292-94)

On this note of sad reluctance the speaker turns to a formulation of past error and present understanding:

> *His problem posed aright*
> *Was—"From the given point evolve the infinite!"*
> *Not—"Spend thyself in space, endeavoring to joint*
> *Together, and so make infinite, point and point:*
> *Fix into one Elvire a Fair-ful of Fifines!"* (2294-98)

The abstractness of this would seem designed to give metaphysical status to the renunciation. The conception is a part of the romantic tradition, but in this poem it is a rationalization and an afterthought. It is enough for the moment, however, and here as throughout the poem, the speaker is capable of rapturous expression of love for the wife, usually when conceived as the phantom wife, as she will soon be here. The next passage contains two quite particular biographical references. In both there is a momentary departure from the symbolism sustained throughout the poem. Elvire has been consistently associated with land, as Fifine with sea. Now, probably in deference to an association with Elizabeth in the love letters, Elvire becomes the sea. It is perhaps also true that the infidelity followed by anger delineated here refers to Browning's relationship with Lady Ashburton:

> *Fifine, the foam-flake, she: Elvire, the sea's self, means*
> *Capacity at need to shower how many such!*

And yet we left her calm profundity, to clutch
Foam-flutter, bell on bell, that, bursting at a touch, ·
Blistered us for our pains. But wise, we want no more
O' the fickle element. Enough of foam and roar!
Land-locked, we live and die henceforth: for here's the villa door.
(2299-2305)

That such an attitude toward the Lady Ashburton affair can be expressed in the renunciatory movement of part 6 is by no means inconsistent with the interpretation here of all that has gone before, and it suggests that the quest might be considered an exploration of personal failure in that affair.

As speaker and wife reach the villa door in the dusk, a striking transformation takes place. The dramatic wife becomes the phantom wife, taking on that guise in which she served the elegiac theme of the poem:

How pallidly you pause o' the threshold! Hardly night,
Which drapes you, ought to make real flesh and blood so white!
Touch me, and so appear alive to all intents!
Will the saint vanish from the sinner that repents?
Suppose you are a ghost! A memory, a hope,
A fear, a conscience! Quick! Give back the hand I grope
I' the dusk for! (CXXX, 2306-12)

Here the phantom wife is saint, as in the elegiac passages, and also ghost as in the epilogue where she is identified with Elizabeth by critics most skeptical of a biographical reading of the rest of the poem. The pressure to symbolize Elizabeth here is conspicuous and obtrusive, for the dramatic wife may be neither ghost nor memory. The poem requires that Elizabeth be understood as "A memory, a hope, a fear, a conscience." And the words "Give back the hand I grope / I' the dusk for" express the anguished need, in renunciation of freedom, that she live again.

Before the poem continues Browning must correct the departure from basic symbolism which has just occurred: "Discard that simile / O' the fickle element! Elvire is land not sea— / The solid land, the safe" (CXXXI, 2313-15). Renunciation now is renunciation of the

sea: "The unlucky bath's to blame" (2316). In Pornic, says the
speaker, the mayor will catalogue him "duly domiciled" and "good-
companion of the guild / And mystery of marriage" (2319-21).[2] But
this is followed by poignant regret for the renunciation of the goal
of the long labor of the poem. The sea, it must be remembered, is
the symbol of sensual reality, of freedom and of life. It is suggested
that the couple should live within the city, somewhat inland. The
tower mentioned in the passage that follows is an image to which
there is no other reference in the poem except in part 1 where the
tent of the carnival performance is stretched beneath a tower. In the
tower image, as in that of the sea, there is thus an association with
Fifine. The speaker in his resolution for inland life and civic serenity speaks as follows:

> *I stickle for the town,*
> *And not this tower apart; because, though, halfway down,*
> *Its mullions wink o'erwebbed with bloomy greenness, yet*
> *Who mounts the staircase top may tempt the parapet,*
> *And sudden there's the sea!* (2321-25)

That plangent memory of the sea is consonant with the failure
of resignation, which will be more violently disturbed by the reas-
sertion of the experiential thrust as the poem draws to a close. The
final expression of resignation within the poem proper is as follows:

> *So shall the seasons fleet, while our two selves abide:*
> *E'en past astonishment how sunrise and springtide*
> *Could tempt one forth to swim; the more if time appoints*
> *That swimming grow a task for one's rheumatic joints.*
> *Such honest civic house, behold, I constitute*
> *Our villa.* (2333-38)

Into the serenity of this, after an observation on the limitations
posed by advancing age there is suddenly interjected a tone of demand and anger: "Be but flesh and blood, and smile to boot! / Enter for good and all!" (2338-39). This anger, a re-emergence of the
ambivalent pattern, dominates the remainder of the poem, in the

obscene cynicism of the speaker in his final lines and in the "savage" mood of the speaker in the epilogue.

In the final lines the failure of the poem to reach a final resolution, the failure of the quest for decision and wholeness, is represented in the ironic contrast of the speaker's harsh voice with the poetry of loving resignation that has gone before. Only here has the dramatic situation been fully restored, and it is the dramatic wife of flesh and blood whom the speaker addresses brutally at the end. In the speaker's harsh bluntness, narrative details are now revealed, or invented, which if presented earlier would have obstructed the symbolic movement of the real substance of the poem:

> *Only,—you do not use to apprehend attack!*
> *No doubt, the way I march, one idle arm, thrown slack*
> *Behind me, leaves the open hand defenceless at the back,*
> *Should an impertinent on tiptoe steal, and stuff*
> *—Whatever can it be? A letter sure enough,*
> *Pushed betwixt palm and glove! That largess of a franc?*
> *Perhaps inconsciously,—to better help the blank*
> *O' the nest, her tambourine, and, laying egg, persuade*
> *A family to follow, the nest-egg that I laid*
> *May have contained,—but just to foil suspicious folk,—*
> *Between two silver whites a yellow double yolk!*
> *Oh, threaten no farewell! five minutes shall suffice*
> *To clear the matter up. I go, and in a trice*
> *Return; five minutes past, expect me! If in vain—*
> *Why, slip from flesh and blood, and play the ghost again!*
> (CXXXII, 2341-55)

Because renunciation is both necessary and impossible, the quest must be both renewed and abandoned. Within the poem the speaker angrily reaffirms the quest. In the epilogue the poet in anger, despair, and final acquiescence, makes a separate peace.

In the epilogue, entitled "The Householder," the wife who comes knocking at the door has realized the speaker's final taunting suggestion that she "slip from flesh and blood, and play the ghost again." The phantom wife, fleeting and enthralling visitant in the

poem, is now at large. To those who are skeptical about the reading
of *Fifine* presented here, the things the poet and the ghostly wife say
to each other in the epilogue must seem improbable in the extreme.
The mood of the "Householder" is continuous with the frustration
expressed in the closing lines of the poem: "Savage I was sitting in
my house, late, lone." When the ghost knocks there is a moment of
unbelieving joy:

> *When, in a moment, just a knock, call, cry,*
> > *Half a pang and all a rapture, there again were we!—*
> *"What, and is it really you again?" quoth I:*
> *"I again, what else did you expect?" qouth She.*

To her question he refuses an answer. Though she was a burden, he in some sense loved her, and for a moment he is delighted.
But he was expecting someone else. There is guilt in this, and he
tries to hurry the pure and potentially accusing spirit away from
the house:

> *"Never mind, hie away from this old house—*
> > *Every crumbling brick embrowned with sin and shame!*
> *Quick, in its corners ere certain shapes arouse!"*

The speaker's next utterance is both defiance and a plea as he attempts to dismiss her again. The plea is not that the evil spirits of
the house depart, but that they continue to attend him. In the "rap-
ping" there is an echo of Elizabeth's interest in spiritualism and so
again as repeatedly in the poem there is a memory of the dead Elizabeth in the world which the speaker attempts to grapple to himself:

> *"Let them—every devil of the night—lay claim,*
> > *Make and mend, or rap and rend, for me! Good-bye!"*

The plea is repeated. This time God is invoked, at least rhetor-
ically, and the plea is now that the evil spirits may continue as long
as he lives:

> *"God be their guard from disturbance at their glee,*
> *Till, crash, comes down the carcass in a heap!"*

The plea is for the joy that has been the eventually frustrated goal of the poem. Joy has become "glee" as impulses to joy are translated into evil spirits in the face of the spiritual purity of the presence of Elizabeth. The plea of the epilogue is really the plea of the entire poem. The Elizabeth now present is that other soul to which the speaker has submitted to bear that "it play master everywhere / In great and small." Elizabeth's reply is a prohibition, the voice of morality and propriety: " 'Nay, but there's a decency required!' quoth She."

Thus the second stanza of the epilogue epitomizes the poem. The third stanza is an apology for it, with perhaps another reference to Lady Ashburton:

> *"Ah, but if you knew how time has dragged, days, nights!*
> *All the neighbor-talk with man and maid—such men!*
> *All the fuss and trouble of street-sounds, window-sights:*
> *All the worry of flapping door and echoing roof; and then,*
> *All the fancies . . . Who were they had leave, dared try*
> *Darker arts that almost struck despair in me?*
> *If you knew but how I dwelt down here!" quoth I:*
> *"And was I so better off up there?" quoth She.*

The final stanza of the epilogue has been misread and sentimentalized as representing joyous union with Elizabeth and affirming the power of spirituality over death.[3] It is rather a consummation of the resolve to "bosom us on death," and it is a reluctant, a painful, consummation. At the end the speaker is occupied chiefly with composing an obituary for himself, and the bosoming on death is depicted in a framework of social expectation, with convention varied, if hardly so, to note that the prospectively deceased suffered much. The last words of the speaker, distraught with preparation for death, are " 'Do end'! quoth I"—and then, finally—"quoth She." She has the last word, and to what she says, without commitment of belief and with weary diffidence, he submits. The renunciation of the final movement of the poem is confirmed:

"*Help and get it over!* Reunited to his wife
        (*How draw up the paper lets the parish-people know?*)
Lies M. or N., departed from this life,
        Day the this or that, month and year the so and so.
What i' the way of final flourish? Prose, verse? Try!
        Affliction sore long time he bore, *or, what is it to be?*
Till God did please to grant him ease. *Do end!" quoth I:*
        "I end with—Love is all, and Death is nought!" quoth She.

10

'Fifine' and Browning's Poetic Structure

A comparison of *Fifine at the Fair* with the body of Browning's work that came before it draws attention to and illuminates characteristics of the poetry which turn out to be fundamental. A number of patterns emerge which are so pervasive that they may be considered prototypal and which in their collective formulation go far toward describing the structure of Browning's poetry. I use the word structure to indicate a central dynamics and a set of configurations which would seem to comprise margins and defining limits of the poet's imagination. One of the advantages of describing such a structure will be to permit a clear identification of the crucial relationship of *Fifine* to the rest of Browning's work.

The structure I will describe might be further elaborated. For instance, one might examine systematically the countervailing imagery with which the structural patterns are often in tension. What I will describe, however, is the essential structure. It reveals a basic dimension of development in Browning's career and provides some understanding of the fact that when we read Browning we always seem to be aware of a drama going on beneath the surface of the poetry. The structure is most conspicuous and most solidly intact in the early work—poetry and plays—down to and including *Pippa Passes*. In *Pippa Passes* the structure is pervasive but it tends to be diffused and transformed and may be less easily recognized than in earlier work. Similar diffusions and transformations of the structure occur in most of the subsequent poetry. In *Men and Women* the structure tends at times to disappear and its manifestations to become vestigial, while in *The Ring and the Book* some of the patterns emerge with renewed clarity.

The central dynamics of Browning's poetry is the dialectic of a radical opposition: love of God and love of the world. Initially the opposition is not only radical but absolute.[1] The love of God is a love absolutely antithetical to love of the world. The world may be taken to include variously or all at once everything that religious asceticism disapproves or finds irrelevant. It includes joy, pleasure, love, the flesh, and affairs of the world. Eventually "the world" means all of the world and all its possibilities. The world always means the world and the flesh. At the center of the world is sexuality and a female image. A ravening appetite for the world confronts an imperious demand for a quality of spirituality the condition of which is innocence. All the controlling patterns of image and action derive from this opposition and vary with its dialectic movement. The eventual goal of the dialectic is a reconciliation which effects an intensification of the world and a diffusion of the character of the God which is the object of the love of God.

The prototypal patterns related to this dynamics are capable of controlling in various dimensions. They may constitute the substance of a brief poem or control the plot of a play or long poem. They may be reflected in sequences of images developed either briefly or extensively. When a pattern is "reflected" in a poem, the imagery in one way or another suggests the pattern and carries its value. The patterns are described below and given names for ease of reference. The lists of the poems in which they appear are by no means exhaustive.

PATTERNS OF COMPROMISE AND PASSIVITY

Five patterns of compromise and passivity develop as sequels to the imminence of love presented in a number of ways—for instance, simply in the appearance of an attractive female image or in a character declared to be the love object of the protagonist.

Objectification of the beloved. The beloved person is trans-

formed into a static entity, usually a corpse, a work of art, an idealization, or a conception of the beloved as having died and existing
now as an immortal soul in heaven. In the latter case both lovers
may have passed into immortality.

The pattern appears in "Porphyria's Lover," "My Last Duchess," "Christina," "Andrea del Sarto," "Evelyn Hope," "Misconcep-
tions," and "The Statue and the Bust." The pattern is present in the
Andromeda passage in *Pauline* and is reflected in the caryatids,
"the silent women," supporting Sordello's Font, and in the por-
phyry statuary in "A Forgiveness."

Flight to finality (the terminal perspective). There is a rapid progression in time arriving at old age, the end of life, or the hereafter,
and permitting the experience of love to be viewed as in the past. In
a later version of this pattern, it is not love but the imminence of
love which is viewed as existing in the past, and it is interpreted as
an opportunity irrevocably lost.

This pattern, in one form or another, is virtually constant in
poems dealing with love. It is effective in the following: *Pauline* (39-
43, 489-90, 617-19, 870-76), "Earth's Immortalities," "Christina," "In
a Gondola," "The Flight of the Duchess," "The Italian in England,"
"The Last Ride Together," "Confessions," "By the Fireside," *The
Ring and the Book*.

Religious transmutation. Erotic or romantic feeling is translated
into religious feeling.

It is important to distinguish this pattern, but it is usually an at-
tendant effect of the first and second patterns described above. It
occurs in "Two in the Campagna" and "The Last Ride Together"
and is especially conspicuous in *Pauline, The Return of the Druses*,
and *The Ring and the Book*.

Recourse to infancy. The protagonist conceives the female love
object as a motherly figure and beseeches her to adopt toward him
a superior or protective relationship. The effect of this pattern is to
be observed in any imagery in which the protagonist is protectively
enfolded—by wings, for instance, as of a bird or angel, or by vegetation.

This pattern occurs in *Pauline* (925-29, 947-49), in the later relationship with Palma in *Sordello*, in the sixth stanza of "Women and

Roses," and at the end of "Fra Lippo Lippi." The fullest expression
of the pattern is "The Guardian Angel," a poem which Betty Miller
considers basically expressive of Browning's personality, a valuably
provocative suggestion though erring in emphasis and not quite fair
to Browning, as will be indicated later.[2]

Abstract option. Love for an individual is translated into, or
supplanted by, love for an abstract or general object or activity.
This takes three forms:

In the *social option* love for an individual is translated into, or
supplanted by, love for society or a condition of social integration.
In the most common form of the pattern the protagonist relinquishes his love for a woman to take a position of leadership in society.

The pattern is dominant in Browning's early work. It occurs in
Pauline (604-8, 689-97) and is a controlling element in *Sordello* and
in all of Browning's plays except *A Blot o' the 'Scutcheon*. It occurs
in "Flight of the Duchess" and in the Luigi episode of *Pippa Passes*
and is reflected in "Prince Hohenstiel-Schwangau" and "In a Balcony." It emerges at the end of "The Englishman in Italy" and in a
combination with the flight to finality comprises the uniting structure of the companion poems "Meeting at Night" and "Parting at
Morning," originally published as one poem.

In the *intellectual option* love for an individual is translated into, or supplanted by, intellectual or scholarly activity.

This pattern, as distinguished from the artistic option (see below), is rare, but it controls one of Browning's most important early works: *Paracelsus*. It is reflected in *Pauline* (639-41) in "Sibrandus
Schafnaburgensis," "One Word More," and "A Grammarian's Funeral."

In the *artistic option* love for an individual is translated into, or
supplanted by, artistic activity, usually poetry. The pattern controls the first part of Sordello's career as the social option does the
second part. It appears in *Pauline* (922-24). It is conspicuous in the
Jules episode in *Pippa Passes* and at the symbolic level may be
taken to explain the denial of the world to Pippa, who represents
the poet in this poem. The pattern provides the theme of "One
Word More," and it is reflected in "Youth and Art," "Dîs Aliter

Visum," "Pictor Ignotus," "A Serenade at the Villa," "The Last Ride Together," "Cleon," "How It Strikes a Contemporary," "Time's Revenges," and "In a Balcony."

The abstract options, especially in the early poetry, are frequently conceived as being in themselves exclusive of, or prohibitive of, love.

The patterns of compromise have their essential function in common. They develop a condition in which love exists but is freed of the tensions inherent in the relationship between lovers, inherent if only because sexuality has always the modality of the future—both desire and fear being concerned with that which has not yet happened. The patterns of compromise achieve a condition of serene passivity by averting or circumventing a condition inherent in love. Yet they never imply a renunciation or total relinquishing of love. The abstract options are conceived in the early poetry as inimical to love, and all the patterns of compromise are conceived at one time or another as resulting in failure, and yet in the moment of choice, in the early poetry, they always sustain an anguished or calmly illusionary potentiality of service to love.

The patterns of compromise as a means of averting or circumventing the tensions of love have eventually the effect of a deprivation of the world. They restrain and limit action. Though they frequently emerge in the configuration of image and metaphor, their most important function is in the control of narrative action and circumstance. They control action and circumstance in most of Browning's poetry and constitute collectively its most conspicuous structural element.

PATTERNS OF ACTION

A number of recurrent patterns involve positive assertion or action and offer the potentiality of fulfillment.

The rescue. A female figure is held in an incarcerating or restraining condition inimical to love. Rescue is anticipated, or actually occurs, the rescuer usually being characterized by his youth or innocence. Frequently the person incarcerating or restraining the victim is older and more powerful than the rescuer, and in such instances the rescue becomes a version of the confrontation of the strong man (see below). A point of essential importance is that the victim of restraint or incarceration is always in some sense a victim of sexuality devoid of love and conceived as obscene. Because we never know anything of the future life of the rescuer and the rescued, the rescue tends to be a movement from a realm of sexuality to a realm of the spirit and thus to be continuous with the effect of the patterns of compromise. The center of interest is in love expressed in the act of rescue. Love so expressed is selfless, but it is also impersonal. It is essentially social, both an evasion and a sublimation of love.

DeVane, who does not observe the sexual implications of the rescue, has identified the pattern as the Perseus-Andromeda motif.[3] He finds that it occurs in *Pauline*, "The Flight of the Duchess," "The Glove," "Count Gismond," and *The Ring and the Book*. It also occurs in *The Return of the Druses* and in *Columbe's Birthday*. In *Pippa Passes* it occurs both in the Jules episode and in the narrative affecting Pippa.

The aerial journey and the mountainous ascent. In the aerial journey, the protagonist is raised high in the air and transported a great distance. This usually occurs through no effort or intent of the protagonist, and he is thus passive in the actual movement. However, the journey is associated, usually as a prelude, with an affirmation of religious faith. The implication of the aerial journey as a flight from the world and the flesh identifies it with the patterns of compromise. The term "mountainous ascent" refers to any imagery of movement up a mountain. The implications here would seem to be identical with those of the aerial journey except that the mountainous ascent involves exertion on the part of the protagonist.

The aerial journey occurs in *Pauline* (478-82), "The Last Ride Together," *Christmas-Eve and Easter-Day*, and *Red Cotton Night-Cap Country*. The mountainous ascent occurs in the final lines of *Sordello* and in "Englishman in Italy," "A Grammarian's Funeral," and *La Saisiaz*. It is reflected in the final lines of *The Return of the Druses* and in "Up at a Villa—Down in the City."

The quest. The quest motif, to be distinguished from the more generalized quest which makes up most of *Fifine*, is expressed as an entering among trees, proceeding inward, and coming upon water. The quest so depicted represents a struggle for freedom, for psychic fulfillment, for sexual realization. The quest is at first recognized for what it is because in one degree or another, in the early poetry, it always fails. The quest is not in itself a pattern of passivity or compromise, but when the trees are especially verdant and seem to enclose protectively there is an affinity between entering among trees and the recourse to infancy, and this suggests the germ of failure. The very pleasantness of the beginning is unpropitious for its ending. When the quest land is conceived as redolent of failure from the beginning, the land is characterized by its bigness and openness; trees becomes less conspicuous or disappear, while towers and mountains may become conspicuous in the landscape. The land becomes rocky and arid. The rugged and barren character of the terrain implies a greater energy in the quest, which paradoxically may be an omen of a measure of success. The quest motif is developed twice in *Pauline* (729-810, 947-71) and twice in *Sordello* (I, 389-415; II, 13-55). It appears in *Paracelsus*, in the Sebald and Ottima episode in *Pippa Passes*, in "The Flight of the Duchess," and in "By the Fire-side." "Childe Roland" must be considered an extraordinary demonic development of this motif.

Confrontation of the strong man. The strong man is to be identified by his relation of dominance to a younger man. The relationship always involves the initial superiority of the strong man, but the content of the relationship, the nature of the power of the strong man over the younger man, varies greatly. It may be physical, moral, or political, or it may consist of superior knowledge or skill; it is usually represented in superiority of rank or station. The strong man is often a feudal or chivalric figure. The basis of the response of the younger man and his hope for controlling the strong man or escaping his dominance is nearly always moral and may involve the abstract option in one form or another. The essential point in the relationship is that the issue of the confrontation for the younger man is his hope of not giving up the world, the world usually having at its center the image of a female. Thus the strong man is usually the antagonist in the rescue. Both within the pattern of the rescue and elsewhere the strong man is usually sexually aggressive and often he is identified with sexuality conceived as obscene.

The pattern is reflected in *Pauline* (1026-27) and constitutes the climactic action in *Sordello*, where it occurs twice, the first instance resulting in psychic castration of the protagonist, the second, in his death. The pattern is a dominant element in all the plays except *Luria*. It occurs in the Sebald episode of *Pippa Passes* and is the dominant element in the Luigi episode; it is also reflected in various other ways in that poem. The pattern is reflected in many later poems, including the most important poems in *Men and Women*, and is singly the most common in Browning's poetry of all the prototypal patterns.

MODES OF DEFEAT AND RESISTANCE

Failure. The protagonist has suffered a profound failure consisting of a giving up or loss of the world. In one degree or another most of Browning's heroes suffer failure, and it is generally the result of the project of the world and of love that is central to Browning's poetry. It has often been noted as a conspicuous characteristic of Browning's work. *Pauline, Paracelsus,* and *Sordello* are studies in failure, as are "Pictor Ignotus," "The Patriot," and "Guido," in *The Ring and the Book*.

Hatred and anger. Hatred and anger are a generalized response to the general condition of failure. Assertive and aggressive modes of resistance to frustration, they are often occasioned by patterns of compromise. They are emphatically and explicitly affirmed as alternative modes of self-expression. Expressions of hatred and anger are usually abrupt and brief, but they may take on volcanic force, becoming major elements or forming the essential substance of a poem.

Anger is affirmed as a positive value in *Paracelsus*, where hatred and anger achieve great magnitude, as they do in "Guido." An interesting example occurs in Phene's song to Jules in *Pippa Passes*. Hatred and anger are also a dominant element in the late poem "A Forgiveness." The meaning of hate whenever it appears in Browning is expressed in "One Word More": "Dante, who loved well because he hated / Hated wickedness that hinders loving."

Before considering the significance of the prototypal structure in the development of Browning's major poetry it is necessary to emphasize two characteristics of the structure. First is the fact that from the beginning the patterns of compromise, the passive patterns, exist under a countervalent pressure. The reason is that these patterns represent a compulsion to stasis and death, the imagery of which is imperatively associated with erotic imagery in Browning's earliest poetry. To suggest, however, that such patterns in themselves typify Browning's temperament, as Miller has done, is to ignore a volcanic dynamism, which may be engendered by a conflict of opposite tendencies. The second characteristic to be emphasized is that the prototypal structure undergoes developmental change. That the passive patterns exist under pressure might be demonstrated by the countervalent imagery with which they are regularly associated—imagery of pagan ritual and myth, for instance—but such a demonstration in any detail would exceed the limits of this study. It is sufficient for present purposes to indicate the pressures reflected in the kinds of changes the structure undergoes in the course of time. Though the structure never entirely disappears from Browning's poetry, the magnitude of its elements often decreases. The tensions between the elements diminish, and the elements take on changed relationships within the structure.

We see early evidence of change when the social option is subsumed in the rescue. In *The Return of the Druses* and in *Colombe's Birthday* single actions have the combined purpose of rescuing a woman and rescuing a social collectivity. And in both *Colombe's Birthday* and *A Soul's Tragedy* the social option is isolated and discredited. In these plays the characters who relinquish love for political power, Berthold and Chiappino respectively, are portrayed as relatively inadequate or villainous, and Valence and Luitolfo, the characters who get the girls, achieve authentic service to society. Norbert, the hero of "In a Balcony," makes a positive choice between clear-cut alternatives, rejecting a role of effective political leadership for romantic love. Here, for once in Browning's poetry, "the world" means affairs of the world; it is conceived as antithetical to love. And never again in Browning's poetry will the social option be treated sympathetically. Repeatedly in other poems in *Men and Women* and thereafter, society is seen as inimical to love, as in "Respectability," and a clear choice is made for love, as in "Love among the Ruins," or the failure to choose is lamented, as in "The Statue and the Bust" and, later, in "Dîs Aliter Visum" and "Youth and Art." In *The Ring and the Book* the antithesis of love and society attains massive dimensions.[4] The social collectivity is omnipresent in the poem and it is treated with consistent contempt or despair. In enmity or ignorance the collectivity is tragically averse to love.

Passive patterns, manifested with extreme subtlety, may be seen under pressure in the early poem "In a Gondola." The love affair would seem to have developed to the point of sexual consummation and the words of "She" can hardly be taken as other than an overt invitation: "What's left but—all of me to take? . . . slake your thirst." "He," however, is distracted, and as "He sings" or "speaks, musing," three especially insignificant images arise. The expressions containing the first two of these images are interrupted by the speaker's words, "Scatter the vision forever." The first image is that of "a feast of our tribe" with which is associated a suggestion of the death of the woman, adumbrating a fusion of the objectification of the beloved and the social option. The second image suggests the religious transmutation, projecting a spiritual exaltation of the speaker with which a vague "withering away" is associated. In the context we may recall the elaborate statement in *Sordello*, VI, of the debilitating effects upon the body of its domination by "the soul." An image of the recourse to infancy follows immediately, the speaker being enwrapped by wings, as in "The Guardian Angel."[5] In the sequel to this image the speaker cries out: "Rescue me thou, the only real? / And scare away this mad ideal." But the impulse to passive patterns prevails, and what follows is built upon the flight to finality. We may assume, ironically, that the rescue comes when the speaker is stabbed by one of "The Three," who have been following. Dying, the speaker tells us that the "best comes now," and to love's having become a matter of retrospect we may attribute the odd complacency with which "He" dies.

The fullest expression of the guardian angel motif is in the poem so titled which appears in *Men and Women;* thereafter it virtually disappears from Browning's poetry. Despite the presence of that rather offensive poem, *Men and Women* reflects a new freedom in dealing with the relationship between men and women, as DeVane has noted.[6] In the collection an impressive number of poems about the love relationship are not controlled by the passive patterns and in them Browning seems to delight in the relationship conceived maturely and realistically. "One Way of Love" suggests an experience of struggle but also of achievement: "My whole life long I learned to love." In "Another Way of Love" the speaker exhibits a commanding masculinity impatient with precisely that quality of necrotic serenity which so often emerged in Browning's earlier poetry: "Well, dear, in-doors with you! / True! serene deadness / Tries a man's temper." "Women and Roses" can be nothing less than a joyous symbolic celebration of sexuality, even though the guardian angel motif appears there. Close Freudian reading of a number of poems in the collection has seen them as symbolizing coitus.[7] In one of Browning's finest poems, "Fra Lippo Lippi," he sustains for the first time a fully developed plea for justification and affirmation of the world and the flesh, though, as will be seen below, this plea is not entirely unqualified.

As has been suggested, an actual reversal of patterns appears in some of the poems in *Men and Women*—"Love Among the Ruins," "In a Balcony," and "The Statue and the Bust." Two other changes are especially significant. Andrea del Sarto is a descendant of Porphyria's lover and the Duke of Ferrara. For him, too, the beloved person has become an object, but there is a difference. The earlier characters are treated with startlingly rigorous objectivity. In the case of the painter, however, the nature of his renunciation of human tensions is made explicit in the resignation of his sexual relationship with Lucrezia to the "cousin" who awaits out-of-doors.

Thus Andrea is made a subject of satire and a despicable figure. His passive mode of being is both given eloquent expression and consciously repudiated. Miller has ignored this point in her treatment of the poem, which is discrediting to Browning.[8]

While Browning in *Men and Women* often achieved expansive freedom from the patterns controlling his earlier poetry, the influence of these patterns continues. A deathly tendency of Browning's imagination, a mode of the objectification of the beloved, is vividly at work in two poems, both necessarily offensive to modern readers. In "Mesmerism" and "Evelyn Hope" there is an uncomfortable suggestion of necrophilia, but in these poems death does not have the stillness, the completeness, which are the values of the static entity. Death has been softened, and, however unpleasantly, it has been humanized. In both poems the conception of life after death confers upon death some of the dynamism in the love relationship which informs *Men and Women* generally.

In even the earliest poetry, the pattern of the failure who gives up the world is accompanied by pressure against the pattern which is expressed in the attitude of the protagonist. When the speaker of "Pictor Ignotus" thinks of the world he might not have given up, symbolized in the worldly art he has forgone, he exclaims, "How my soul springs up!" Paracelsus, prime embodiment of the intellectual option, is eventually the victim of "some innate and inexplicable germ / Of failure" (I, 184-85). He recalls that "there came a slow / And strangling failure" (I, 501-2). His failure may be explained only as the effect of his vocation, the career of knowledge implying for him the rejection of love, of joy, and, quite specifically, of the flesh. The world that is alien to him is imaged as a world of pagan joy in which "savage creatures seek / Their loves in wood and plain—and God renews / His ancient rapture" (V, 679-81).

The most extreme effect of his failure is an outburst of savage hostility: "I will exterminate the race" (V, 328). With great consistency Browning in *Paracelsus* affirms hatred as an authentic mode of self-assertion: "To hate? / If that be our true object which evokes / Our powers in fullest strength, be sure 't is hate!" (IV, 149-51).

With an idea in mind of the pressures associated with the proto-typal structure and of the kind of changes it undergoes, it is possi-ble to examine aspects of the structure as they appear developmen-tally in some of Browning's major works.

The history of Sordello's soul is a long history of successive fail-ures. Here there seems to be established most fully the meaning of certain of the prototypal patterns in Browning's poetry. Sordello's first sense of failure comes with the discovery, mistaken as it even-tually turns out, that he is of humble birth. His persisting failure, however, is associated with other things. As in *Paracelsus*, failure seems essentially inexplicable. It is vaguely connected with a reason for "his difference from men" which "surprised him at the grave" of Eglamore, the troubador who dies when Sordello has defeated him in poetic competition (II, 316-17). As in *Paracelsus* failure is seen not as an end result of vocation, but as its corollary. Poetry means for Sordello a giving up of the world, a choice of "Song, not deeds" (II, 440). The effect of his poetic vocation is to exclude him from hu-man joy. He is one "conceiving all / Man's life, who see[s] its blisses, great and small, / Afar—not tasting any" (II, 425-27).

The prohibition of joy seems also implicit in the intensity of imagined joy: "each joy must he abjure / Even for love of it" (II, 554-55). Sordello says, "Blisses strong and soft / I dared not enter-tain, elude me" (III, 156-57). The prohibition is especially identified with vocation, and Sordello experiences "the Poet thwarting hope-lessly the Man" (II, 659). The vocation is defective also because of special qualities which Sordello brings to it; for this reason his art is without a guiding emotional or intellectual orientation: "he loves not, nor possesses One / Idea that, star-like over, lures him on / To its exclusive purpose" (II, 395-97).

The psychological corollary of this appears in Sordello's expla-nation that "no machine / To exercise my utmost will is mine: / Be mine mere consciousness!" (II, 427-29).

This, obviously, is a succinct statement of the ontological diffu-sion J. Hillis Miller has found central to Browning's art.[9] Eventually a sense of complete ontological dissolution results. "And lo, Sor-dello vanished utterly, / Sundered in twain" (II, 656-57). As for "the complete Sordello, Man and Bard," says the narrator, he "was gone" (II, 690, 693). In the narrator's words, Sordello thinks that, entering into the world and thus learning joy, he might,

> *foreswearing bard-craft, wake*
> *From out his lethargy and nobly shake*
> *Off timid habits of denial, mix*
> *With men, enjoy like men.* (II, 703-6)

Eventually Sordello concludes, with resolution, that self-realization must be linked with an embrace of the world and the flesh: "I must, ere I begin to Be, / Include a world, in flesh, I comprehend / In spirit now" (III, 172-74).

After abandoning poetry Sordello turns to the social collectivity, aspiring to leadership. That this decision has as its purpose the fulfillment of Sordello's own needs is repeatedly emphasized. The narrator says:

> *For thus*
> *I bring Sordello to the rapturous*
> *Exclaim at the crowd's cry, because one round*
> *Of life was quite accomplished; and he found*
> *Not only that a soul, whate'er its might,*
> *Is insufficient to its own delight,*
> *Both in corporeal organs and in skill*
> *By means of such to body forth its Will.* (III, 561-68)

The need to be fulfilled by a change of careers is a need for exercise of the "will" expressive of the personality, but the original attraction to the social body involves more than this. It behooves Sordello to think of "men, and take their wants . . . / As his own want" (IV, 266-68). This does not mean that Sordello observes and sympathizes with the deprivations and injustices suffered by the collectivity. On the contrary, he sees in others a capacity for joy he cannot share except by identification with them. Unmistakably Sordello is aware of being deprived of something that other people have, and the value he places upon the collectivity is derived from a very special case of achievement of being by becoming what one sees. Sordello sees the crowd as "all these livers upon all delight" (IV, 196). It is under the impress of this conception that he realizes

> *he must impress [their will]*
> *With his own will, effect a happiness*
> *By theirs, —supply a body to his soul*
> *Thence, and become eventually whole.* (IV, 201-4)

The idea that integration with the social entity can serve as a surrogate for erotic or romantic love is formulated in the words of the narrator. He has just recalled a girl he loved, one

> *I looked should foot Life's temple-floor.*
> *Years ago, leagues at a distance, when and where*
> *A whisper came, "Let others seek!—thy care*
> *Is found, thy life's provision; if thy race*
> *Should by thy mistress, and into one face*
> *The many faces crowd?"* (III, 750-55)

The point receives much emphasis. Sordello's decision to serve the people did not result from a "claim / On their part, nor was virtue in the aim / At serving them on his" (IV, 271-73).[10] Only after making his decision does it occur to Sordello that his service to men could "be fraught / With incidental good to them as well, / And that mankind's delight would help to swell / His own" (IV, 278-81). Eventually the condition of Sordello's embracing the world is that he succeed in influencing the formidable worldling and great warrior Taurello Salinguerra, who turns out to be Sordello's father. With "consummate rhetoric" he would "bind / Taurello body with the cause and mind" (V, 329-30).[11] In this too he fails, and the result of his confrontation of Salinguerra is that Sordello dies. Having followed the spritual conflicts of Sordello to the end, the poem turns back to interpret his failure: "What made the secret of the past despair?" The explanation is to be found in that description of psychological repression using the word *soul* as we would use *the unconscious* (see p. 13). The explanation ends, "And the result is, the poor body soon / Sinks under what was meant a wonderous boon" (VI, 547-48). The failure is a failure to "shake / Off timid habits of denial, mix / With men, enjoy like men" (II, 704-6). The explanation must be taken as relevant to the tradition of the failure throughout Browning's work.

The implications of the structure in *Pippa Passes* are of very great interest. The patterns are sometimes obvious, as in Luigi's projected assassination of the strong man, for which he must surely die—"The dying is best part of it"—or as in the Monsignor's rescue of Pippa from sexuality conceived as obscene, the Monsignor being, as a fusion of hero and priest, of the world and faith, a foreshadowing of Caponsacchi. It is not so obvious that the aging Luca, whom Sebald kills in order to possess his wife (a deed for which Sebald must kill himself), should be associated with the strong man. He has, however, the power of wealth; his relation to Sebald is paternal, and he "says he would like to be Prince Metternich." In *Pippa Passes* the prototypal structures most often appear with the kind of subtlety seen in "In a Gondola." Close examination would indicate that the poem has the most various and complex prototypal structure of any of Browning's works and that it derives its special character specifically from a new strategy—the strategy of the female protagonist—for reconciling the love of God and the love of the world. To demonstrate these points, however, would require a much more elaborate argument than is possible here.

What is possible here is to show the general course of development of the structure in some of the poetry of Browning's years in Italy. This may be achieved by giving special attention to the confrontation of the strong man while neglecting, relatively, the other patterns.

Christmas-Eve and Easter-Day gives extended discursive treatment to the radical opposition between the love of God and the love of the world. "Christmas-Eve," the first of the two companion poems, examines three religious alternatives—Roman Catholicism, the mythic conception of German higher criticism, and a dissenting Christian faith of childhood, affirming the last of these. The effect of "Easter-Day" is to undermine that affirmation profoundly, first by the examination of intellectual and temperamental obstacles to

faith and then by elaboration of a dream-vision articulating metaphysical conceptions as an alternative to Christian orthodoxy. If
we conceive these conceptions as nothing more than a rational
transformation of orthodoxy, achieving a successful reconciliation
to Christianity, then much of the dream-vision will be unintelligible. It must be understood that the dream-vision proposes not a
compromise but an alternative and that the alternative requires not
only rational choice but a loss of innocence of profound significance for the future of Browning's poetry.

The poem begins in a dialogue with an unidentified person, the
theme of which is "How very hard it is to be a Christian!" The protagonist avers that he could accept faith as a probability but points
out that there are other difficulties. The modern imagination does
not lend itself to faith; in effect the modern temperament is an obstacle, and it is especially so because faith requires that one give up
the world—"renounce it utterly." In this dialogue the issue is traditional Christian faith, and the opposition of love of God and love
of the world is conceived as absolute. The rest of the poem develops in a dream-vision. The speaker imagines the approach of Judgment Day in spite of which he finds himself "Choosing the world."
His awareness that he should "renounce it utterly" is not "authentically deep and plain enough" to lead him to such renunciation
though he has tried all his life to reconcile himself to it. A voice indicates that he is " 'judged for evermore.' " The speaker is surprised
to find, however, that the orthodox manifestations of the Judgment
Day, such as the white throne and the rising of the dead, do not occur. Instead "HE" appears, an awesome version of the strong man
before whom the speaker experiences an unmanning reminiscent of
Sordello's first confrontation of Salinguerra. The speaker "fell before His feet, a mass, / No man now."

The substance of the long speeches of HE may be briefly summarized. The orthodox judgment, HE says, was for those in whom
only terror could inspire an apprehension of truth. The speaker,
however, must be concerned with a conception of God as an absolute, relevant to the entire human race, and, by implication, not peculiarly Christian. For the speaker there is a measure of redemption
in the fact that he is of a race in which scarcely one in a million can

feel "that any marvel lay / In objects round his feet all day." But because the speaker has chosen "this finite life" in disbelief of revelation, because "Thy choice was earth," the world is his, he must take it, and he may not again enter into the condition of innocence in which the faith of orthodoxy was possible:

> *"So, once more, take thy world! Expend*
> *Eternity upon its shows,*
> *Flung thee as freely as one rose*
> *Out of a summer's opulence,*
> *Over the Eden-barrier whence*
> *Thou are excluded. Knock in vain!"*

The earth and the realms of art and the mind which the speaker so prizes must, indeed, be his. Life as embrace of the world is to be considered as preparatory to a transcendent heaven which will be a heightened continuation of life in this world.

At first pleased by this revelation, the speaker then feels that he has been excluded from love and falls into despair, protesting, "I let the world go, and take love!" Expecting pity and approval, the speaker is shaken to see in HE the attitude of an executioner and he falls "prone, letting Him expend / His wrath." "His" response, however, is to explain that the world the speaker has embraced is "curled / Inextricably round about" with love, which he could not perceive. HE then rebukes the speaker, not for rejecting "the tale" of orthodox faith, but for his reason for doing so: his inability to believe the magnitude of love symbolized in the story of Christ. Cowering under this rebuke, the speaker pleads to be permitted to continue in hope. There follows a reconciliation:

> *Then did the form expand, expand—*
> *I knew Him through the dread disguise*
> *As the whole God within His eyes*
> *Embraced me.*

HE has affirmed "natural supernaturalism" and a conception of heaven which, being only a magnification and intensification of the world, has as its most significant effect a consecrating of the world as it is. The proposal is truly radical, and what is at issue is a literal, fundamentalist faith and a loss of innocence—"the Eden-barrier whence / Thou art excluded." For a long time that innocence will remain for Browning both necessary and oppressive.

Following the dream-vision, the speaker questions the validity of its meaning: "And commonly my mind is bent / To think it was a dream—be sure / A mere dream and distemperature." Then he denies that innocence is irretrievable: "Thank God, no paradise stands barred / To entry." But the poem ends in uncertainty—"and who can say?" The antithetical ending, the ending which as afterthought, irony, or a turning to countervailing imagery, either questions or denies the direction taken in the main body of a poem is frequent in Browning's poetry hereafter. Thus Fra Lippo, embracing the world, is returned to innocence. Bishop Blougram, arguing faith, is endowed with doubt and associated, not with heaven, but with hell. Cleon is undercut by irony. Caponsacchi, renouncing the world, ends by imagining a life with Pompilia in the world. Guido's fury and hatred end with a plea to Pompilia. Fra Celestino ends with an afterthought about the asceticism of his entire life. And in *Fifine* the quest is abandoned. Browning's poems are excursions into dangerous territory, and they end in retreat. The antithetical ending is a mark of the dynamism of which each poem is an expression, being an exploration of a possibility not fully realized but never without its significance for the future.

The confrontation of the strong man in the dream-vision of "Easter-Day" is an initiation ceremony that does not quite succeed, and yet *Christmas-Eve and Easter-Day* is the matrix of much that appears in *Men and Women*, in which individual poems explore possibilities proposed in the earlier work. Of most pervasive importance for *Men and Women* is that reconciliation in which the anthropomorphic God as strong man tends to disappear in an abstraction of love. When religion is affirmed in *Men and Women*, it tends to be the religion articulated by HE in "Easter-Day," and a correlative continuity exists in the fact that in *Men and Women* the confrontation of the strong man tends to lose its virulence.

The persistence of the pattern of the confrontation of the strong man may be seen in the frequency with which poems in *Men and Women* bring into some kind of conflict a character representing either power or formal authority and a character of relative weakness or formal subordination. The pattern is reflected when in the sexual competition portrayed in "A Light Woman," the dominating character is called an "eagle" and the weak competitor, with "maiden face," is called a "wren." Fleetingly the pattern is glimpsed in "De Gustibus—" when "a girl bare footed" brings the speaker green melons and news of the attempted assassination and maiming of the king. More often the pattern is more obvious, and its varied treatment suggests that its persistence is accompanied by a diminution of its urgency. The confrontation is the subject of casual third-person narration in the poem "Protus," and the strong man figure in "Cleon," referred to as "Protus in his Tyranny," is not physically present. In "Fra Lippo Lippi" the strong man image is refracted into three separate authority figures—the police (or members of the watch), Cosimo de Medici, and the prior. In "How It Strikes a Contemporary" the relationship of the youthful speaker and the power figure, the poet called the "Corregidor," is indirect and entirely impersonal. In "Protus" there is an interchange of characteristics between roles. Protus, the lawful emperor, descendant of a god, is distinguished for his youth and beauty and is in a number of ways reminiscent of Sordello, while John the Pannonian, formally the inferior, has the massive masculinity and the crude abruptness associated with the strong man seen heretofore in formal authority. The fate of Protus, after his throne has been usurped by John, is to revert to interests similar to those associated in earlier poems with the youthful protagonist. It is rumored that he became a tutor and a writer and died a monk. There is a note of special disdain in the line, "I deduce / He wrote the little tract 'On Worming Dogs.' " John in his role as emperor has all the qualities of the prototypal strong man. The poem, inspired by admiration of "the crown-grasper," ends with the words, "What a man!" More frequently than before the strong man in *Men and Women* tends to be benefic: John, in holding off the Huns; the Protus of "Cleon," in his munificence, his solicitude, and his sympathetic curiosity. The strong men now are essentially untainted by sexual aggressiveness. The "eagle" wins the lover of his friend, the "wren," but he does so in his friend's interest; only afterwards is he tempted by his prize.

In two dramatic monologues of *Men and Women* the speaker is the strong man and the point of view his. That had occurred before in "The Bishop Orders His Tomb," where perhaps the feat was made possible only by the vantage point of the terminal perspective. In "Instans Tyrannus" the ruler of a "million or two, more or less" recounts his experience with a lowly subject who was obdurate in the face of physical abuse, temptations of the flesh, and plots against his life. Then he describes this man's religious fervor in skirts-of-God imagery recalling "Christmas-Eve," ending:

> *The man sprang to his feet,*
> *Stood erect, caught at God's skirts, and prayed!*
> *So, I was afraid!*

Bishop Blougram, too, is unmistakably a strong man, and the issue of his monologue embodies another significant transformation of the type—in that he is seen in roles previously associated with the youthful protagonist. Bishop Blougram has as his project the reconciliation of the radical opposition fundamental to Browning's poetry. The primary argument of his monologue is that one may have both faith and the world. The bishop's faith is very close to that spirituality condoning flesh and earth eventually permitted by the HE of "Easter-Day." If he believed half of what he said, as indicated in the antithetical ending, then he believed very little indeed. In "How It Strikes a Contemporary," the "Corregidor," who does not experience the joys of the flesh, is a poet and his orientation is to God. He is also an unacknowledged ruler of men, which is to suggest that religion and the abstract options are no longer necessarily interpreted as resulting in failure. Even the intellectual option in "A Grammarian's Funeral" does not leave the grammarian without honor among his peers, though the satirical intent of the poem is clear.[12]

The most significant development in the confrontation of the strong man in *Men and Women* is a marked attenuation of its consequences. The results are never fatal, and when the confrontation involves a loss or giving up of the world circumstances usually in some way compensate. More important, the confrontation for the protagonist—youthful or of inferior status—usually results in success, at least to the extent that the balance tips in his favor. He gains freedom from restrictive forces or from some element of influence or control.

Among Browning's protagonists in *Men and Women*, there are only two in whom failure approaches in magnitude that of the early confrontations. Andrea del Sarto has objectified his beloved and has lost her as a sexual being. Though he retains compensatory pride in his craftsmanship, his life and his art are devoid of power, and he suffers failure of filial, sexual, and religious love. And for Andrea there is no confrontation. Rather his failure dates from his betraying and abandoning his relationship to a strong man, Fancis I, a benevolent power under whose auspices his art had flourished—"A good time, was it not, my kingly days?"

In a single instance in *Men and Women* a confrontation has immediately grave results, and the pattern conforms closely to earlier instances, the failure resulting directly from the confrontation. "In a Balcony" is built around a confrontation, and yet we may feel a parallel with the absence of confrontation in "Andrea del Sarto," for in this instance, uniquely, the authority figure is not a man but a woman—the queen, who has mistaken Norbert's love for Constance for love for herself. The object of the confrontation is to disabuse the queen and claim Constance. The value of the confrontation is emphasized by the fact that it is not needed in order to gain Constance as a sexual object, for she urges Norbert to maintain the secrecy of their relationship. Here the confrontation has taken on new meaning. Norbert fully recognizes that to confront the queen means to assert his claim to Constance and at the same time to renounce his position of political leadership, or in structural terms, to reject the social option, an option which in the course of Norbert's discussion is equated with the artistic option, so that, by implication, both are rejected. In the earliest confrontations the abstract options provided the moral basis for the confrontation and the means intended for controlling the strong man. "In a Balcony" clearly isolates the sexual issue as the issue of the confrontation. In the early confrontations the sexual issue was always obscured in other issues—political, religious, or moral. It is perhaps because of the isolation of the sexual issue that the outcome of the confrontation is graver here than anywhere else in *Men and Women*. At the end with the approach of the guards, it is clear that Norbert falls into the malefic power of the queen.[13]

The most dramatic confrontation in *Men and Women* occurs in "Saul." It is also the most successful: the spiritual power of the youthful protagonist prevails. Of all the strong men in Browning, Salinguerra and Saul are the most awesome, and there are parallels of imagery and theme between the confrontations in *Sordello* and "Saul." Sordello confronts Salinguerra with a moral but worldly cause, essentially social and political though touched with religious associations. The mediating principle in "Saul" and the theme of the first part of David's appeal to Saul is a reconciliation of the spirit and the world which seems coherent with that proposed in "Easter-Day": "How good is man's life, the mere living! how fit to employ / All the heart and the soul and the senses, for ever in joy!" In response to this Saul begins to awaken from his despair and there occurs an element of rapprochement that was impossible for Sordello, who could not bear the gaze of Salinguerra. David says, "I looked up and dared gaze at those eyes, nor was hurt any more / Than by slow pallid sunsets in autumn."

In the first phase of David's song, the world and the spirit coexist in space, as it were. In the next phase they have a relationship in time, and the effect is an attenuation of their compatibility. In substance, Saul may glory in, and need not renounce, the worldly joys in which he has lived in the past, but should turn now to spirit: "Leave the flesh to the fate it was fit for! the spirit be thine!" In structural terms, David advocates the terminal perspective: "Carouse in the past! / But the licence of age has its limit; thou diest at last." In response to the conception of spirit as an augmentation of life as it approaches its end, Saul returns to vitality—"he slowly resumed / His old motions and habitudes kingly." David now addresses Saul as "Father," and imagery develops a relationship not only filial but infantile. The image of David between Saul's knees suggests parturition. Physical contact becomes almost terrifying, though gentle—"and he bent back my head with kind power." This is the dramatic expression of a reconciliation expressed otherwise in the fact that the poetry revels in Saul's world, not only a world which he possesses, but one with which he is symbolically identified. The image of Saul is not referred to again, though he is repeatedly addressed. The remainder of the poem depicts the development of David's faith and the sequel to the confrontation. David's faith continues to be in a cosmos interfused by spirit and touched by indication of a kind of antinomianism, recurrent in Browning, that suggests a faith without either form or content: "It is by no breath, / Turn of eye, wave of hand, that salvation joins issue with death!" Here, however, a deepened natural supernaturalism, or pantheism, gives rise to the idea of an incarnation, not so much of God in Christ as of Christ in man. It is "my flesh" says David, "that I seek / In the Godhead!" His vision culminates abruptly in the words, "See the Christ stand!"

While this is explicitly a Christian affirmation, it is the climax of a development within the poem of thought profoundly divergent from traditional Christianity and deeply informed by the alternative to innocence posed in "Easter-Day." Thus intellectually diluted, the love of God here affirmed retains, nevertheless, the prototypal tension with the love of the world, as will become clear upon examination of the sequel to the confrontation.

The sequel is another form of the antithetical ending, giving rise to imagery expressive of discords generated by the direction of thought and temperament in the main body of the poem. Departing from the presence of Saul, David enters a realm of landscape alive with meaning. At one level the poetry here must be taken as expressive of nature startled, riven, by the anticipatory revelation of Christ. And the recurrence of serpent imagery, associated at the beginning of the poem with Saul, asserts the power of spirit and suggests the exorcism of the malefic aspects of the strong man: "E'en the serpent that slid away silent—he felt the new Law." Thus the ending is integral with the poem at the dramatic level. And yet a strangeness about the imagery of the ending (stanza XIX) requires that we read also at another level of meaning. There arises a question of "Life or death." David is impelled, obscurely, by a supernatural "Hand." In the awakened earth, "hell" is "loosed with her crews." The evening is infused with "trouble." The stars "tingled and shot / Out in fire the strong pain of pent knowledge." With the dawn the "trouble had withered from earth," and we come to recognize a negation of elements that were in "tumult" in the night. The last nine lines of the poem are configured by the quest motif in imagery the import of which becomes clearest by comparing it with that of the earliest appearance of the motif, in *Pauline* (729-810). The common images are those of tree, snake, bird, beast, and water. In *Pauline* the "tall trees overarch to keep us in," suggesting the protectedness of infancy. The arrival point of the quest is "a small pool whose waters lie asleep." The serpent nearby is quiescent: "The pale-throated snake reclines his head." But the scene is redolent with a sense of something startling, new, and strange, and a suggestion of a potential awakening in which intimations of delight and of the ominous are mingled. Near the "dreamy waters" are "two or three strange trees." They are "wondering at all around, as strange beasts herd / Together far from their own land: all wildness." Close at hand "the wild hawks" fly. Though the small pool lies asleep, it is also "this silent depth" which "lies / Still, as but let by sufferance," and over it the trees bend "as wild men watch a sleeping girl." In this earliest appearance of the quest motif in his poetry, Browning captures with almost preternatural efficacy an anticipation of awakening in the deepest, most subtle stirrings of adulthood.

At the end of "Saul," as the effect of a religious regression, these imagistic elements of *Pauline* are stricken and dispersed. The "shuddering" forest feels "new awe." Animals depart the scene in instinctive fear and alienation—"the startled wild beasts that bore off, each with eye sidling still / Though averted with wonder and dread." The birds "stiff and chill" can hardly fly; they "rose heavily." The departure of the serpent "that slid away silent" is followed by a suggestion of nature debilitated, in "the white humid faces upturned by the flowers." The central water, shallow, dispersed in "little brooks," affirms the religious regression in "obstinant, all but hushed voices." In "Saul" the malefic power of the strong man has yielded to spirituality, but the reconciliation, which is always at issue in the confrontation, is unstable.

The religious center of "Fra Lippo Lippi," like that of "Saul," sustains simultaneously both the love of the world and the love of God, but while the movement in "Saul" is from the flesh to the spirit, the movement in "Fra Lippo Lippi" is from the spirit to the flesh: "What would men have? Do they like grass or no— / May they or mayn't they? all I want's the thing / Settled for ever one way." And here, as in *Fifine*, uncertainty means a falsification and vitiation of art—"As it is, / You tell too many lies and hurt yourself."

The three images of authority in the poem—the members of the watch collectively, Cosimo de Medici, and the prior—all serve within the dramatic dimension to represent prohibition of the flesh. Lippo's advocacy of the flesh prevails, though uncertainly. The members of the watch, obscurely differentiated except for the indication of a leader, are first represented by an exposing light in Lippo's face and a hand on his throat. Like HE in "Easter-Day," the watch is associated with the image of an executioner—"the slave that holds / John Baptist's head a-dangle by the hair." This image is replaced, as Lippo's prestige and his arguments gain ground, with "your cullion's hanging face." Cosimo has had Lippo incarcerated where for three weeks he has been "a-painting for the great man, saints and saints / And saints again." And Cosimo must not know of Lippo's fleshly escapade. But Cosimo represents the world— "trash, such as these poor devils of Medici / Have given their hearts to"—and it is because of his patronage that Lippo may say, "I'm my own master, paint now as I please." It is only the prior, as representative of religious prohibition, whose influence Lippo never quite escapes: "And yet the old schooling sticks, the old grave eyes / Are peeping o'er my shoulder as I work."

"Fra Lippo Lippi" is Browning's most direct and sustained celebration of the world before *Fifine*. Its affirmation, however, is qualified. The thesis of the world and the flesh has its most obvious dramatic expression in Lippo's personal sensuality. His escapade in the red-light district is excused as the product not of lust, but of "pure rage" against a prohibitive cultural milieu. Lippo's sensuality is softened by an endearing, spontaneous cuteness, a suggestion of infantilism, which characterizes him at both the beginning and the end of the poem. In deep consistency with this, symbolism preserves Lippo in a state of innocence. A part of this sybolism is a subtle emergence of the pattern of the rescue. Among the myriad realistic images in Lippo's "pictures of the world" is that of "the Prior's niece who comes / To care about his asthma." The "nieces" of high churchmen are suspect in the Renaissance and in Browning's poetry, and there is thus a hint of a parallel with Fifine conceived as a prostitute. The prior's response to this image echoes the executioner theme which appears in connection with the watch at the beginning of the poem, and it associates with the prior as strong man the motif of sexuality as obscene. The prior says,

> *"Oh, that white smallish female with the breasts,*
> *She's just my niece . . . Herodias, I would say, —*
> *Who went and danced and got men's heads cut off!"*

To Lippo the prior's niece is "the little lily thing"; he sees her as a "patron saint" and compares her to Saint Lucy, the virgin saint, martyred perhaps because of her virginity. At the end of the poem the prior's niece is with Lippo under the form of Saint Lucy, and if this suggests rescue, it is of a mutual sort, the female being the rescuer in a way that parallels the rescue motif as it appears in *Fifine*. The closing lines of the poem are a cinematization, as it were, of Fra Lippo Lippi's *Coronation of the Virgin*. Lippo is imagined as rising abruptly into the "pure company" of Madonna and saints in the painting, by which he is "mazed, motionless, and moon-struck." A "sweet angelic slip of a thing" takes him by the hand, defends him as the one who " 'devised you, after all,' " and leads him out of the divine realm of the painting. In the final lines of the cinematized sequence, the image of "the cover of a hundred wings" reflects the recourse to infancy. The immediate religious association is transformed in the flow of metaphor to sexual imagery, again beguilingly cute, and both the religious and the sexual associations are endowed with innocence.

The condition of faith in "Saul" and the recourse from sexuality in "Fra Lippo Lippi" is innocence. The poet Cleon stands in contrast. In "Cleon" the confrontation of the strong man, after a long history in Browning's poetry, comes to a unique stasis. Basic elements of the prototypal pattern are present. The protagonist, the poet, addresses Protus, who is a possessor of the world. One aspect of the protagonist's utterance is a protest against his being deprived of the world. His vocation as poet is a factor in this deprivation. He articulates conceptions which have the potentiality of endowing life with joy and, if not restoring the world, compensating for its loss, but these conceptions fail to achieve such an end. The prototypal pattern, however, has been radically attenuated: the strong man is not physically present; in addition the protagonist is not young and in various respects, including their ages, the protagonist and the strong man are equals. Furthermore, it is not the strong man who has deprived the protagonist of the world. Rather his gifts to the poet are symbolic of the world, especially as they include "one white she-slave," and imagery tends to associate with the gifts an idea of the strong man's giving of himself and of the diffusion of his image:

> Gift after gift; they block my court at last
> And pile themselves along its portico
> Royal with sunset, like a thought of thee.

Men will interpret the gifts as an "act of love." It is, however, a dispassionate act, expressive of "thy munificence." Symbolism suggests that between the protagonist and the strong man there exists a relationship of sexual parity. Mediating this relationship is the "one white she-slave":

> One lyric woman in her crocus vest
> Woven of sea-wools, with her two white hands,
> Commends to me the strainer and the cup
> Thy lip hath bettered ere it blesses mine.

Protus rather than Cleon is the supplicant and the relationship is devoid of tension, its quietude symbolized in "this settle-down of doves" on Cleon's court and coherent with the classic calm of Cleon's utterance. The occasion for Cleon's utterance is a need the two men share.

The relationship of Cleon to the strong man is a correlative of Cleon's spiritual condition. That condition as a human possibility appears for the first time in Browing's work as the proposal of HE in "Easter-Day." Cleon is excluded from innocence. Significantly, he is the oldest of all Browning's major protagonists thus far, with the possible exception of Bishop Blougram. Except insofar as has been indicated, the passive patterns, which are strategies for sustaining innocence, do not appear in the poem.

Cleon has all the intellectual characteristics serving to exclude from innocence. While he is in possession of those conceptions by which Browning has attempted to reconcile faith and the world, these do not avail, and sometimes conflicting implications contradict them. The pantheistic concept—"Zeus' self, the latent everywhere"—is part of "a dream." The possibility is raised "that imperfection means perfection hid, / Reserved in part, to grace the after-time." But for the first time in Browning's poetry, it is proposed that the realm of perfection lies below man, in animal life in which consciousness has not been achieved. A general evolutionary process is recognized. In intellect it results in "greater mind," and in art it results in a heightened consciousness; yet consciousness as the culmination of evolution is portrayed, cogently, as failure. Perhaps most telling of all the intellectual aspects of Cleon's condition is the fact that he has imagined the Christian myth: he "wrote the fiction out." Though this provides a link with the ironic effects of the quotation heading the poem—" 'As certain also of your own poets have said' "—Cleon's claim is in no way discredited. His "fiction" is portrayed as an almost inevitable response to a need. The import of this is in implications lying beyond Cleon's consciousness: religious truth capable of being produced by the poetic imagination may have had its origin as poetry. The idea that religion, myth, and poetry are identical in their origins—a commonplace of the age—is given dignity by Cleon's conception of poetry as a gift of the gods.

The conception is compatible with some kind of Christian affirmation, but this only gives emphasis to the fact that for Browning in *Men and Women*, the possibility of innocence is contingent upon the possibility of literal belief. Our response to Cleon's position can hardly fail to be influenced by the fact that it is consistent with the higher criticism, Browning's acceptance of which is later revealed in "A Death in the Desert."[14] Cleon's intellectual position is impressively coherent.

Clearly irony undercuts Cleon's position. This is anticipated in the quotation at the beginning and achieved at the end when Cleon, who has independently imagined a Christ, spurns the message brought by Christian missionaries. Yet we may hardly think of the values of the poem as consisting solely in that irony. The irony corresponds to the antithetical ending and the willful rejection of HE and of the dream-vision in "Easter-Day." The final irony may be taken as satire of Cleon's position, but that position retains a strength given it by the commanding presence of the poet.

Cleon is free of human weakness that could make him an object of satire or compromise the universality of his meaning. The power of his appeal both to respect and to sympathy exists in his capacity for pain and his ability to recognize the limits posed against desire. His anguish is acute, but he will not accept the solace of illusions by which he is tempted. The failure he experiences is the failure of the human condition. His "I ask—and get no answer" is the cry of the century. True to the message of HE in "Easter-Day," Cleon, at the door of paradise, must "knock in vain." In his agony he adumbrates the existential conception of consciousness as an irremediable flaw, an incompleteness, inseparable from pain. Here, for the first time in Browning, death becomes something other than an artistic recourse for the management of sex. Death as finality is accepted as integral with life: "the throbbing impulse we call death." Cleon's art has compromised his possession of the world; it is not a substitute for life and is inadequate to joy, but he maintains the dignity of its unique achievement against the overpowering models of the past and affirms its consonance with the heart of things: "Refer this to the gods / Whose gift alone it is!" Identifying with his achievement amidst metaphysical desolation, he affirms the authenticity of his being: "I stand myself." Never before in a Browning character has there been such intellectual rigor, such honesty, or such quiet constancy in suffering. Cleon is Browning's first adult.

The emotional power of *The Ring and the Book* is generated in four central monologues: "Caponsacchi," "Pompilia," "The Pope," and "Guido." The first three are united by common values and to these the fourth stands in awful antithesis. The pro-Pompilia monologues develop a quality of passion peculiarly possible in that nineteenth-century condition of society in which the family had become the central institution. They develop that passion, however, with both an earthy solidity and a spiritual dignity which make it seem the substance of civilization. The explanation in broadest terms is that while the poem keeps steadily in view the realities of life arising from the fact that we are physical beings possessed of imperative appetites, it develops a quality of love to which that fact is irrelevant. Inherent in this achievement is a development of structures which had been present in Browning's poetry from the first.

The central rhetorical fact of the poem is the terminal perspective: Pompilia is dying and all her life lies in the past. The perspective holds for all the major speakers, all of whom have either given up the world or are at the point of death. In "Pompilia" the fear that is the meaning of death is muted by the fact that Pompilia has experienced a deliverance, so that in the prospect of death there is quietude. It is from a life of pain and fear of death that she has been delivered. The conspicuousness in the poem of the Perseus-Andromeda motif in the form of the cognate myth of Saint George has been often remarked. There are in fact two rescues. Pompilia's perilous final decision to escape Guido at any cost came "at the first prompting," says the Pope, "of what I call God / And fools call Nature" (X, 1073-74). Her decision was "to save the unborn child, / As brute and bird do, reptile and the fly" (1076-77). The context of her action is cosmic, impersonal, and in this sense divine. Her action is social and thus selfless, and it is impersonal because prompted by an instinctual loyalty to the order of things. As it turns out in the foreshortened perspective of the past, she gave her life for that loyalty, a sacrifice for which there can be no rational, earthly explanation. Heretofore in the rescue pattern, escape has been from sex conceived as obscenity. Pompilia did not escape that. It is there as a reality in her past. She says, "One cannot both have and not have, you know." Yet she is "purged of the past, the foul in me, washed fair" (VII, 352-53). So the reality of Guido does both exist and not exist. It has burned away in the hatred that is "the truth of Guido," and Gaetano is not "Count Guido Franceschini's child at all" (1763). Guido and his harsh sensuality are alien to the realm of love in which she briefly lives. Dying, she holds the realm of love on the verge of heaven, for only there can it remain immune to appetite without repudiation of the flesh. Pompilia's is not a realistically drawn portrait, and she does not represent life, which is an obscure continuum. Pompilia is a convincing lyric; she incarnates a fragile human possibility which is the artistic rationale of the poem.

"Caponsacchi" is the climactic development in Browning's poetry of the rescue, and, in a way implicit in that fact, it is the climactic development of the religious transmutation of love. The notion of the rescue as an end in itself becomes explicit: " 'Always, my life long, thus to journey still!' " (VI, 1312). And for Caponsacchi the rescue is conspicuously rescue from sexuality conceived as obscene. During the journey Pompilia speaks in her sleep resisting the sexual claims of Guido: " 'Never again with you! / My soul is mine, my body is my soul's' " (1295-96). Caponsacchi responds with a prayer: " 'Let God arise and all his enemies / Be scattered!' " (1302-3). Pompilia, defying Guido at the inn, cries out in an exorcism of Guido as sexuality:

> "Hell for me, no embracing any more!
> I am God's, I love God, God—whose knees I clasp,
> Whose utterly most just reward I take,
> But bear no more love-making devils: hence!" (1529-32)

Repeatedly there emerges the confrontation of the strong man. This informs Caponsacchi's memory of his ancestors:

> *. . . we Aretines*
> *Had tied a rope about the neck, to hale*
> *The statue of his father from its base*
> *For hate's sake.* (251-54)

Caponsacchi's first direct encounter with Pompilia results from his response to an indirect challenge from Guido, described as " 'a formidable foe' " who " 'will stick at nothing to destroy you' " (641-42). During the journey, they pass the estate of a bishop from whom Caponsacchi had been advised to seek preferment, and Caponsacchi is amused by the idea of confronting him with insolence and rebuke (1249-65). At the inn Guido appears as the diminished strong man of the later poetry: "There posed the mean man / As master" (1434-35). Caponsacchi distinguishes only "the redoubtable Tommati" (133) among the members of the court, which for both Caponsacchi and Guido has the functon of the restraining strong man as auditor.

Fundamental to the entire monologue of Caponsacchi, controlling his attitudes and underlying everything he says, is the religious transmutation of love. Pompilia on his first glimpse of her at the theater becomes a religious image, a madonna by Raphael (406). At the window in Guido's house she is "Our Lady of all the Sorrows" (707). She becomes Christ: while she is dying "they are now casting lots" for her garmet (57). The most concentrated development of the religious transmutation occurs in imagery interfusing the objectification of the beloved and the flight to finality. As soon as Caponsacchi is alone with Pompilia in the intimacy of the coach, the following occurs to him:

> *I said to myself—"I have caught it, I conceive*
> *The mind o' the mystery: 't is the way they wake*
> *And wait, two martyrs somewhere in a tomb*
> *Each by each as their blessing was to die;*
> *Some signal they are promised and expect,—*
> *When to arise before the trumpet scares:*

> *So, through the whole course of the world they wait*
> *The last day, but so fearless and so safe!*
> *No otherwise, in safety and not fear,*
> *I lie, because she lies too by my side.* " (1183-92)

Reflecting on this Caponsacchi says to the court, "You know this is not love, Sirs,—it is faith" (1193). He thus echoes a line from *Pauline*: "And thou art to receive not love but faith." Because this "is faith," the quality of feeling developed around Pompilia is both tender and exalted, and dissociation of the flesh from the love of Pompilia is given great emphasis:

> *I never touched her with my finger-tip*
> *Except to carry her to the couch, that eve,*
> *Against my heart, beneath my head, bowed low,*
> *As we priests carry the paten.* (1617-20)

The depth of this is reflected in subtle ways. There is perhaps a reflection of the recourse to infancy when Pompilia addresses Caponsacchi by the name of her unborn child (1388-89). Imagery descriptive of the flight suggests a circumvention of the quest and arriving at a realm of spirit. At one point Caponsacchi says they have "gone round by the wood, / Not through, I seem to think,— and opposite / I know Assisi; this is holy ground" (1203-5).

Caponsacchi's monologue is drenched with a quality of feeling achieved in the religious transmutation and the escape from a realm of the flesh to a realm of spirit. The mode of spiritual exaltation makes the monologue distinctive in Browning's work. Nevertheless, here, as in some of the poems in *Men and Women*, a rapprochement occurs between the love of the world and the love of God. This monologue is the point in Browning's poetry at which religious feeling becomes nearly compatible with worldliness. We may note that the religious transmutation, which is instantly implicit in Caponsacchi's relation to Pompilia, first deepens and then changes direction. After seeing Pompilia for the first time, at the theater, Caponsacchi experiences an access of religious seriousness.

He foreswears the frivolity of his life as a worldly churchman and taunts his religious superior: " 'Sir, what if I turned Christian?' " (474). After the first actual meeting with Pompilia, when he agrees to take her to Rome, Caponsacchi is deeply moved: "powerless, all that night / I paced the city: it was the first Spring" (945-46). The first spring is followed soon by a thought of death, and as for earlier Browning heroes, such as the speaker of "In a Gondola," there is an identification of death and happiness, this combines with a suggestion of the aerial journey: "Death meant, to spurn the ground, / Soar to the sky,—die well and you do that. / The very immolation made the bliss" (951-53).

Caponsacchi is aware that he is undergoing a transformation, passing "into another state, under new rule" (964). The transformation leads him for the first time to take seriously his vow as priest to whom "fleshly woman" is forbidden. This is associated with a deathly impulse, and it leads him to the conclusion: " 'Duty to God is duty to her' " (1030). After delaying for two days, he resolves not to take Pompilia to Rome and to minister to her only as priest: " 'Advise her seek / Help at the source' " (1059-60). The psychological component of this decision would seem to be emphasized when it is characterized, not in Christian, but in classical imagery. Caponsacchi says that, having reveled in the superficial joys of "the fabeled garden," he then came on "the thing of perfect gold, / The apple's self: and, scarce my eye on that, / Was 'ware as well o' the seven-fold dragon's watch" (1007-9).

When he next meets Pompilia, however, her rebuke for his delay is decisive, and Caponsacchi prepares for action, closing the "Summa"—which symbolized his original access of religious feeling—and calling for " 'laic dress' " and a sword. The faith to which Caponsacchi now turns is one in which we may not easily distinguish Pompilia form the deity. It would be a mistake to think of Caponsacchi's religious faltering and his later spiritualized resolution as a protestantizing of Catholic local color. The alternatives are more closely related to those posed in the dialogue with HE in "Easter-Day." The religious transmutation has been modified.

While the center of Caponsacchi's faith gravitates toward the world, the monologue in a variety of ways, massive in their effect, seeks accommodation with the world. Caponsacchi is given the feudal status usually reserved for strong men. A "younger son" of the oldest family in Arezzo, he recognizes "no equal there" (222-24). "A Tuscan Noble," he might have been "the Duke" (1582) had he not chosen the Church. And the choice of the Church was hardly a religious choice at all. He had recognized himself incapable of being true to religious vows, and worldly prelates had reassured him: " 'Renounce the world? Nay, keep and give it us!' " (309). By implication he would have seen religious obeisance as an impossible humiliation. Of the worldly version of Churchly life, he says, "I could live thus and still hold head erect" (338). Before meeting Pompilia, he leads a life of sophisticated elegance, writes madrigals, plays cards, indulges in flirtation and, it is suggested, in more than flirtations. At the theater his friend Conti assumes his interest in " 'the shapely nether limbs of Light-skirts there' " (429). The world in which he moves is contemptuous of serious commitment, and Caponsacchi's exemption from any such commitment is repeatedly emphasized. The bishop tells him that he keeps " 'a heavy scholar' " locked up ghostwriting for him and confined for diverson to " 'catching his own fleas' " (321-27). There is reference to " 'our lump of learning, Brother Clout, / And Father Slouch, our piece of piety' " (373-74). It is only for a few hours after his first sight of Pompilia that Caponsacchi is quite a Christian. When he at first withdraws from her in deepened piety, his new condition weakens his hold on the world. He is anxious lest she have " 'the fantastic notion that I fear / The world now!' " (1043-44). Testifying at the end he is concerned to scorn the conception of himself as "a priest who fears the world" (88). During the journey to Rome Caponsacchi is displeased when Pompilia refers to his priestly function, as she asks " 'wherefore do you not read / The service at this hour?' " (1270-71). And yet, aware of the incredulity of the court concerning the innocence of his relationship to Pompilia, Caponsacchi acknowledges the human and fleshly element in his motivation:

> *If I pretended simply to be pure*
> *Honest and Christian in the case, —absurd!*
> *As well go boast myself above the needs*

> *O' the human nature, careless how meat smells,*
> *Wine tastes, —a saint above the smack!* (1717-21)

In any effort to understand the relationship between Caponsacchi and Pompilia we must eventually recognize a certain strangeness. Pompilia declares, "He was mine, he is mine, he will be mine" (VII, 1457). Caponsacchi avers a union with her of great emotional intensity—"when at the last we did rush each on each" (VI, 1812). And, yet, for this the word love is proscribed in a way that irony does not entirely neutralize:

> *As for love, —no!*
> *If you let buzz a vulgar fly like that*
> *About your brains, as if I loved, forsooth,*
> *Indeed, Sirs, you do wrong! We had no thought*
> *Of such infatuation, she and I.* (1969-73)

For Caponsacchi the explanation is clear and simple: "That I assuredly did bow, was blessed / By the revelation of Pompilia" (1864-65). To find a rationale for the identification of God and Pompilia we will turn in vain to any reference outside the poem. We may argue reasonably that Caponsacchi is a realistic psychological portrait, a victim of illusionary passion in extremity of circumstance whose theology is not to be taken seriously. But if we do so, we may not feel that we have arrived at reality until we come to "Guido." It must be understood that the resolution is artistic: "She's dead now, Sirs!" (1982). And, logic notwithstanding, Caponsacchi is splendid, an artistic triumph having as its purpose that reconciliation of faith and the world epitomized when he is called by Pompilia "soldier-saint" (VII, 1786) and by the Pope "warrior-priest"(X, 1096). Caponsacchi, who is no failure, is a climactic expression, and a vindication, of a tendency of passion present in Browning's poetry from the beginning. Caponsacchi is a climactic and illusionary triumph of Browning's lifelong effort to have it both ways, to embrace the world in innocence. Finally Caponsacchi's spiritual exaltation of Pompilia, of her "revelation," is not enough, and his proposal to give up the world does not quite succeed. He has an afterthought, his imagination turning back to the world and a life lived with Pompilia "unfettered by a vow" (VI, 2082). He ends, "O great, just, good God! Miserable me!" His despair would be a fit introduction to "Guido," which, however, lies four monologues away.

The Pope proposes a theological rationale which justifies Caponsacchi's heroic usurpation of the world in the rescue. His essential arguments, however, have no special relevance to the equation of Pompilia with God. More important, they have the effect, almost decisively, of dispelling the imperious demand for innocence which has controlled Browning's previous poetry.

For the Pope, the question of sexual innocence, ambiguous in Caponsacchi's life generally and so precise and urgent for Caponsacchi in his relation to Pompilia, is of diminished importance. As a general principle, he discredits sexual restraints upon the young and gives approval to the sowing of wild oats (X, 1100-1115). He finds it easy to believe that Caponsacchi's relationship to Pompilia was entirely innocent, but is unabashed by the possibility that it was not. In this instance, noninnocence would have been only (and somewhat vaguely) to "release too much / The perfect beauty of the body and soul." This, while urging the importance of resisting temptation (1180-88).

The Pope's radical theology is developed as the sequel to a question concerning the validity of his judgment of Guido: What if, having judged Guido on the basis of Christian faith, he should find cause to doubt that faith (1265-84)? Acknowledging the basis for doubt, he refers to God as "our known unknown" and insists only that he is "existent somewhere, somehow, as a whole" (1315-16). Previously he has identified that which "fools call Nature" with God (1074). He turns now to the question of revelation, a "tale of Thee," which he says "I find credible: / I love it with my heart" (1348-50). The Pope then considers "the tale" (1351-69), intending to "try it with my reason." He examines the mind of man as the highest form of existence known to us and finds him "strong, intelligent, and good." Though "mind is not matter, nor from matter," it has the relation of effect to cause in a totality, part of which we can examine. In the world we find strength and intelligence, but not "goodness in a like degree." What is missing, then, is "just the instance which this tale supplies / Of love without limit." Thus "is the tale true and God shows complete." The conclusion that revelation is true leaves open the queston as to the kind of truth it expresses, whether "fact" or "truth reverberate" (1388-1407). The Pope, at this point, discounts the importance of the question. He thus implies, however, his receptivity to the idea of scripture as expressing symbolic or poetic truth, and it is perhaps for this reason that he may express indifference to questions concerning "the transmitting of the tale," or, ahistorically, such questions raised by the higher criticism as those concerning the authorship of the Gospels. The idea that "revelation" is not "fact" but "truth reverberate" becomes of great importance later in the Pope's monologue. Before proceeding to substantially new arguments, he expresses two of the religious ideas most often appearing in Browning's poetry, bringing them together in a way which would seem to clarify them definitively: "Life is probation and the earth no goal / But starting-point of man: compel him strive, / Which means, in man, as good as reach the goal" (1436-38).

We may note that if striving is as good as reaching the goal, then the goal need not be reached at all and is equally effective whether real or fictitious. The idea that life is probation is justified insofar as it does "compel him strive" and beyond meeting that requirement need not affirm the life for which this one is probation. The idea that life is probation thus takes on symbolic value and need not, any more than scripture, be taken as expressing fact.

The Pope next treats at great length (the passage extends from line 1440 to line 1630) a question profoundly prejudicial to Christianity: What have been its actual effects in history? The spectacle of Christianity in its historical effects leads to the question: "Well, is the thing we see, salvation?" and the Pope answers, "I put no such dreadful question to myself" (1630-31). He turns back to the subjective basis of spiritual certainty (1632-39). Though the Pope will not accept the evidence of history against Christianity, he is soon listening to an imagined voice of superior spirituality from beyond the Christian realm, the voice of Euripides (1667-1790). Assertion of the spiritual authority of Euripides is Browning's most emphatic return thus far to the conception articulated by HE in

"Easter-Day" of a deity contrasting in universality with the cultural parochialism of Christian orthodoxy. The indictment of Christianity by the Pope's Euripides is strong. Christians have failed,

> *"Though just a word from that strong style of mine,*
> *Grasped honestly in hand as guiding-staff,*
> *Had pricked them a sure path across the bog,*
> *That mire of cowardice and slush of lies*
> *Wherein I find them wallow in wide day!"* (1786-90)

The image of "wide day" contrasted with "dawn" in the lines that follow (1791-1850) will make it clear that Euripides speaks for the modern world and that what he calls "slush of lies" is Christian doctrine literally interpreted. The Pope asks, "How should I answer this Euripides," but does not in fact answer him. He imagines wishing back the power of primitive literalism in "that thrill of dawn," but recognizes that as a possibility "only allowed [to] initiate" historical beginnings. The power of early faith enabled men to follow "the true way" in the beginning, but the true way, presumably in its tendency to truth, eventually requires our "bearing to see the light from heaven still more / And more encroached on by the light of earth" (1818-19).

The effect of the conflict between science and religion is to reduce Christian revelation to myth, comparable "to a mere Druid fire on a far mount." What is needed is a realization transcending both the light of science and the light of orthodoxy: "More praise to him who with his subtle prism / Shall decompose both beams and name the true." This will be achieved by the modern world, soon to arrive with the eighteenth century (1851-1954). In that century belief in literal revelation ("the report") will be supplanted by belief in a spiritual reality superior to that of revelation, a belief in "the thing reports belie." The effect will be that some will realize a new and superior spirituality but "the many" will "fall away." Both spirituality and morality will be diversely experienced. Some few will hold on to Christian fundamentalism and moral absolutism. Pompilia is in some sense like these. Her intuition leading her to action harmonious with Christianity, she wonders "wherefore change?" (1887). The harbinger of the new age is Caponsacchi, "the first experimentalist / In the new order of things" (1910-11). Though he stands to the new age as Augustine did to the last, he is an "experimentalist" and there is danger and uncertainty in his example. We "must thank the chance that brought him safe so far." Caponsacchi has been guided by "his own mere impulse." Others, making a similar claim, will follow "the lowest of life's appetites." Thus Guido is also a harbinger of the new, he and his brother the Abate representing the new order working in "the world"—"such make the world." The Pope's final judgment of Guido is moral and has no clear basis in the new metaphysics he has adumbrated and welcomed.

The Pope's radical theologizing is not a Protestantizing of Christianity. It is a de-Christianizing of spiritual truth. His arguments in "answer" to Euripides and his affirmation of Caponsacchi's sensuality (factual or hypothetical) are an elaborate justification of the alternative to innocence posed by HE in "Easter-Day" and constitute an assimilation of Cleon. The Pope's turning back to affirm his judgment of "the world" and of Guido (1955-2134) from the perspective of Christianity, "the old coarse oracle" (1979), corresponds to the antithetical ending characteristic of most of Browning's greatest dramatic monologues. And *The Ring and the Book* has yet to run its course.

Before the end of Caponsacchi's testimony, when all is over and Pompilia is dying, he says: "My part / Is done; i' the doing it, I pass away / Out of the world. I want no more with earth" (VI, 167-69).

This is the condition of all the speakers who love Pompilia—Caponsacchi, the Pope, Fra Celestino—the Pope because he "may die this very night" (X, 2133), Fra Celestino who has "long since renounced your world, ye know" (XII, 614). The condition of those who love Pompilia is that they have no needs, and perhaps only thus can they enter into her realm of love.

Standing against them all is the murderer of Pompilia, embodiment of a ravening need, "the inexorable need in man for life" (XI, 1982). Waiting to die, Guido speaks his only love: "Life! / How I could spill this overplus of mine" (143-44). For him "life, without absolute use / Of the actual sweet therein, is death, not life" (1487-88). His faith is "Faith in the present life, made last as long / And prove as full of pleasure as may hap, / Whatever pain it cause the world" (725-27).

Guido is a failure. For reasons genuinely incomprehensible to him he has been deprived of the world and now it is to be taken from him with his life. He has been "the muzzled ox that treadeth out the corn" (1469), denied "the taste of the green grass in the field!" (1471). Like Paracelsus (III, 713-20) he imagines the world that is denied him as a chivalric troop that has passed him by: "Where is the company? Gone! / A trot and a trample!" (112-13). Against his fate "the angry heart explodes" (466). His anger is "the honest instinct, pent and crossed through life, / Let surge by death into a visible flow / Of rapture" (2064-66). He raises in protest an implacable hatred—"this tenacious hate of fortune, hate / Of all things in, under, and above earth" (1798-99). "Morality and Religion conquer me" (508), cries Guido, and his hatred rises to exhaustive denunciation. He despises Christianity for "substituting death for life" (1985) and because its meaning for him has been: " 'Suppression is the word' " (1514). He declares himself "a primitive religionist" (1919) and affirms his brute nature: "Let me turn wolf. . . . Grow out of man, / Glut the wolf-nature" (2056-60). This involves a process, a change moving toward realization. By his culture he has been "deformed, transformed, reformed, informed, conformed!" (2063). He is now reversing the process, "unmanned, remanned" (2393). He becomes thus a man facing death totally without the palliatives which human culture may provide. Asserting only what he has as man alone—his volcanic, protesting anger—he comes, at least in moments, to knowledge. The single certainty expressed by the Pope is a sense of being, shared by himself and God. What he dares "think we know, indeed" is "That I am I, as He is He" (X, 380-81). Guido uses a metaphor for knowledge— "something like a foothold in the sea" (XI, 2297)— which echoes the Pope's (X, 1659, 1886-87) and comes also to a sense of ontological certainty:

Unmanned, remanned: I hold it probable—
With something changeless at the heart of me
To know me by, some nucleus that's myself:
Accretions did it wrong? Away with them. (XI, 2393-96)

Like Caponsacchi, Guido learns " 't is death that makes life live, / Gives it whatever the significance" (2376-77). Like both Pompilia and the Pope, He affirms the metaphysical principle that will not permit his exclusion from the order of being: "All that was, is; and must forever be" (2399). For a hundred lines near the end Guido seems to triumph over death: "I begin to taste my strength, / Careless, gay even" (2330-31). Before his final cry to Pompilia he achieves tragic dignity: "I have gone inside my soul / And shut its door behind me" (2291-92). Pride rises into hubris. The pressure of death creates the illusion of life. For a moment near the end Guido is the possessor of the world: "Who are these you have let descend my stair?" (2414). It is the company of death. At the end, inevitably, Guido is unprepared. His collapse into a final, miserable cry, "Pompilia, will you let them murder me?" (2427) is thoroughly consistent with the meaning of Guido as he rejects his passing knowledge of the significance of death, crying, "Life is all!" (2421).

After Guido we may not wonder that the last of the credible fictional speakers in the book, Fra Celestino, one of those who loved Pompilia and have given up the world, has an afterthought:

"*I have long since renounced your world, ye know:*
Yet what forbids I weigh the prize forgone,
The worldly worth? I dare, as I were dead,
Disinterestedly judge this and that
Good ye account good: but God tries the heart.
Still, if you question me of my content
At having put each human pleasure by,
I answer, at the urgency of truth:
As this world seems, I dare not say I know
—Apart from Christ's assurance which decides—
Whether I have not failed to taste some joy.
For many a doubt would fain perturb my choice—

Many a dream of life spent otherwise—
How human love, in those varied shapes, might work
As glory, or as rapture, or as grace:
How conversancy with the books that teach,
The arts that help,—how, to grow good and great,
Rather than simply good, and bring thereby
Goodness to breathe and live, nor, born i' the brain,
Die there,—how these and many another gift
Of life are precious though abjured by me." (XII, 614-34)

In Guido and the speaker of *Fifine*, especially considered in his identification as Don Juan, common characteristics and circumstances, though they differ in magnitude and significance, constitute collectively a striking parallel. While all the relevant circumstances in *The Ring and the Book* may not be fully documented here, they are readily apparent even to the casual reader. The following common profile emerges (numbers in parenthesis are lines in "Guido" or other books of *The Ring and the Book* as indicated):

A disreputable nobleman is an extreme case, all odds discrediting the cause of his verbal struggle. He deliberately identifies himself with criminality and conceives himself as in sustained conflict with society. He persistently protests his desire for truth (171). He is preoccupied with two modes of woman—one of chaste purity and pallor, the other a sensual object (2183-227). He is haunted by the memory of a dead woman. The potential meaning for him of woman as a sensual object is his own revitalization. He acknowledges that pleasure is always achieved at the expense of others (530). He is held in a restraining condition, and a woman is conceived of as his rescuer. Age is an issue in his frustration (998). He acknowledges and is reconciled to the brute aspect of his nature. He identifies death as a stimulus to life. He identifies his values with those of a primitive religion (1919) and interprets Christianity as having suppressed an older faith that must inevitably reassert itself (1975-86). The truth which he celebrates without question is a sense of ontological certainty, and this he realizes by the exercise of resources of the world and the flesh.

The two poems also show striking correspondences of imagery. A stream with a kingfisher flying over it (12) is associated with life and happiness. (The image appears also in *Paracelsus* and in the "Parleying with Francis Furini.") The new moon (259) is associated with life and happiness. Life is identified with carnival (582). Flesh as sensual pleasure is associated with grass (152). The speaker describes his condition of sensual deprivation as that of a beast of burden confined to treading corn in a mill (1469; the image appears also in "Fra Lippo Lippi.") Sex is designated by reference to a "word" that is not uttered (V, 595). The wife is associated with sainthood (2110) and with a Raphael painting (2117). Pompilia, like both the Saint and the phantom wife in *Fifine*, is described as "half on earth / Half out of it" (1726-27). Describing his discovery that Pompilia has absconded with Caponsacchi, Guido uses the phrase "head of me, heart of me" (V, 1040). The speaker of *Fifine* uses the phrase at the beginning of the epilogue, which records his ultimate relinquishment of the quest of Fifine.

The continuity of *Fifine* with *The Ring and the Book* provides support for Guido's claim to a share of truth and suggests the organic relationship of *Fifine* with Browning's work as a whole. Possibly the best key of all to *Fifine* is the point that the speaker is both Guido and Caponsacchi.

It will now be possible to explore a definition of the status of *Fifine* in Browning's work as a whole. In *Sordello* confrontation of the strong man results first in psychic castration and then in death. In *Fifine* the image of the strong man is vestigial. It appears early in the poem after Fifine has appeared, "bringing up the rear" of the pageant of women worthies. (The pageant is foreshadowed in the caryatids around Sordello's font, in the "girl show" in *Pippa Passes*, and in "Women and Roses.") The strong man now is the "Strong Man" of the fair, simply an ominous embodiment of physical strength barring passage to Fifine. He looms " 'twixt fold and fold of [the] tent" (XXV, 286) the occupant of which is Fifine. Tent and dolmen in conjunction, respectively, with tower and menhir, are cognate symbols in the poem for the female. We do not see the "Strong Man" again, and at the beginning of the culminating movement of the quest the speaker's imagination penetrates the tent and claims Fifine (XCI, 1600-1610).

The appearance of the quest motif, as distinguished from the larger quest that makes up the poem, is also vestigial, but its configuration suggests a magnitude of change. The goal of the quest in *Pauline* is first "a small pool whose waters lie asleep" (752), then "solid azure waters" beneath which "fern-ranks, like a forest spread themselves" (792-4), a realm where "the quick glancing serpent winds his way" (796). Paracelsus, "in autumn woods / Where tall trees used to flourish," finds "chill mushrooms, coloured like a corpse's cheek" (III, 540-43). He says, "I sicken on a dead gulf streaked with light / From its own putrefying depths alone!" (II, 175-76). In *Sordello* the entering among trees leads in one instance to the "font" which we later learn to be the burial place of Sordello's mother (I, 410; V, 795), and in another instance to a marsh or "great morass" where one is endangered by "circling blood worms" (II, 31). The body of water in "Childe Roland" is a little river "as unexpected as a serpent comes." It "might have been a bath / For the fiend's glowing hoof—to see the wrath / Of its black eddy bespate with flakes and spumes." It is "the river which had done them all the wrong, / Whate'er that was" and it is filled with ambiguous horrors. The entering among trees in *Fifine* (LXII-LXIII) follows the elegiac movement and is introductory to the affirmation of the world and the flesh in part 3. The body of water is the sea where the waters "freshen as they haste" (LXIII, 988). The sea is, of course, a central image of the poem, symbolic of the world, and it is the element in which the speaker learns "the truth more true . . . than any truth beside— / To wit, that I am I" (LXVI, 1064-65).

Significantly, the passive patterns appear most conspicuously as part of the elegiac process. The beloved is objectified as the painting by Raphael symbolizing an immutable relationship finally seen in terminal perspective, as the love between wife and speaker survives death by fire (XXXVI, 570-77). The wife is also objectified as the statue by Michelangelo and then more specifically as the statue becomes Eidotheé symbolic of the idealization of the beloved. After the statue is destroyed, says the speaker, that idealization is "recalled the same to live within his soul as heretofore" (LVII, 870). From the images of the painting and the statue the poem moves to the heavenly vision in which are fused a spiritualized objectification of the beloved and the religious transmutation. Inherent in the elegiac process, however, is the need to realize such patterns in order to move beyond the finality they imply, and this occurs when into the white light of the heavenly vision there emerges the massive image of Glumdalclich. Here a prototypal pattern designed for completion, permanence, and stasis becomes part of a movement from death into life. In Browning's early poetry the imminence of love was followed in the flight to finality by a movement to death; death was the recourse of love, the condition of its possibility. It is fundamental to *Fifine* that this relationship is reversed, and images of life emerge repeatedly from images of death.

In "Cleon" and *The Ring and the Book* death takes on a significance clearly distinguished from its function as the recourse and condition of love. Both Caponsacchi and Guido see death in a dialectical relationship generative of life. For Caponsacchi, however, this conception comes at that point in his response to Pompilia's plea in which romantic feeling is being transmuted into religious feeling and is part of the compulsion taking him back to the Church. It is a conception that Guido inevitably rejects as the urgency of his need dramatizes its validity in his anguished "Life is all!" In *Fifine* death is a dialectical principle, a matter now not of concept, but integral with intuitive knowledge; it is experienced calmly in symbolic expression: "Thither the waters tend; they freshen as they haste" (LXIII, 988).

The extensive discourse in *Fifine* on "Man" and "Woman" elaborates the abstract option in order to reject it. The alternative to woman is social, the role of leadership,—and, less obviously, artistic. Here, however, the artistic option is seen as exclusive of woman only in the devitalization of art which results from social conformity. As early as the Jules episode in *Pippa Passes*, art, though treated as an option, is seen as potentially a path to the eventual achievement of love. "Fra Lippo Lippi" achieves a bold, though deeply qualified, association of sensual and artistic vitality. In *Fi-*

fine the rejection of the social and artistic options as options issues in the symbolic identification of sexual and artistic power celebrated in the triumph of Arion. *Fifine* does not deal with the intellectual option in the deliberate way in which it deals with the social and artistic options, and yet it is notable that the speaker exults in his role as metaphysician, even as scientist, and is "elate" in "tracing each effect back to its cause" (CIII, 1810). It is in this role that he comes to the fulfillment and self-knowledge associated with the cultural vision.

In a more general way as well, *Fifine* reverses directions taken in the earlier poetry. Beginning with *Paracelsus*, Browning's work was a search for society in the sense that it was a search for historical forms to clothe the structures arising from personal and artistic motives. A great diversity of historical and cultural forms, focusing chiefly in the art and late feudal organization of the Renaissance, provided a panoply of opportunities to explore the possibilities of love as variegated by dynamics of the spirit and the flesh. Identification of the speaker of *Fifine* as Don Juan and as "Don and Duke, and Knight of the Golden Fleece" is also a historical recourse, but it is inherent in the poem that here for once historicity is purely transparent, a thin and indeed irrelevant disguise for a conflict and a thesis that have little to do with history beyond their special significance in the history in which Browning lived. The defoliation of history, removal of its varid forms to discover and affirm its primordial energies, is the continuing process of the quest in *Fifine*. The pageant of women worthies would be found by analytical psychology to represent a psychological configuration, but the women of the pageant are given historical identification and they are a part of a process decomposing "the impudence of history" and reducing what the women have in common, their womanhood, to its immediate and present embodiment in Fifine.

The aerial journey, like the abstract options, appears in *Fifine* so that its implications may be rejected. Suddenly the speaker is "pinnacled" above Saint Mark's square only to find that "the proper goal for wisdom was the ground / And not the sky" (CVIII, 1867-68), and the immediate sequel is the assimilation of man's brute nature.

Hatred-anger, early affirmed as an authentic mode of self-expression, was perhaps a surrogate for joy. In its periodic recurrence in *Fifine* it becomes a motive force of the quest. Guido's affirmation of his brute nature was an act of explosive hatred and anger discredited by the glare of his blatant immoraltiy. In *Fifine* the affirmation of man's brute nature occurs in the calm of the Venetian vision and as part of the culmination of the poem in intellectual realization. This affirmation is the basis of the speaker's reconciliation with the human collectivity, a reconciliation anticipated in the epiphany of Fifine, which precedes the dream-vision.

The rescue, or the Andromeda motif, which achieves its fullest expression in *The Ring and the Book*, has its obvious correlate in the Prometheus myth. The captive chained to the rocks by the sea and awaiting deliverance is not a female figure but a male. The object of rescue had been deliverance from sexuality conceived as obscene. The possibility of rescue now is the possibility of sexuality as the basis of love. So radical is the reversal that we may indeed be tempted to discredit it except that it is part of a massive pattern of reversals the collective implication of which is a unified conception of man reconciling, briefly, but with poetic power, the love of God and the love of the world.

With part 6 and the epilogue, the pattern of the failure with his regret and his anger is reasserted. For one to whom all truth is relative, temperament must be decisive. The denouement is peculiarly personal, and we may easily understand that important reasons for it were quite objective. Elizabeth was a real woman; she had died and had been loved; and Browning was sixty years old. And yet, despite the anticlimactic failure, it is unquestionable that in *Fifine* there occur a resolution of conflicts and a consummation of tendencies fundamental to Browning's art from the beginning, and the significance of this is suggested by the changed nature of Browning's poetry after *Fifine*. The prototypal patterns will recur, but with a difference. For instance, the aerial journey comprises the climax of the *Red Cotton Night-Cap Country*, but here it is suicidal and absurd. The plot of *The Inn Album* is a transmuted version of the confrontation of the strong man in which the strong man has shriveled up, the youthful protagonist has taken on the proportions of a giant, and the denouement consists in the killing of the diminished strong man. The point of importance in these works, as in all Browning's work after 1872, is a reduction of tensions and a prevailing detachment of treatment which are a measure of the culminating function of *Fifine* in Browning's poetry.

11
Background and Milieu

That Browning should have arrived at a theory of culture as an elaboration of libido comes to seem more probable in the light of the history of his intellectual experience and in the light of aspects of the intellectual history of his time. The cultural reduction becomes possible when ideas are available to explain it, and, as we know, conceptions which will explain it are those of the unconscious, of repression, and of sublimation.

We may note, to begin with, a special tendency of Browning's mind. In *Sordello* as in *Fifine*, we are repeatedly impressed with the idea that the product of Browning's imagination must have its origin in the unconscious. We may also conclude that his power to translate experience emanating from the unconscious into vivid correlative imagery tends to make such experience available for intellectual comprehension. One example may be examined. We do not know anything about what happens in Sordello's first interview with Salinguerra, but the effect for Sordello is psychologically devastating:

> *Scarce an hour had past*
> *When forth Sordello came, older by years*
> *Than at his entry. Unexampled fears*
> *Oppressed him, and he staggered off blind, mute*
> *And deaf. . . . (IV, 331-35)*

Another writer would rest with "blind" and perhaps not recognize it as symbolic of castration. Characteristically Browning presses symbolism toward explicit analysis. He adds ". . . like some fresh-mutilated brute."

In a letter of 1876 Browning made it clear that he had been in possession of the idea of the unconscious from his earliest youth and that it had been of vital importance for his life and art. In his last important book, in the "Parleying with Francis Furini," he defined "soul" in a thoroughly secular way: "Call consciousness the soul, some name we need." In the "Parleying with Charles Avison" Browning proposes another definition of "Soul" as "the absolute fact underlying that same other fact." That "same other fact" he calls mind and provides "an illustrative image" which is a remarkable description of the unconscious:

> *We see a work: the worker works behind,*
> *Invisible himself. Suppose his act*
> *Be to o'erarch a gulf: he digs, transports,*
> *Shapes and, through enginery—all sizes, sorts,*
> *Lays stone by stone until a floor compact*
> *Proves our bridged causeway. So works Mind—by stress*
> *Of faculty, with loose facts, more or less,*
> *Builds up our solid knowledge: all the same,*
> *Underneath rolls what Mind may hide not tame,*
> *An element which works beyond our guess,*
> *Soul, the unsounded sea—whose lift of surge,*
> *Spite of superstructure, lets emerge,*
> *In flower and foam, Feeling from out the deeps*
> *Mind arrogates no mastery upon—*
> *Distinct indisputably.* (151-65)

"Soul," Browning says, "has its course 'neath Mind's work overhead,— / Who tells of, tracks to source the founts of Soul?" (181-82). If Browning was not sure of the source, his conception of its direction was strikingly in advance of his time.

According to Lancelot Law Whyte, "the conception of unconscious mental process was *conceivable* (in post-Cartesian Europe) around 1700, *topical* around 1800, and *fashionable* around 1870-1880."[1] Some distinctions are needed. Whyte's evidence indicates that the subject was occasionally a topic for physicians and philosophers around 1800; around 1870-1880 it was fashionable for highly educated people in general. By 1800 the unconscious had been linked with a "formative principle, with the organs of generation and the élan of desire, and with illness."[2] That is to say, historical investigation reveals that someone or other, here or there, had proposed such links. J. G. Cabinas had in 1799 proposed that the condition of the mind was influenced by the condition of the "organs of generation." Sometime after 1800 Maine de Biran proposed that medicine was the key to mental health, thus linking consciousness and unconscious somatic processes. According to Whyte, the possibility of the importance of the unconscious for mental and physical health "became a practical issue for a few physicians around 1820-30."[3] J. F. Hebart in Germany proposed a conception of "inhibited" ideas becoming obscured to consciousness and remaining in conflict with conscious ideas, but this proposal had no immediate response, and few thinkers, according to Whyte, were willing to accept it. However, Sir William Hamilton lectured in 1836 and thereafter on ideas of the unconscious promoted in Germany, and his influence on Browning in other respects is not improbable. Relativism was a part of Browning's thought from the beginning. Sordello says: "Why must a single of the sides be right? / What bids choose this and leave its opposite?" (VI, 445-46). If we should look for a single influence for Browning's relativism, Hamilton would be a very likely candidate. He was an acquaintance of Carlyle's in Edinburgh. John Stuart Mill, who wrote a book on Hamilton, said that he was the only English metaphysician of his generation who had gained a European reputation. Hamilton's thought was like Browning's in that he considered belief, or intuitive perception, prior to, and the ground of, knowledge rationally realized and his relativism affirmed the existence of an absolute that was unknowable.

Sordello was published in 1840. Browning had been working on it for seven years. "In *Sordello*," says DeVane, "Browning almost discovered psychoanalysis."[4] DeVane has in mind the work of S. W. Holmes, who proposed Browning's anticipation of Jung's theory of the collective unconscious and his theory of types.[5] If DeVane's conclusion is exaggerated, it is not pointless. In the passage from *Sordello* quoted in part in the Introduction Browning describes repression. We need not be put off by the fact that for the unconscious Browning used the word "Soul." According to Whyte, so did Ralph Cudworth in the seventeenth century and so did Eneas Dallas as late as 1866. Both in 1840 and in 1877 the word "soul" for Browning stands for a highly secularized conception.

From the discussion of *Sordello* thus far surely it is clear that Browning understood that he was describing sexual repression. If we substitute the Freudian allegory for the allegory of soul and body, Browning's analysis means that the superego has overwhelmed the efforts of the ego to negotiate the needs of libido. Browning's description is not incidental. It is his explanation of the life, the failure, and the death of the hero. It is the intellectual center of *Sordello*, to which Sordello's politics are incidental. It would be another sixty years before Freud would conceive repression so clearly as Browning did in 1840. In the meantime, the lonely knowledge that Browning gained in *Sordello* had thirty years to ferment before the writing of *Fifine*. These years were crucial for the growth of interest in the idea of the unconscious.

Schopenhauer's *The World as Will and Idea* was first published in 1818 but attracted little attention until it appeared in its greatly expanded version of 1844. Browning could have obtained an enlarged conception of the significance of sexuality from Schopenhauer, for whom "will" which underlies all things has its focus in the genital organs. Browning, however, like Freud, did not read Schopenhauer, although both men may have been influenced by him indirectly. When a friend gave Browning a study of Schopenhauer's life and thought, he replied peevishly but convincingly that he found nothing new in it. He wrote that what Schopenhauer "considered his grand discovery— and which *I* had been persuaded of from my boyhood—and have based my whole life upon—[is] that the soul is above and *behind* the intellect which is merely its

servant. . . . The consequences of this doctrine were so momentous to me—so destructive of vanity, on the one hand,— or undue
depression at failure, on the other—that I am sure there must be
references to and deductions from it throughout the whole of my
works."[6]

Given Browning's penchant for unusual reading, one may easily
imagine his thought having been influenced by Richard Payne
Knight, whose *A Discourse on the Worship of Priapus* was published in 1786 and reissued in 1818 under the more genteel title, *The
Symbolic Language of Ancient Art and Mythology.*[7] This possibility is especially interesting because Browning's most obvious symbol in his central symbolic statement is an ancient fertility rite.
Knight argues that from just such rites, employing symbols of male
and female genitalia, all myth including the Christian was derived.
Quite specifically Knight identified the cross as a development from
the phallic symbol. It is possible too that Browning knew *Re-
cherches sur l'origine, l'espirit, et le progrès des arts de la Grèce*
(1785) by Pierre d'Hancarville. Even if Browning knew only
Knight, Hancarville could be the somebody "pert from Paris," for
Knight mentions him as an important source. The implications of
Browning's symbolism are obviously far more comprehensive than
the theses of Knight and Hancarville, and yet to speculate upon
such influences is to envision just such fusion of psychological theory as is implicit in Browning's anthropological conceptions.

According to Whyte, the growth of the idea of the unconscious
accelerated with a rush in the 1850s. W. B. Carpenter coined in
1853 the phrase "unconscious cerebration," which was in common
usage in 1870. A number of publications in the five-year period before the publication of *Fifine* indicate the importance the idea of the
unconscious had achieved. In 1867 W. Griesinger's *Mental Pathology and Therapeutics* was translated into English, and H. Mauds-
ley's *Physiology and Pathology of the Mind* summarized English
contributions to the subject. E. V. Hartmann's massive *Philosophy
of the Unconscious*, appearing in German in 1868, surveyed past
ideas of the unconscious. "The unconscious was in the air," says
Whyte, and "it was already fashionable talk for those who wished

to display their culture."[8] In the year of the publication of *Fifine* there appeared W. B. Carpenter's *Unconscious Action of the Brain* and, in German, *Das Unbewusste und der Pessimismus* of J. Volkelt. The idea of the unconscious was, of course, constantly implicit in the literature of the romantic period.

Works in another area of knowledge are perhaps more likely than works on psychology to have influenced Browning directly. Sir John Lubbock's *The Origin of Civilization and the Primitive Condition of Man* (1870) reinforced interest in primitive man. More important was Edward Burnett Tylor's *Primitive Culture: Researches into the Development of Mythology, Philosophy, Religion, Language, Art, and Custom*, which, published in 1871 and still in print, established the modern science of anthropology.[9] There is some basis for assuming that Browning read Tylor, who could have influenced *Fifine* in a number of ways. Tylor distinguished between progress and evolution to the extent of acknowledging that primitive institutions were sometimes healthier than modern institutions and that vital beliefs and customs sometimes disappear to be revived again in later periods. While Browning even as early as *Paracelsus* tended to see primitive cultures as conditions of health, Tylor may have reinforced these intuitions. The wide range of modern culture which Tylor associates with primitive origins is suggestive—especially his connection of myth and modern poetry and his emphasis upon the relativism of morality seen in anthropological perspective. In the light of Browning's female sexual imagery we will be interested in Tylor's emphasis upon the importance of the Earth Mother and upon the Earth as mother in primitive myth.[10] Tylor also comments upon Christian suppression of primitive forms of worship and upon the survival of these forms against suppression.[11] Tylor uses an unusual word which does not appear in Browning's immense vocabulary before *Fifine*. (XXXI, 381). The word is "nautch." It will be remembered, too, that Browning's peasant lad deals with the idea of God in these words: "Earth did not make itself, but came of Somebody" (CXXIII, 2074). "We come and go, outside there's Somebody that stays" (2082). Commenting on primitive conceptions of God, Tylor says, "Thus it has come to pass that one of the leading personages to be met with in the tradition of the world is really no more than—Somebody. There is nothing this wondrous creature cannot achieve, no shape he cannot put on."¹²

Time and a propitious intellectual ambience are needed for the maturation of ideas. Between Freud's first use of the term "repression" in *Studies in Hysteria*, written with Breuer in 1895, and his systematic application of the conception to cultural theory in *Totem and Taboo*, in 1913, there elapsed a period of eighteen years. When Browning came to write *Fifine* all the elements of a comparable reduction were available. Tylor had provided a conception of pervasive continuity between primitive and modern culture. Knight, whose theory of myth is yet undisproved, could have suggested the unifying concept. Within the Victorian milieu, the younger poets of "the fleshly school of poetry" must have seemed evidence of "something new / Inside, that pushed to gain an outlet" (CX, 1900-1901). The idea of the unconscious was now in the air, and for thirty-two years Browning had lived with both a firmly described conception of unconscious repression and the fact of it. In the passage in *Fifine* beginning "A poet never dreams: / We prose-folk always do" there is clearly adumbrated the conception of sublimation. The cultural reduction articulated symbolically in part 5 of *Fifine* comes to seem almost inevitable.

Whether or not the cultural reduction either in Freud's or Browning's version is true is not so important as the fact that the idea comprised a massive cultural transcendence. In a crucial respect Browning's vision went far beyond Freud's, for Browning envisioned a condition of man unified, his spiritual and his instinctual needs in harmony. Swinburne too, as early as 1866, had seen the repressive power of Christianity and had looked back to an older harmony, but a more consistent parallel with Browning's thought lay in the future. Morse Peckham, among others, has pointed out that there are similarities between Browning and Nietzsche, whose *The Birth of Tragedy* appeared in the same year as *Fifine*.¹³ The cyclical conception of history posed in the idea that the phallic stone bides its time to rise again has something in common with Nietzsche's eternal recurrence and provides a measure of the distance between Browning at this time and what may be considered

Christianity in anything but name. In *The Birth of Tragedy* Nietzsche maintained, as he said later, "a wary and hostile silence on the subject of Christianity," his open rejection coming later. Fundamental to *The Birth of Tragedy*, however, is the conception of vitality in human culture as stemming from a force embodied in primitive myth and ritual celebrating procreative powers. It is a striking fact that when Browning looked to the past for an image of vitality, he, like Nietzsche, came to the Dionysian myth which is the early subject matter of "the shattering dithyramb" as developed by Arion, Browning's actor in his celebration of the unity of poetic and sexual vitality. Nietzsche, like Browning, anticipated a renewal and saw the substance of that renewal embodied in primitive religious forms. For Nietzsche, as for Browning, the liberation of man's basic energies implied an achievement of ontological certainty, a participation in "primal being," to use Nietzsche's terms. *The Birth of Tragedy* was Nietzsche's first book. *Fifine at the Fair* was Browning's last important poem, except for the retrospective *Parleyings*; in *Fifine*, for a moment at least, Browning joined hands with Nietzsche and became part of a continuum leading to the twentieth century. The claim the Victorians made for Browning as an original thinker is best supported by *Fifine at the Fair*, which Browning, laboring in need, dared not let them understand.

Fifine at the Fair is a descriptive-meditative poem which may be seen to resemble what M. H. Abrams has called "the Greater Romantic Lyric," providing we recognize that a fundamental shift has occurred in the meaning of "nature." In Wordsworth and Coleridge nature is represented as landscape and elemental forces of weather. In *Fifine at the Fair* the central representation of nature is Fifine, or woman as sexuality, and Browning's landscape is filled both with symbols of human culture and with animal life. The vision of unity achieved is between subjectivity and objectivity, but it is not, as in the Greater Romantic Lyric, a unity between mind and a chaste landscape theistically conceived; it is the twentieth-century synthesis of human culture and nature as biological reality in man himself and in the totality of animal life.

In *Fifine at the Fair* the romantic synthesis has been deepened, and that synthesis was inherently incompatible both with lingering feudal aspects of society and with middle-class institutions and attitudes inspired by a conception of spirit as autonomous and alien to matter and the flesh. In the Victorian period the Puritan elements of middle-class culture had in some respects intensified and they had vastly extended the range of their influence. Browning, despite his brief Shelleyan apostasy, was formed by middle-class culture in his youth, and in the maturity of his later London years he was avidly engaged in living a role in society. Like most of the major mid-Victorians, and unlike the great romantics, Browning was unwilling to be an outcast from society even though its culture was profoundly inadequate to his needs. The relation of Victorian propriety to the volcanic energies of the epoch is the relation in *Fifine at the Fair* of the dramatic structure and the strategy of disguise to the inner surge of symbol. As in the general condition often called the Victorian compromise, the pressure of energy against form sometimes created grotesque distortion. *Fifine at the Fair* is preeminently a Victorian poem, both in its defects and in its revolutionary implications. And "compromise," suggesting complacency, is not the word for either the culture or the poem. The internal pressures are intense and generative. In *Fifine at the Fair* luminous tensions rise eventually in a fusion of thought and sensate form that is both art and vision, witnessing the death of a culture and asserting the birth of a new one from perennial sources of vitality. But Browning had come to the extreme and precarious limits of his temperament and his art.

Notes

Chapter 1

1. N.S. 42 (October 1, 1872): 545-46, reprinted in *Browning: The Critical Heritage*, eds. Boyd Litzinger and Donald Smalley (New York: Barnes & Noble, 1970), p. 377.

2. See Mrs. Sutherland Orr, *A Handbook to the Works of Robert Browning*, 6th ed. (London: G. Bell and Sons, 1892), p. 150. The worst impressions of Browning's earliest critics have been confirmed in the twentieth century by William Clyde DeVane, who refers to the "mass of very dubious sophistry which makes up the main poem." See *A Browning Handbook*, 2d ed. (New York: Appleton-Century-Crofts, 1955), p. 368. Park Honan, however, considers it at least "as fine a work as [Browning] wrote in his later years." See William Irvine and Park Honan, *The Book, the Ring, and the Poet: A Biography of Robert Browning* (New York: McGraw-Hill Book Co., 1974), p. 463. (Irvine wrote chapters 1-21; Honan, chapters 22-27.) Another critic finds *Fifine* "the last of Browning's really interesting and important poems." See "A Poet's Poet," *Times Literary Supplement*, May 28, 1970, p. 574.

3. Roma A. King, Jr., *The Focusing Artifice: The Poetry of Robert Browning* (Athens: Ohio University Press, 1968), p. xiv; Morse Peckham, *Victorian Revolutionaries: Speculations on Some Heroes of a Culture Crisis* (New York: George Braziller, 1970), p. 85.

4. Edward C. McAleer, ed., *Dearest Isa: Robert Browning's Letters to Isabella Blagden* (Austin: University of Texas Press, 1951), p. 376 (March 30, 1872).

5. Quoted by W. H. Griffin and H. C. Minchin, *The Life of Robert Browning, with Notices of His Writings, His Family and His Friends*, rev. ed. (London: Methuen and Co., 1938), pp. 248-49.

6. Except as otherwise indicated, all quotations of Browning's poetry are from Frederick G. Kenyon, ed., *The Works of Robert Browning* (London: Smith, Elder, and Co., 1912). In references to *Fifine* roman numerals not otherwise identified represent Browning's divisions of the poem, which

will be referred to as sections; arabic numerals represent the lines numbered consecutively throughout the poem.

7. *Handbook*, p. 370. The first of the quotations is from Aeschylus's *Choephoroe*; the second is from Aristophanes' *Thesmophoriazusae*.

8. King, pp. 179-85, divides the poem into three parts as follows: I-LXXXVII, LXXXVIII-CXXIII, CXXIV-CXXXII. King's part 1 corresponds essentially to parts 1 through 4 in this study.

9. Stopford A. Brooke, *The Poetry of Robert Browning* (1902; reprint ed., New York: AMS Press, 1965), p. 422; King, *Focusing*, pp. 174-75; Irvine and Honan, *Book, Ring, and Poet*, p. 463.

10. Edward Dowden, *Robert Browning* (1904; reprint ed., New York: Kennikat Press, 1970), p. 303; King, *Focusing*, p. 173.

11. Betty Miller, *Robert Browning: A Portrait* (London: John Murray, 1952), pp. 207-17.

12. *Symposium*, trans. Benjamin Jowett, in Irwin Edman, ed., *The Works of Plato* (New York: Random House, 1928), p. 369.

13. The quotations here from *Sordello* follow the text of 1840. Of the revisions made by Browning in 1863 and retained in subsequest editions, three seem to me to reduce the secular implications of Browning's original use of the word *soul*: in line 494 "Soul" became "Soul's"; in 495 "its" became "the"; in 564 "More than" became "Beyond." See *The Complete Works of Robert Browning*, ed. Roma A. King, Jr., et al. (Athens: Ohio University Press, 1970), 2: 321-23. This edition is referred to hereafter as *Variorum*. Quotations of *Sordello* are from the text of this work, or, as indicated, the text of 1840 is reconstructed from variants recorded in this work.

14. Miller, *Portrait*, pp. 9-11; W. S. Swisher, "A Psychoanalysis of Browning's 'Pauline,' " *Psycho-Analytic Review* 7 (1920): 126-30. John Maynard, dissenting, assures us that "Browning may be exonerated from the charge of oedipal fixation." See *Browning's Youth* (Cambridge, Mass.: Harvard University Press, 1977), p. 46.

15. King, *Focusing*, p. 177. Of the various readings of *Fifine*, King's (pp. 172-88) is incomparably the most sensitive, thorough, and reliable. The present study agrees with King's on the following important points: a) association of the speaker with Don Juan, to use King's words, "encourages misunderstanding"; b) characterization is minimal and the central development is little related to the dramatic situation—"Space and time are scarcely the setting for this poem," says King; c) the discourse of the speaker is essentially serious; d) the key terms *soul*, *true*, and *false* are used "in an untraditional manner"; e) the speaker's objective and his ultimate vision are affirmative and the eventual renunciation of the quest is "negation, not affirmation; spiritual death, not moral achievement"; f) the

speaker's ultimate vision is not renounced with the renunciation of the quest. Despite these points of agreement, however, the method and the conclusions of the present study depart widely from those of King. According to King, the poem is an "exploration of the problem of being," and "the speaker gropes for reality of self." King does not recognize that the speaker's sense of ontological certainty is achieved only as a by-product of the quest and of enthusiasm in anticipation of its profound intellectual achievement. In describing the speaker's final condition, King says, "His failure to achieve complete freedom is paradoxically his victory." His "new vision," according to King, is a kind of *via media* or balance between elemental aspects of life, a vision of "the necessary tension between spirit and sense, law and lawlessness, restraint and freedom, death and life—Elvire and Fifine." I find the poem intellectually much more interesting than that.

Philip Drew's reading, in *The Poetry of Browning: A Critical Introduction* (London: Metheun & Co., 1970), pp. 303-21, is harmonious with King's. Drew discounts the speaker's identification with Don Juan and the relevance of the dramatic structure to the central symbolic development. He also rejects older interpretations of the poem as satire, such as that of Charlotte Watkins. According to Watkins—"The 'Abstruser Theme' of Browning's *Fifine at the Fair*," *PMLA* 74 (1959): 426-37—the thought of the poem corresponds to that of the early Pater and is satirized by being put into the words of the disreputable Don Juan. A very different treatment of the poem as satire is that by DeVane in "The Harlot and the Thoughtful Young Man: A Study of the Relation between Rossetti's *Jenny* and Browning's *Fifine at the Fair*," *Studies in Philology* 29 (July 1932): 463-94. He feels that Rossetti's paranoiac conclusion that the poem satirized him was not without some basis. DeVane's argument seems now quite speculative. Surprisingly, Park Honan, in *Book, Ring, Poet*, pp. 463-70, has recently treated Don Juan as literally Don Juan and the poem as satirical.

The most extended treatments of the poem before Raymond (see note 17, below) and DeVane were those of Mrs. Sutherland Orr, *Handbook*, and J. T. Nettleship, *Robert Browning: Essays and Thoughts* (London: John Lane, 1895). Orr is still of value. Nettleship, who provides an extensive but superficial prose summary, pp. 223-56, considers the work thoroughly Christian.

Barbara Melchiori, in *Browning's Poetry of Reticence* (New York: Barnes & Noble, 1968), pp. 158-87, accepts all the older criticism and subjects the poem to Freudian observation in a way which seems random and perhaps somewhat careless. She sees the poem as pervasively autobiographical, but consigns the intellectual content to "grey wastes of casuistry," for which she has been justly reproved by Philip Drew. Yet she is one of the few readers to understand the tone of the epilogue, and she recognizes the presence of the dead wife in the main poem. She also recognizes that *Fifine* "is a poem in which the imagery is more obviously sexual than anywhere else in Browning." In standard psychoanalytic fashion, Melchiori assumes that Browning is unconscious of his sexual imagery. However, she ignores entirely the most conspicuous sexual imagery in the poem, and it is this symbolism, inseparable from Browning's major symbolic statements, with which I am concerned.

A study by Claudette Kemper Columbus—"*Fifine at the Fair*: A Masque of Sexuality and Death Seeking Figures of Expression," *Studies in Browning and His Circle* 2 (Spring 1974): 21-38—reads *Fifine* as total nihilism, which has some point but is at best misleading.

Clyde de L. Ryals, in *Browning's Later Poetry: 1871-1889* (Ithaca, N.Y.: Cornell University Press, 1975), pp. 59-82, affirms the unity of the prologue and epilogue with the body of the poem. His study, often sensitive and valuable, is quite traditional. For instance, he finds the poem making the point that "no matter how much a man may try to suppress his biological (and descendental) nature, it is always there waiting to exert its claims." Ryals, in effect, accepts W. O. Raymond's reading of the final stanza of the epilogue. (See note 3, chapter 9, below.)

16. Orr, *Handbook*, p. 150; Dowden, *Robert Browning*, p. 301; an anonymous reviewer may have recognized this when he wrote, "The epilogue is utterly unworthy of Browning. There is to our mind something akin to profanation about it" (Litzinger and Smalley, *Critical Heritage*, p. 377).

17. Raymond, "Browning's Dark Mood: A Study of *Fifine at the Fair*," *Studies in Philology* 31 (1934): 578-99, reprinted in W. O. Raymond, *The Infinite Moment and Other Essays in Robert Browning*, 2d ed. (Toronto: University of Toronto Press, 1965), pp. 105-28; Whitla, "Browning and the Ashburton Affair," *Browning Society Notes* 2 (July 1972): 12-41; Thurman L. Hood, ed., *Letters of Robert Browning Collected by Thomas J. Wise* (London: John Murray, 1933), p. 155 (April 4, 1972).

18. Elvan Kintner, ed., *The Letters of Robert Browning and Elizabeth Barrett, 1845-1846* (Cambridge, Mass.: Belknap Press, Harvard University Press, 1969), 1: 214 (September 25, 1845).

19. Hood, *Letters*, pp. 163, 249, 265.

20. Raymond, *Infinite Moment*, p. 122; DeVane, *Handbook*, p. 367.

21. According to DeVane, the poem was written between December 1871 and May 11, 1872 (*Handbook*, p. 364); Maisie Ward, who read Whitla's essay in manuscript, speculates provocatively in *Robert Browning and His World: Two Robert Brownings?* (New York: Holt, Rinehart,

and Winston, 1969). She suggests that it may have been Lady Ashburton, not Browning, who proposed marriage (p. 71) and in a note she suggests yet another possibility. Pointing to differences in moral tone between the aristocracy and Browning's middle class, Miss Ward says, "*If* Louisa had been suggesting an affair while Browning thought she was proposing marriage they would certainly have been talking at cross purposes" (p. 307). Park Honan rejects the idea that Lady Ashburton proposed and accepts entirely the interpretation of the affair by W. O. Raymond (Irvine and Honan, *Book, Ring, and Poet*, p. 575)

22. DeVane, *Handbook*, p. 367.

23. See *Sordello*, VI, 237-41 (reading of 1840, *Variorum*, pp. 311-12). This passage is one of the first in which Browning addressed directly, that is, nondramatically, the counterclaims of the spirit and the flesh, and it establishes the extreme dialectical strategy by which he would usually confront the question. The passage imposes a radically Puritan meaning of "Good" and "Evil" and, by implication, affirms "Evil," leaving the reader bewildered:

> *Evil's beautified*
> *In every shape! But Beauty thrust aside*
> *You banish Evil: wherefore? After all*
> *Is Evil our result less natural*
> *Than Good?*

Chapter 2

1. Kintner, *Letters*, 1: 555 (March 24, 1846).

2. Ibid., 1: 270, 432, 555, 556; 2: 586, 597, 641, 646, 647, 689, 753.

3. Ibid., 2: 773 (June 12, 1846).

4. Ibid., 1: 32 (March 1, 1845). See also 1: 20, 29, 72-73, 99.

5. Ibid., 1: 204 (September 17, 1845). See also 2: 686.

6. McAleer, *Dearest Isa*, p. 282 (September 19, 1867). See also p. 283, n. 9.

7. Kintner, *Letters*, 1: 195 (September 16, 1845). See also 2: 662-63 and 1013.

8. Ibid., 2: 696 (May 11, 1846); 1: 335 (December 21, 1845). See also 2: 664, 689.

9. Ibid., 2: 763 (June 7, 1846).

10. Ibid., 1: 7 (January 13, 1845); 2: 732 (May 25, 1846).

11. Duckworth, *Browning: Background and Conflict* (1931; reprint ed., Hamden, Conn.: Archon Books, 1966), pp. 193-94.

12. Kintner, *Letters*, 2: 637 (April 18, 1846) (See also 2: 820); 1: 217 (September 27, 1845); 2: 736 (May 28, 1846).

13. Ibid., 1: 274 (November 17, 1845); 2: 664 (April 28, 1846); 2: 737 (May 28, 1846); 2: 740 (May 29, 1846).
14. Ibid., 2: 933 (August 5, 1846); 2: 937 (August 5, 1846).
15. Ibid., 1: 349, 352, 357. There are references to the siren in more than twenty of the love letters. For the prophetic interpretation of Landor's lines see ibid. 1: 273, n.6. Landor's lines are as follows:

> There is delight in singing, though none hear
> Beside the singer; and there is delight
> In praising, though the praiser sit alone
> And see the prais'd far off him, far above.
> Shakespeare is not our poet, but the world's.
> Therefore on him no speech; and short for thee,
> Browning! Since Chaucer was alive and hale,
> No man hath walk'd along our roads with step
> So active, so inquiring eye, a tongue
> So varied in discourse. But warmer climes
> Bring brighter plumage, stronger wing; the breeze
> Of Alpine heights thou playest with, borne on
> Beyond Sorrento and Amalfi, where
> The Siren waits thee, singing song for song.

16. Ibid., 1: 543 (March 17, 1846); 1: 540 (March 16, 1846); 2: 686-87 (May 7, 1846).
17. Ibid., 1: 46 (April 15, 1845).
18. Ibid., 2: 623 (April 14, 1846); 1: 46 (April 15, 1845).
19. Ibid., 1: 359; 2: 723 (May 22, 1846).
20. DeVane, *Handbook*, p. 353.
21. Kintner, *Letters*, 1: 554 (March 24, 1846).
22. Ibid., 1: 216 (September 26, 1845).
23. DeVane, *Handbook*, p. 515.
24. Kintner, *Letters*, 1: *xxvi*.
25. Ibid., 1: 30-31 (February 27, 1845).
26. Ibid., 1: 34 (March 5, 1845); 1: 36-38 (March 11, 1845); 1: 43 (March 20, 1845).
27. Ibid., 1: 85 (June 6, 1845). The next day Robert provided further comment; see 1: 89 (June 7, 1845).
28. Ibid., 1: 15 (February 3, 1845); 1: 30 (February 27, 1845). The latter reference is to *Prometheus Bound*, lines 336-38 of Elizabeth's translation.
29. Ibid., 2: 592 (April 5, 1846); 1: 91 (June 9, 1845); 1: 100 (June 22, 1845); 1: 182 (September 5, 1845).

30. Ibid., 2: 644 (April 22, 1846). The translation, provided by Kintner, is line 1150 of Elizabeth's translation.

31. Ibid., 2: 1025 (August 30, 1846).

32. Ibid., 1: 517 (March 5, 1846). Elizabeth translated *Bia* as *Force*. The character, or personification, would seem to be symbolic of the element of necessity in the world.

33. Lines 128-37, trans. David Grene, in *The Complete Greek Tragedies*, vol. 1, *Aeschylus*, ed. David Grene and Richmond Lattimore (Chicago: University of Chicago Press, 1959), p. 316. © 1942 by The University of Chicago.

34. Kintner, *Letters*, 1: 303 (December 2, 1845).

35. DeVane, *Handbook*, p. 172.

36. Fred Manning Smith, "Elizabeth Barrett and Browning's *The Flight of the Duchess*," *Studies in Philology* 39 (1942): 102-17; and "More Light on Elizabeth Barrett and Browning's *The Flight of the Duchess*," *Studies in Philology* 39 (1942): 693-95.

37. Kintner, *Letters*, 1: 267 (November 12, 1845).

Chapter 3

1. Morse Peckham says of Browning that one "learns to respond to the appearance of the word 'truth' in his poetry as to a flag of warning" (*Victorian Revolutionaries*, p. 98).

2. Even Pompilia, who is "held up amidst the nothingness / By one or two truths only" (VII, 603-4), says, "Let us leave God alone" (1759).

3. Philip Drew writes that the import of this is not clear: "It may be put forward in sincerity: it may be as disingenuous as the special pleadings of Guido" (*Critical Introduction*, p. 312).

4. A sense of ontological certainty is the meaning of truth for Sordello, the Pope, and Guido.

5. *The Form of Victorian Fiction* (Notre Dame, Ind.: University of Notre Dame Press, 1968), p. 45.

6. The emphasis here on sight may reflect the romantic tradition described by M. H. Abrams, *Natural Supernaturalism* (New York: W. W. Norton & Co., 1971), pp. 375-77. The shift from sound to sight, from speech to vision, is a corollary of the collapse of the dramatic monologue.

7. Robert Langbaum, *The Poetry of Experience* (1957; reprint ed., New York: W. W. Norton & Co., 1963), pp. 109-36.

Chapter 4

1. *Oeuvres de Molière*, eds. Eugène Despois and Paul Mesnard (Paris: Librairie Hachette et Cie, 1912), 5: 98.

2. The suggestion that Browning's speaker reflects the verbal agility of Molière's Don Juan has been made by Clyde de L. Ryals, "Browning's *Fifine at the Fair*: Some Further Sources and Influences," *English Language Notes* 7 (September 1969): 46-51. There may be also influences of a more specific sort. The wife's appearance as a ghost in the epilogue may have been suggested by Molière's play. Just before Don Juan is consumed by fire, his final warning and opportunity for repentance is presented in the form of a ghost of a veiled woman, who is probably Donna Elvire, for Don Juan thinks he recognizes her voice. There may be another parallel between the dramatic situations of the epilogue and the opening of act 1, scene 3 of *Don Juan*, the scene from which Browning took the headnote. In both cases the wife, in an unexpected visit, is met at the door, and the confrontation involves surprise and a question of recognition.

One may also see parallels between Molière's Elvire and Browning's Elizabeth. Both have a strong religious faith and both were stolen by their husbands from secluded conditions—Elvire from a convent, Elizabeth from long seclusion in her sickroom under the religious auspices of her father.

3. Roma King says of the prologue and epilogue that "it is not at all clear that they are thematically and structurally related to the poem itself." They are "either unrelated or tangentially related" (*Focusing*, p. 187). King would seem to be forced into this position by his rejection of the biographical content of the main poem.

4. Elizabeth's translation of the line tends to bowdlerize: "And struck the red light in a blush from my brow" (*Prometheus Bound and Other Poems* [New York: C. S. Francis & Co., 1851], p. 14).

5. The imagery here of the mill animal symbolic of deprivation of sensual joy occurs again later in this poem as well as in "Fra Lippo Lippi" and in "Guido."

6. Barbara Melchiori, in *Poetry of Reticence*, p. 169, has read the phrase "sexless and bloodless sprite," which immediately precedes the words quoted here, as referring to Fifine. The passage is difficult and clarification requires examination together of the end of section XV and the beginning of section XVI:

> *for with breasts'-birth commence*
> *The boy, and page-costume, till pink and impudence*
> *End admirably all: complete the creature trips*
> *Our way now, brings sunshine upon her spangled hips,*
> *As here she fronts us full, with pose half-frank, half-fierce!*

XVI

Words urged in vain, Elvire! You waste your quarte and tierce,
Lunge at a phantom here, try fence in fairy-land.
For me I own defeat, ask but to understand
The acknowledged victory of whom I call my queen,
Sexless and bloodless sprite: though mischievous and mean,
Yet free and flower-like too, with loveliness for law,
And self-sustainment made morality. (XV, 164-XVI, 175)

The lines following the colon in XVI are parallel with the last two and a half lines of XV, both in structure and in the themes of completeness and self-sustainment. At line 169 it is obvious that the wife has expressed disapproval of Fifine, and the speaker replies to her in the first four and one half lines of XVI. Then following the colon in line 173 the speaker resumes his characterization of Fifine.

7. Gypsies were at first thought in England to have come from Egypt: hence the name.

8. *Handbook,* p. 457.

9. M.-L. von Franz, "The Process of Individuation," in *Man and his Symbols,* ed. Carl G. Jung (1964; reprint ed., New York: Dell Publishing Co., 1968), p. 195.

10. The mythological correspondences suggested here would seem to be justified by the treatment of the subject by Erich Neumann, *The Great Mother,* trans. Ralph Manheim, Bollingen Series 47, 2d ed. (Princeton, N.J.: Princeton University Press, 1963), pp. 75-83.

11. Obviously this provides a point of support, perhaps the only point of any substance, for DeVane's argument that Rossetti's conclusion that the poem was about him had some reasonable basis. See *Handbook,* pp. 366-67.

12. *The Origins and History of Consciousness,* trans. R. F. C. Hull, Bollingen Series 42, (Princeton, N.J.: Princeton University Press, 1954), p. 198.

13. Miller, *Portrait,* pp. 196-217.

Chapter 5

1. Betty Miller suggests that the poem provides a key to Browning's temperament, a suggestion which will be referred to below, in chapter 10. See *Portrait,* p. 145.

2. Kintner, *Letters,* 1: 195 (September 16, 1845).

3. Ibid., 1: 335 (December 21, 1845).

4. Maisie Ward, *Robert Browning and His World: The Private Face* (New York: Holt, Rinehart, and Winston, 1967), pp. 221, 224.

5. Humanities Research Center, University of Texas.

6. Browning had met the painter Jean Leon Gérôme (1824-1904) in Paris in 1869. See McAleer, *Dearest Isa*, p. 317 (May 16, 1869).

7. The length of hair suggests that the person is a woman. That she is so is confirmed by the fact that the image is one of "three prime types of beauty."

8. Ward, *Two Robert Brownings*, p. 35.

9. The painting is reproduced in Gardner B. Taplin, *The Life of Elizabeth Barrett Browning* (New Haven, Conn.: Yale University Press, 1957), frontispiece.

10. Kintner, *Letters*, 1: 3 (January 10, 1845).

11. Photographs of these works appear in Martin Weinberger, *Michaelangelo the Sculptor*, vol. 2, *Plates and Indexes* (New York: Columbia University Press, 1967). See the series of plates 60.1-65.2.

12. Irvine and Honan, *Book, Ring, and Poet*, p. 249.

13. I am grateful to Mr. E. V. Quinn, Librarian of Balliol College, for making available to me a microfilm copy of the manuscript.

14. McAleer, *Dearest Isa*, pp. 200-201 (December 19, 1864).

Chapter 6

1. She was not insensitive to music. On the contrary, she sometimes found the effect of music so powerful as to be unbearable, and on occasion it was necessary for her to leave a performance before it had been completed. See Taplin, *Life of Elizabeth Barrett Browning*, p. 150.

2. There would seem to be other echoes of the *Rubaiyat*: the phrase "paradise i' the waste" (IX, 97); the phrase "or else a bungler swerves" (XLIII, 666); the discussion ending with the line, "I, he made, vindicate who made me" (LVI, 850-58); the wording "or twist of nose,—that proved a fault in workmanship" (XCIX, 1752).

3. DeVane, *Handbook*, p. 365. The passage echoed and satirized by Browning is *Childe Harold*, canto IV, stanza 180. In a letter Browning commented on the passage in *Fifine* as follows: "I never said nor wrote a word against or about Byron's poetry or power in my life; but I did say, that, if he were in earnest and preferred being with the sea to associating with mankind, he would do well to stay with the sea's population; thereby simply taking him at his word, had it been honest—whereas it was altogether dishonest, seeing that nobody cared so much about the opinions of mankind, and deferred to them, as he who was thus posturing and pretending to despise them." See Hood, *Letters*, p. 159 (August 16, 1873).

DeVane feels that Browning's real target was not Byron but Alfred Austin, who worshiped Byron and was contemptuous of Browning. See *Handbook*, p. 365. This is consistent with the fact that Browning seems to be satirizing Austin elsewhere in the poem. See LXXIX and my discussion.

4. E. D. H. Johnson, *The Alien Vision of Victorian Poetry* (Princeton, N.J.: Princeton University Press, 1952).

5. The image of the stream with a kingfisher flying over it occurs three times elsewhere in Browning's work: in *Paracelsus* (V, 431-46), in "Guido" in *The Ring and the Book* (XI, 5-12), and in the "Parleying with Francis Furini," where it appears in connection with a reference to Joan of Arc, the subject of a painting by Pen Browning, much criticized for its frank treatment of nudity. In each case the symbolism seems to be of life.

6. A comparable image appears in *Pauline* (77-79): "and I ne'er sung / But as one entering bright halls where all / Will rise and shout for him."

7. Alfred Austin's treatment of Browning in *The Temple Bar* had been abusive. The essay had been reprinted in a collection of Austin's criticism, *The Poetry of the Period* (London: Richard Bentley, 1870). In *Pacchiarotto*, where the object of the attack is unmistakable, Browning made brutal capital of Austin's five-foot stature.

Chapter 7

1. The meaning of "poetry" and "prose" as interpreted in this context corresponds closely to a meaning established in *A Soul's Tragedy*, published in 1845 and probably written in 1843. The closet drama is written in two acts, the first in poetry, the second in prose. The first act portrays Chiappino's pretension to love; the second act depicts the default of that pretension. Thus poetry is associated with hope and illusion, and prose is involved in a failure and a renunciation. For further comment on this play see chapter 10, below.

Chapter 8

1. In light of the evidence of Browning's power to excavate primitive levels of human consciousness one may find relevance in Claude Levi-Strauss's observation of "the very profound analogy which people throughout the world seem to find between copulation and eating." See *The Savage Mind* (Chicago: University of Chicago Press, 1966), p. 105. The suggestion is supported by the relationship of Schumann's music to the banquet. Symbolically they are the same. Schumann's music sustains "the certitude I yet may hardly keep" that is the central realization achieved symbolically in part 5. The speaker, addressing Schumann, says

"thou as well / Wast certain of the same" (XC, 1583-84). Browning's special knowledge in this poem concerns the importance of sexuality to all of human life.

2. Sordello's dream of success also involves an image of falling architecture (V, 75-78).

3. "No one, it seems to me, has penetrated so deeply into the dilemma of culture transcendence as Robert Browning" (Peckham, *Victorian Rebels*, p. 129).

4. Six years before writing *Fifine*, Browning wrote to Isabella Blagden that his only interest was in discovering "the proof of certain great principles, strewn in the booths at a fair." See McAleer, *Dearest Isa*, p. 201 (December 19, 1864).

5. Langbaum, *Poetry of Experience*, pp. 35 and 210-35.

6. *The Sacred and the Profane*, trans. Willard R. Trask (New York: Harcourt, Brace & World, 1959), p. 155.

7. Various writers have had difficulty in distinguishing the two configurations within the poem of ancient stone monuments and particularly in describing the structure containing the caverned passage. Mrs. Orr, who purports to be reporting Browning's explanation, describes this first structure as cross-shaped (Orr, *Handbook*, p. 159). Roma King is under the impression that there are two structures very similar to each other, one "a standing tower" and "the other, fallen by order of the priest" (*Focusing*, p. 184). A tower does appear in the poem (V, 36, and CXXXI, 2322) but it is not a part of the symbolism of part 5. Some of the confusion arises perhaps because Browning identifies the two relevant structures symbolically, and for good reason. The two shapes, however, are very different. First appear "these piled stones" (CXXII, 2049) and the "mass and mass, strange quality of stone" (2060). Later, in the same perspective, the structure is "magnificently massed" as "the mound you see" (CXXIV, 2164) and "those mammoth stones" are "piled . . . Temple-wise" (2165-66). The other shape, later introduced, is quite simply "a huge stone pillar" (CXXII, 2104), or, in archeological terms, a menhir. We see it first "laid at length" (2105); later it is imagined in the past as upright (2136-51). Obviously the first structure is a dolmen, represented by the central standing structures of Stonehenge and in more common form by many examples in France. A dolmen consists of several megaliths arranged so as to form a chamber. A dolmen, sometimes partly covered with earth, may have the appearance of a mound; it may not be considered a tower, and it cannot be cross-shaped. It is clear that the cross is experienced within the caverned passage.

The mystery may be cleared up by a book published in the same year as *Fifine* and probably before *Fifine*, which appeared at midyear. The book is James Fergusson's *Rude Stone Monuments in All Countries* (London: John Murray, 1872). Fergusson describes a dolmen called "Dol ar Marchant," near Mane Lud, as "the most interesting, if not the finest, free standing dolmen in France." In his treatment of this dolmen, pp. 361-63, Fergusson draws on the work of a Mr. Ferguson (with one "s") in *Proceedings of the Royal Irish Academy* 7 (1864): 298 ff. Fergusson reproduces a drawing by Ferguson of the back wall of the interior of the dolmen. In the drawing, the wall has drawn or carved on it a cross with two crossarms. Fergusson himself was unable to see this cross but acknowledges that the darkness of the interior makes it difficult to see anything within. Closely related to the dolmen, according to Fergusson, is a giant fallen "obelisk," measuring 64 feet in length and 13 feet across at its greatest diameter. The site is 43 kilometers (farther by road) from Le Croisic, where Browning spent the autumn of 1867. Browning may have seen the "Dol ar Marchant," as he made many sight-seeing excursions during his vacations on the coast of France. We know that he had seen similar structures in France. He may also have seen Fergusson's book. Fergusson's preface is dated December 1, 1871, and the book could well have been in print before mid-year. The realism of Browning's description does not, of course, alter its symbolic value.

8. Female images or suggestions of sexuality are often associated with tents, veiled enclosures, grottoes, vaults, mines, pits, or caverns in Browning's work. For instance: *Pauline*, 328-35 (deep groves, wet caves), 963-70 (mind's cave); *Paracelsus*, IV, 539-43 (dark cell), V, 192-205 (cave); *Sordello*, I, 325-32 (arras), I, 389-427 (corridor, dim-gallery, vault), II, 41, 45 (pavilion, curtain); in *The Return of the Druses*, I (huge veil suspended before "chamber of delight"); in "Count Gismond" (canopy); in "The Flight of the Duchess" (mine); in *The Ring and the Book*, XII, 492-553 ("rites obscene" in cavern).

9. Hood, *Letters*, p. 106 (February 19, 1867).

10. *Myths, Dreams, and Mysteries*, trans. Philip Mairet (New York: Harper and Row, 1960), p. 171.

11. A comparable image becomes conspicuous in *Sordello*. After the recognition scene when Palma and Taurello leave Sordello alone in the room where he dies, Palma sings a fragment from the earliest song Sordello ever wrote. It is made up chiefly of the following words: " 'the few fine locks / Stained like pale honey oozed from topmost rocks / Sun-blanched the livelong summer' " (V, 907-9). The lines are repeated near the end of the poem (VI, 867-69).

12. In *The Return of the Druses*, act 2, "word" is also associated with love and the unattainable. Djabal says, "To yearn to tell her, and yet have no one / Great heart's word that will tell her! I could gasp / Doubtless one such word out, and die!"

13. Eliade, *Myth and Reality*, trans. Willard R. Trask (New York: Harper and Row, 1963), pp. 171-72.

14. The central deficiency of Roma King's interpretation of the poem is that he ignores this crucial relationship entirely. The link between the falling architecture of the dream vision and the stone monuments is essential. The relationship is defined by the question introducing the symbolism of the stone monuments. When that symbolic display has been completed, the relationship is restated at the beginning of section CXXXIV.

15. It has been argued that such a conception informs *Sordello*. See S. W. Holmes, "Browning's *Sordello* and Jung: Browning's *Sordello* in the Light of Jung's Theory of Types," *PMLA* 56 (September 1941): 758-96.

Chapter 9

1. *Victorian Revolutionaries*, p. 87.

2. In 1865 and on a previous occasion at Sainte Marie, near Pornic, Browning occupied the house of the mayor. See Miller, *Portrait*, p. 235.

3. Of the final stanza Raymond writes, astonishingly, as follows: "In one of those flamelike bursts of emotion through which the poet is wont to voice the supreme conviction of his life and art, Browning anticipates the joyous freedom of the spirit, and the rapture of indivisible communion with the soul of his wife, forever blended with his soul in Love" (*Infinite Moment*, p. 125).

Chapter 10

1. "The heart of Browning remains a struggle of irreconcilable forces." See J. Hillis Miller, *The Disappearance of God* (Cambridge, Mass.: Belknap Press, Harvard University Press, 1963), p. 86.

2. Miller, *Portrait*, pp. 145-47.

3. DeVane, "The Virgin and the Dragon," *Yale Review* 37 (1947): 33-46.

4. For an interesting discussion of society as expressed in the omnipresent crowd in *The Ring and the Book*, see Richard D. Altick and James F. Loucks, *Browning's Roman Murder Story* (Chicago: University of Chicago Press, 1968), pp. 281-326.

5. "The Guardian Angel" was written in 1848, before the publication of *Christmas-Eve and Easter-Day*, and should perhaps be associated psychologically with the phase of Browning's life which produced the longer poem.

6. *Handbook*, p. 209.

7. Karl Kroeber, "Touchstones for Browning's Victorian Complex-

ity," *Victorian Poetry* 3(Spring 1965): 101-7; and Russell M. Goldfarb, "Robert Browning's 'The Last Ride Together,' " in *Sexual Repression in Victorian Literature* (Lewisburg, Pa.: Bucknell University Press, 1970), pp. 66-81.

8. *Portrait*, pp. 175-76.

9. *Disappearance of God*, pp. 81-156.

10. The words quoted are from the version of 1840. The revision of 1863 obscures the meaning relevant to the point being made here. On the other hand, in the next quotation used, this same point is strengthened by addition of the word "incidental."

11. Version of 1840. The revision of 1863 destroys the relationship of body (Taurello) and "mind and cause" (Sordello) so pointedly made in 1840.

12. In *"A Grammarian's Funeral*: Browning's Praise of Folly?" *Studies in English Literature* 3(1963): 449-60, Richard D. Altick argues that the poem satirizes the grammarian. As satire, the poem rejects the prototypal pattern.

13. Browning's comment many years later need not be taken to prevail against this interpretation. He is reported to have said that the queen "would have died, as by a knife in the heart. The guard would have come to carry away her dead body" (DeVane, *Handbook*, p. 253). This is a particularly awkward suggestion, for we do not learn in the poem that the queen has died. In the nature of Browning's progress as reflected in the changing prototypal patterns, the meaning of the confrontation for him would have changed, and if the report of what he said is true, we may assume that he was rewriting the poem.

14. Elinor Shaffer, "Browning's St. John: The Casuistry of the Higher Criticism," *Victorian Studies* 16 (December 1972): 205-21.

Chapter 11

1. Whyte, *The Unconscious before Freud* (1960; reprint ed., London: Social Science Paperbacks and Tavistock Publications, 1967), p. 163. All data on the history of the idea of the unconscious are taken from this work.

2. Ibid., p. 129.

3. Ibid., p. 140.

4. *Handbook*, p. 87, n. 24.

5. "Browning's *Sordello* and Jung," pp. 758-96.

6. Edward C. McAleer, *Learned Lady: Letters from Robert Browning to Mrs. Thomas FitzGerald* (Cambridge, Mass.: Harvard University Press, 1966), pp. 34-35 (August 28, 1876). McAleer identifies the "Life" referred

to as Helen Zimmern, *Arthur Schopenhauer, His Life and Philosophy* (London: Longmans, Green, 1876).

7. Burton Feldman and Robert D. Richardson, *The Rise of Modern Mythology: 1680-1860* (Bloomington: Indiana University Press, 1972), pp. 249-56.

8. Whyte, *Unconscious*, p. 163.

9. Tylor, *Primitive Culture*, 2 vols. (1871; reprint ed., New York: Harper & Brothers, 1958).

10. Ibid., 1: 29; 1: 137; 2: 532-35; 1: 326.

11. Ibid., 1: 333; 2: 299, 314.

12. Ibid., 2: 256-57; 1: 394.

13. *Victorian Revolutionaries*, p. 127.

Index